THE TOP 10 OF SPORTS

THE TOP 10 OF SPORTS

Russell Ash and Ian Morrison

CONTENTS

London, New York, Munich, Melbourne, and Delhi

Senior Editor Nicki Lampon
Senior Art Editor Anna Benjamin
DTP Designers Sonia Charbonnier, Rajen Shah
Production Heather Hughes
US Editor Margaret Parrish
Managing Editor Sharon Lucas
Managing Art Editor Marianne Markham
Category Publisher Stephanie Jackson

Produced for DK Publishing, Inc. by
Design Revolution Ltd,
Queens Park Villa,
30 West Drive,
Brighton BN2 0QW

Senior Designer Becky Willis
Designer Michael Lebihan
Project Editor Julie Whitaker

First American Edition, 2002
00 01 02 03 04 05 10 9 8 7 6 5 4 3 2 1

Published in the United States by
DK Publishing, Inc.
375 Hudson Street
New York, New York 10014

Copyright © 2002 Dorling Kindersley Limited
Text copyright © 2002 Russell Ash and Ian Morrison

DK Publishing offers special discounts for bulk purchases for
sales promotions or premiums. Specific, large-quantity needs
can be met with special editions, including personalized
covers, excerpts of existing guides, and corporate imprints.
For more information, contact Special Markets Department,
DK Publishing, Inc., 375 Hudson Street,
New York, New York 10014 Fax: 212-689-5254.

A Cataloging in Publication record is available
from the Library of Congress

ISBN 0-7894-8927-9

Reproduction by Colourscan, Singapore

Printed and bound in Slovakia by Neografia

See our complete product line at
www.dk.com

Track & Field 8
Olympic Champions 10
Fastest Men & Women 12
Jumping Giants 14
World Champions 16
Record-Breakers 18
The World Mile Record 20
Marathons 22

Golf 24
The Ryder Cup 26
Tournament & Money Winners 28
The Major Records 30
The US Masters 32
The British Open 34
The US Open & the US PGA 36
Miscellaneous Records 38

Boxing 40
Heavyweight Boxing 42
Heavyweight Champions 44
Boxing Greats 46
Boxing Firsts 48
Titles & Records 50

Tennis 52
Grand Slam Champions 54
US Open Records 56
Wimbledon Records 58
Australian & French Open Records 60
The Davis Cup 62
ATP & WTA Record Breakers 64

Football 66
Super Bowl Records 68
Championship & Post-Season Games 70
Record-Breakers 72

Season Records 74
Coaches, Drafts & Most Valuable Players 76
Teams, Franchises & Stadiums 78
College Football 80

Baseball 82
World Series Records 84
Championship Series & Divisional Winners 86
Batting Heroes 88
Pitching Greats 90
Single-Season Records 92
Managers, Awards, & Other Records 94
Teams & Ballparks 96

Basketball 98
NBA Finals & Playoffs 100
Teams & Arenas 102
Single-Season Record-Breakers 104
All-Time Greats 106
Coaches, Awards & Drafts 108
ABA, WNBA, World Championships & Olympics 110
College Basketball 112

Hockey 114
Stanley Cup Records 116
Season Record-Breakers 118
All-Time Hockey Greats 120
Coaches, Awards & Stadiums 122
Around the World 124
NCAA Hockey 126

Auto Sports 128
NASCAR Records 130
CART Records 132
Indianapolis 500 Records 134
Formula One Records 136
Endurance Races & Rallying 138
On Two Wheels 140

Olympics — 142
The Olympic Champions — 144
Medal-Winning Countries 1896–1928 — 146
Medal-Winning Countries 1932–1968 — 148
Medal-Winning Countries 1972–2000 — 150
The Winter Games — 152
Paralympics — 154

Water Sports — 156
Olympic Swimming Greats — 158
World Champions & Record-Holders — 160
Yachting & Water-Skiing — 162
Canoeing & Rowing — 164

Horse Racing — 166
Triple Crown — 168
Breeders' Cup — 170
Champion Jockeys — 172
Racing in the UK — 174
Harness Racing — 176

Other Sports — 178
Cycling — 180
Gymnastics — 182
Badminton, Table Tennis & Squash — 184
Weight Lifting, Wrestling & Judo — 186
Archery, Fencing & Shooting — 188
Soccer — 190

Skiing — 192
Skating & Bobsledding — 194
Bowling, Triathlon, Field Hockey,
   Hurling, Gaelic Football & Handball — 196
Australian Rules Football — 198
Sporting World — 200
Awards — 202

Index — 204
Acknowledgements — 208

INTRODUCTION

Top 10 lists

There are certain subjects that naturally benefit from being presented in the form of lists. Sports, with its focus firmly on winning, and hence comparison between the relative success of one individual or team against another, is among the most fitting. Indeed, there are some sports—most notably baseball in the United States and cricket in the United Kingdom—whose statistics captivate their followers almost as much as the sports themselves.

Sports coverage

The Top 10 of Sports presents the 10 (or sometimes, in view of the presence of several of equal standing, more than 10) leaders in innumerable aspects of every major sport, including national and international competitions, and major divisions within each, as well as those that attract fewer followers. We have tried to be even-handed about what to include and what to omit, but if you are passionate about one of the more minority sports and distressed by its absence, please accept our apologies.

▼ Golfing superstar Tiger Woods. His appearance on more than one list in this book emphasizes his status as one of the top golfers of all time.

Made to measure

The Top 10 of Sports contains a mixture of hard statistical facts and trivia, while the "At the Start" entries briefly detail the origins and developments of each sport. Quotations by and about sportspeople provide the only detour into personal opinion, since all the Top 10 lists that follow are entirely quantifiable—highest scorers, leading award- or money-winners, and so on—or rank the 10 first achievers in a particular area of sporting endeavor. Cutoff dates in most instances are as of the end of the latest season, but inevitably some seasons were in progress as we went to press. Equal entries are generally listed alphabetically, unless a goal differential or similar offers some distinction between those of otherwise equal standing.

Sports superstars

One of the things Top 10 lists do is to highlight just how far ahead of their competitors certain superstars of sports are. When we see exponents such as Tiger Woods in golf or Wayne Gretzky in hockey appear so prominently in so many lists, it further emphasizes their status within their respective fields.

World class

The many Olympic lists offer country comparisons, while those within sports indicate national skills and enthusiasms. While large countries—especially the former Soviet Union and the United States—dominate many sports, it is notable that small countries such as Hungary figure prominently in sports like fencing and table tennis, while, perhaps surprisingly, Cuba matches Japan in women's judo.

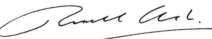

Record-breakers

Top 10 lists provide a perspective where the achievements of individuals can be seen alongside those of their rivals, so we can see at a glance just how unassailable their leads appear to be. However, even though so many are hard acts to follow, it would be short-sighted to say that they will never be beaten: the once "impossible" four-minute-mile record now stands at 3 minutes 43.13 seconds, and although there are world records that have stood for almost 20 years, they are in the minority as new sporting generations challenge the records of their predecessors.

Contact us

If you have any comments or corrections, or ideas for new lists for a future edition of The Top 10 of Sport, please contact us at: ash@pavilion.co.uk (Russell Ash) or igm@atlas-iap.es (Ian Morrison).

TRACK & FIELD

At the Start

The origin of running competitions can be dated back to 3800 BC in Egypt. At the first Olympic Games, the athletes (from the Greek, *athlos*, a contest) competed in running, jumping, discus and javelin throwing, wrestling, and boxing. The earliest recorded winner of a track and field competition was Coroebus of Elis, who won the stadium-length sprint race at the Olympics in 776 BC. His prize was an apple. Modern additions to track and field events include the Marathon, which commemorates the run of Pheidippides from Marathon to Athens in 490 BC, bringing news of a victory over the invading Persians. After breaking the news, he dropped dead.

OLYMPIC CHAMPIONS

- Longest-standing current Olympic records
- Most track & field gold medals in men's events
- Most track & field gold medals in women's events
- Countries with track & field golds in men's events
- Track & field medal winners at one Olympics
- Countries with track & field golds in women's events

> Perhaps there's no such thing as an unbeatable performance, but for a reasonable facsimile thereof, Beamon's leap of 29 feet 2½ inches at the Mexico City Olympics October 1968 does nicely.
>
> **Red Smith**, sports writer

Top 10 Longest-standing current Olympic records

	Event	Athlete/country	Winning distance/time/score	Date
1	Men's long jump	Bob Beamon, US	8.90 m	Oct. 18, 1968
2	Women's shot put	Ilona Slupianek, East Germany	22.41 m	July 24, 1980
3	Women's 800 meters	Nadezhda Olizarenko, USSR	1 min 53.42 sec	July 27, 1980
4	Women's 4 x 100 meters	East Germany	41.60 sec	Aug. 1, 1980
5	Decathlon	Daley Thompson, UK	8,847 points	Aug. 9, 1984
6	Men's 5,000 meters	Saïd Aouita, Morocco	13 min 5.59 sec	Aug. 11, 1984
7	Men's marathon	Carlos Lopes, Portugal	2 hr 9 min 21 sec	Aug. 12, 1984
8	Men's shot put	Ulf Timmermann, East Germany	22.47 m	Sep. 23, 1988
9 =	Women's 100 meters	Florence Griffith-Joyner, US	10.54 sec	Sep. 24, 1988
=	Women's heptathlon	Jackie Joyner-Kersee, US	7,291 points	Sep. 24, 1988

Bob Beamon's record-breaking jump in 1968 is regarded as one of the greatest achievements in athletics. He was aided by Mexico City's rarefied atmosphere, but to add a staggering 22½ in (55 cm) to the old world record and win the competition by 28 in (71 cm) was no mean feat. At 29 ft 2½ in, Beamon's jump was the first to exceed 28 feet, let alone 29 feet. The next jump to exceed 28 feet in the Olympics was not until 1980, 12 years after Beamon's leap.

Top 10 Most track & field gold medals in men's events*

	Athlete/country	Golds
1	Ray Ewry, US	10
2 =	Carl Lewis, US	9
=	Paavo Nurmi, Finland	9
4 =	Michael Johnson, US	5
=	Ville Ritola, Finland	5
=	Martin Sheridan, US	5
7 =	Harrison Dillard, US	4
=	Archie Hahn, US	4
=	Hannes Kolehmainen, Finland	4
=	Alvin Kraenzlein, US	4
=	Eric Lemming, Sweden	4
=	Jim Lightbody, US	4
=	Al Oerter, US	4
=	Jesse Owens, US	4
=	Myer Prinstein, US	4
=	Mel Sheppard, US	4
=	Lasse Viren, Finland	4
=	Emil Zatopek, Czechoslovakia	4

* Including relays

Top 10 Most track & field gold medals in women's events*

	Athlete/country	Golds
1 =	Evelyn Ashford, US	4
=	Fanny Blankers-Koen, Netherlands	4
=	Betty Cuthbert, Australia	4
=	Bärbel Wockel (née Eckert), East Germany	4
5 =	Valerie Brisco-Hooks, US	3
=	Olga Bryzgina, USSR/ Unified Team	3
=	Shirley de la Hunty-Strickland, Australia	3
=	Gail Devers, US	3
=	Florence Griffith-Joyner, US	3
=	Marion Jones, US	3
=	Jackie Joyner-Kersee, US	3
=	Tatyana Kazankina, USSR	3
=	Marie-Josè Perèc, France	3
=	Tamara Press, USSR	3
=	Wilma Rudolph, US	3
=	Renate Stecher, East Germany	3
=	Irena Szewinska-Kirzenstein, Poland	3
=	Gwen Torrence, US	3
=	Wyomia Tyus, US	3

* Including relays

Bob Beamon nearly didn't make the 1968 Olympic long jump final. His first two qualifying jumps were "no jumps"—one more and he would have been out.

Top 10 Countries with track & field golds in men's events

	Country	Golds
1	US	265
2	Finland	48
3	UK	43
4	USSR/Unified Team/Russia	38
5	Sweden	17
6	Kenya	15
7 =	East Germany	14
=	Germany/West Germany	14
9	Italy	13
10 =	Canada	12
=	Poland	12

Top 10 Track & field medal winners at one Olympics

	Athlete/country	Year	Gold medals	Silver medals	Bronze medals	Total
1	Ville Ritola, Finland	1924	4	2	0	6
2 =	Irving Baxter, US	1900	2	3	0	5
=	Marion Jones, US	2000	3	0	2	5
=	Paavo Nurmi, Finland	1924	5	0	0	5
=	Martin Sheridan, US	1906	2	3	0	5
6 =	Erik Backman, Sweden	1920	0	1	3	4
=	Fanny Blankers-Koen, Netherlands	1948	4	0	0	4
=	Florence Griffith-Joyner, US	1988	3	1	0	4
=	Hannes Kolehmainen, Finland	1912	1	0	3	4
=	Alvin Kraenzlein, US	1900	4	0	0	4
=	Eric Leeming, Sweden	1906	1	0	3	4
=	Carl Lewis, US	1984	4	0	0	4
=	Jim Lightbody, US	1904	3	1	0	4
=	Paavo Nurmi, Finland	1920	3	1	0	4
=	Jesse Owens, US	1936	4	0	0	4
=	Stanley Rowley, Australia	1900	1	0	3	4

Ritola's medals of 1924 were as follows: Gold: 10,000 meters, 3,000 meters steeplechase, 3,000 meters track team race, cross-country (team). Silver: 5,000 meters, cross-country (individual).

Top 10 Countries with track & field golds in women's events

	Country	Golds
1	US	44
2	USSR/Unified Team/Russia	39
3	East Germany	25
4	Germany/West Germany	17
5	Australia	11
6	Romania	10
7	Poland	7
8 =	France	6
=	Netherlands	6
=	UK	6

◄ Bob Beamon on the way to his world record leap at the 1968 Mexico Olympics. It was his first jump of the competition.

FASTEST MEN & WOMEN

- Fastest women's 400-meter runners of all time
- Fastest men's 400-meter runners of all time
- Fastest women's 200-meter runners of all time
- Fastest women's 100-meter runners of all time
- Fastest men's 200-meter runners of all time
- Fastest men's 100-meter runners of all time

"The ones who believed in themselves the most were the ones who won.
— Florence Griffith-Joyner"

Top 10 Fastest women's 400-meter runners of all time*

	Athlete/country	Date	Time (sec)
1	Marita Koch, East Germany	Oct. 6, 1985	47.60
2	Jarmilla Kratochvilova, Czechoslovakia	Aug. 10, 1983	47.99
3	Marie-Josè Perèc, France	July 29, 1996	48.25
4	Olga Bryzgina, USSR	Oct. 6, 1985	48.27
5	Tatyana Kocembova, Czechoslovakia	Aug. 10, 1983	48.59
6	Cathy Freeman, Australia	July 29, 1996	48.63
7	Valerie Brisco-Hooks, US	Aug. 6, 1984	48.83
8	Chandra Cheeseborough, US	Aug. 6, 1984	49.05
9	Falilat Ogunkoya, Nigeria	July 29, 1996	49.10
10	Olga Nazarova, USSR	Sep. 25, 1988	49.11

* Outdoor performances; only the best performance for each athlete is included
Source: IAAF

Marita Koch set her world-best mark during the 1985 IAAF World Cup in Canberra. Since then, only one woman has come within a second of her record time.

Top 10 Fastest men's 400-meter runners of all time*

	Athlete#	Date	Time (sec)
1	Michael Johnson	Aug. 26, 1999	43.18
2	Harry Reynolds	Aug. 17, 1988	43.29
3	Quincy Watts	Aug. 5, 1992	43.50
4	Danny Everett	June 26, 1992	43.81
5	Lee Evans	Oct. 18, 1968	43.86
6	Steve Lewis	Sep. 28, 1988	43.87
7	Larry James	Oct. 18, 1968	43.97
8 =	Alvin Harrison	June 19, 1996	44.09
=	Jerome Young	June 21, 1998	44.09
10	Derek Mills	June 4, 1995	44.13

* Outdoor performances; only the best performance for each athlete is included
\# All US
Source: IAAF

The fastest 400 meters by a non-US athlete is 44.14 seconds by Cuba's Roberto Hernandez at Seville on May 30, 1990.

◄ The 2000 Sydney Olympics 100-meter champion Maurice Green of the US proudly celebrates his win.

Top 10 Fastest women's 200-meter runners of all time*

	Athlete/country	Date	Time (sec)
1	Florence Griffith-Joyner, US	Sep. 29, 1988	21.34
2	Marion Jones, US	Sep. 11, 1998	21.62
3	Merlene Ottey, Jamaica	Sep. 13, 1991	21.64
4 =	Heike Drechsler, East Germany	June 29, 1986	
		Aug. 29, 1986	21.71
=	Marita Koch, East Germany	June 10, 1979	
		July 21, 1984	21.71
6 =	Grace Jackson, Jamaica	Sep. 29, 1988	21.72
=	Gwen Torrence, US	Aug. 5, 1992	21.72
8 =	Silke Gladisch-Möller, East Germany	Sep. 3, 1987	21.74
=	Marlies Oelsner-Göhr, East Germany	June 3, 1984	21.74
10	Juliet Cuthbert, Jamaica	Aug. 5, 1992	21.75

* Outdoor performances; only the best performance for each athlete is included
Source: IAAF

Top 10 Fastest women's 100-meter runners of all time*

	Athlete/country	Date	Time (sec)
1	Florence Griffith-Joyner, US	July 16, 1988	10.49
2	Marion Jones, US	Sep. 12, 1998	10.65
3	Christine Arron, France	Aug. 19, 1998	10.73
4	Merlene Ottey, Jamaica	Sep. 7, 1996	10.74
5	Evelyn Ashford, US	Aug. 22, 1984	10.76
6	Irina Privalova, Russia	July 6, 1994	10.77
7	Dawn Sowell, US	June 3, 1989	10.78
8 =	Xuemei Li, China	Oct. 18, 1997	10.79
=	Inger Miller, US	Aug. 22, 1999	10.79
10	Marlies Oelsner-Göhr, East Germany	June 8, 1983	10.81

* Outdoor performances; only the best performance for each athlete is included
Source: IAAF

Since "Flo-Jo" became the first woman under 10.50 seconds, no other woman has gone below 10.60 for the 100 meters. Her record time was set in the quarter-finals of the 1988 Seoul Olympics.

Top 10 Fastest men's 200-meter runners of all time*

	Athlete/country	Date	Time (sec)
1	Michael Johnson, US	Aug. 1, 1996	19.32
2	Frank Fredericks, Namibia	Aug. 1, 1996	19.68
3	Pietro Mennea, Italy	Sep. 12, 1979	19.72
4	Michael Marsh, US	Aug. 5, 1992	19.73
5 =	Joe DeLoach, US	Sep. 28, 1988	19.75
=	Carl Lewis, US	June 19, 1983	19.75
7	Ato Boldon, Trinidad	July 13, 1997	19.77
8	Tommie Smith, US	Oct. 16, 1968	19.83
9	Francis Obikwelu, Nigeria	Aug. 25, 1999	19.84
10	John Capel, US	July 23, 2000	19.85

* Outdoor performances; only the best performance for each athlete is included
Source: IAAF

Pietro Mennea's world record stood for nearly 17 years. When it was broken, two men went under his mark on the same day.

Top 10 Fastest men's 100-meter runners of all time*

	Athlete/country	Date	Time (sec)
1	Maurice Green, US	June 16, 1999	9.79
2 =	Donovan Bailey, Canada	July 27, 1996	9.84
=	Tim Montgomery, US	July 13, 2001	9.84
=	Bruny Surin, Canada	Aug. 22, 1999	9.84
5	Leroy Burrell, US	July 6, 1994	9.85
6 =	Ato Boldon, Trinidad	Apr. 19, 1998, June 17, 1998	
		June 16, 1999, July 2, 1999	9.86
=	Frank Fredericks, Namibia	July 3, 1996	9.86
=	Carl Lewis, US	Aug. 25, 1991	9.86
9 =	Linford Christie, UK	Aug. 15, 1993	9.87
=	Obadele Thompson, Barbados	Sep. 11, 1998	9.87

* Outdoor performances; only the best performance for each athlete is included
Source: IAAF

At the age of 16, Canadian-born Donovan Bailey ran 100 meters in 10.65 seconds. Before turning his attention full-time to track, he had worked as a stockbroker.

◄ The world's fastest woman, Florence Griffith-Joyner, who died of heart failure in September 1998 at the age of just 38.

JUMPING GIANTS

- Women's high jumpers of all time
- Men's high jumpers of all time
- Men's triple jumpers of all time
- Women's long jumpers of all time
- Men's long jumpers of all time

Top 10 Women's high jumpers of all time*

	Athlete/country	Date	Height (meters)
1	Stefka Kostadinova, Bulgaria	Aug. 30, 1987	2.09
2	Lyudmila Andonova, Bulgaria	July 20, 1984	2.07
3 =	Inha Babakova, Ukraine	Sep. 15, 1995	2.05
=	Tamara Bykova, USSR	June 22, 1984	2.05
=	Heike Redetzky-Henkel, Germany	Aug. 31, 1991	2.05
6 =	Hestrie Cloete, South Africa	Aug. 4, 1999	2.04
=	Silvia Costa, Cuba	Sep. 9, 1989	2.04
=	Venelina Veneva, Bulgaria	June 2, 2001	2.04
9 =	Tatyana Babashkina, Russia	May 30, 1995	2.03
=	Ulrike Meyfarth, West Germany	Aug. 21, 1983	2.03
=	Louise Ritter, US	Aug. 7, 1988	2.03
=	Niki Bakoyiánni, Greece	Aug. 3, 1996	2.03

* Outdoor performances; only the best performance for each athlete is included

Source: IAAF

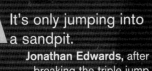

It's only jumping into a sandpit.
Jonathan Edwards, after breaking the triple jump world record, 1995.

◀ Javier Sotomayor of Cuba, the high jump world record-holder.

Top 10 Men's high jumpers of all time*

	Athlete/country	Date	Height (meters)
1	Javier Sotomayor, Cuba	July 27, 1993	2.45
2	Patrik Sjöberg, Sweden	June 30, 1987	2.42
3	Igor Paklin, USSR	Sep. 4, 1985	2.41
4 =	Charles Austin, US	Aug. 7, 1991	2.40
=	Sorin Matei, Romania	June 20, 1990	2.40
=	Rudolf Povarnitsyn, USSR	Aug. 11, 1985	2.40
=	Vyacheslav Voronin, Russia	Aug. 5, 2000	2.40
8 =	Hollis Conway, US	July 30, 1989	2.39
=	Jianhua Zhu, China	June 10, 1984	2.39
10 =	Gennadiy Avdeyenko, USSR	Sep. 6, 1987	2.38
=	Sergey Malchenko, USSR	Sep. 4, 1988	2.38
=	Dragutin Topic, Yugoslavia	Aug. 1, 1993	2.38

* Outdoor performances; only the best performance for each athlete is included
Source: IAAF

Top 10 Men's triple jumpers of all time*

	Athlete/country	Date	Distance (meters)
1	Jonathan Edwards, UK	Aug. 7, 1995	18.29
2	Kenny Harrison, US	July 27, 1996	18.09
3	Willie Banks, US	June 16, 1985	17.97
4 =	James Beckford, Jamaica	May 20, 1995	17.92
=	Khristo Markov, Bulgaria	Aug. 31, 1987	17.92
6	Vladimir Inozemtsev, Ukraine	June 20, 1990	17.90
7	João Carlos de Oliveira, Brazil	Oct. 15, 1975	17.89
8	Mike Conley, US	June 27, 1987	17.87
9	Charles Simpkins, US	Sep. 2, 1985	17.86
10	Yoelbi Quesada, Cuba	Aug. 8, 1997	17.85

* Outdoor performances; only the best performance for each athlete is included
Source: IAAF

When Willie Banks set the triple jump world record at Indianapolis in 1985, he became the first American since Daniel Ahearn 74 years earlier to set the record. Like Ahearn, Banks also never won Olympic gold.

Top 10 Women's long jumpers of all time*

	Athlete/country	Date	Distance (meters)
1	Galina Chistyakova, USSR	June 11, 1988	7.52
2	Jackie Joyner-Kersee, US	May 22, 1994, July 31, 1994	7.49
3	Heike Dreschler, East Germany	July 9, 1988, July 8, 1992	7.48
4	Anisoara Cusmir-Stanciu, Romania	June 4, 1983	7.43
5	Yelena Belevskaya, USSR	July 18, 1987	7.39
6	Inesa Kravets, Ukraine	June 13, 1992	7.37
7 =	Marion Jones, US	May 31, 1998, Aug. 12, 1998	7.31
=	Yelena Kokonova-Khlopotnova, USSR	Sep. 12, 1985	7.31
9	Maurren Higa Maggi, Brazil	June 26, 1999	7.26
10	Larisa Berezhnaya, Russia	May 25, 1991	7.24

* Outdoor performances; only the best performance for each athlete is included
Source: IAAF

While she has not managed to break Chistyakova's world-best mark in the long jump, Jackie Joyner-Kersee did set the world heptathlon record during the 1988 Seoul Olympics.

Top 10 Men's long jumpers of all time*

	Athlete/country	Date	Distance (meters)
1	Mike Powell, US	Aug. 30, 1991	8.95
2	Bob Beamon, US	Oct. 18, 1968	8.90
3	Carl Lewis, US	Aug. 30, 1991	8.87
4	Robert Emmiyan, USSR	May 22, 1987	8.86
5 =	Larry Myricks, US	July 18, 1988	8.74
=	Erick Walder, US	Apr. 2, 1994	8.74
7	Ivan Pedroso, Cuba	July 18, 1995	8.71
8	Kareem Streete-Thompson, US	July 4, 1994	8.63
9	James Beckford, Jamaica	Apr. 5, 1997	8.62
10	Yago Lamela, Spain	June 24, 1999	8.56

* Outdoor performances; only the best performance for each athlete is included
Source: IAAF

Going into the 1968 Olympic Games, the men's long jump Olympic record stood at 8.12 meters. Bob Beamon shattered that mark, but it was also broken by runner-up Klaus Beer (East Germany) and the joint world record holder at the time, Ralph Boston (US).

◀ Jonathan Edwards, triple jump Olympic champion in 2000 and the first male British jumper to win Olympic gold since Lyn Davies in the long jump in 1964.

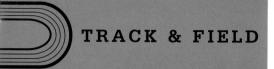
WORLD CHAMPIONS

- Oldest World Championship records

- Athletes with most World Championship gold medals

- Athletes with most IAAF Grand Prix titles

- Medal-winning countries at the World Championships

- First athletes to win three consecutive individual titles at the World Championships

HOW DID IT BEGIN?

The first official IAAF World Championships were held in Helsinki in 1983. They were originally held every four years between Olympic celebrations, but since 1991 have been a biennial event. The venues for all official events have been: 1983: Helsinki, Finland; 1987: Rome, Italy; 1991: Tokyo, Japan; 1993: Stuttgart, Germany; 1995: Gothenburg, Sweden; 1997: Athens, Greece; 1999: Seville, Spain; 2001: Edmonton, Canada. The 2003 Championships will be held in Paris.

Top 10 Oldest World Championship records

	Event	Athlete/country	Winning time/distance/points	Date
1	Women's 800 meters	Jarmila Kratochvilova, Czechoslovakia	1 min 54.68 sec	Aug. 9, 1983
2	Women's 400 meters	Jarmila Kratochvilova, Czechoslovakia	47.99 sec	Aug. 10, 1983
3	Men's marathon	Rob de Castella, Australia	2 hr 10 min 3 sec	Aug. 14, 1983
4 =	Men's shot put	Werner Günthör, Switzerland	22.23 m	Aug. 29, 1987
=	Women's marathon	Rosa Mota, Portugal	2 hr 25 min 17 sec	Aug. 29, 1987
6	Women's high jump	Stefka Kostadinova, Bulgaria	2.09 m	Aug. 30, 1987
7	Women's discus	Martina Opitz, East Germany	71.62 m	Aug. 31, 1987
8 =	Heptathlon	Jackie Joyner-Kersee, US	7,128 pt	Sep. 1, 1987
=	Men's 800 meters	Billy Konchellah, Kenya	1 min 43.06 sec	Sep. 1, 1987
10	Women's 200 meters	Silke Gladisch, East Germany	21.74 sec	Sep. 3, 1987

Source: IAAF

Top 10 Athletes with most World Championship gold medals*

	Athlete/country	Total
1	Michael Johnson, US	9
2	Carl Lewis, US	8
3	Sergey Bubka, USSR/Ukraine	6
4 =	Maurice Greene, US	5
=	Marion Jones, US	5
=	Lars Riedel, Germany	5
7 =	Gail Devers, US	4
=	Haile Gebrselassie, Ethiopia	4
=	Jackie Joyner-Kersee, US	4
=	Ivan Pedroso, Cuba	4
=	Antonio Pettigrew, US	4
=	Calvin Smith, US	4

* Including relays

Despite all his world titles, Michael Johnson had still not broken the world 400-meter record despite 10 years of trying. However, that came to an end when he won his fourth consecutive 400-meter world title in Seville in 1999, and in a new world best.

◄ Sergey Bubka, the winner of the first six pole vault World Championship titles, 1983–97.

Top 10 Athletes with most IAAF Grand Prix titles

	Athlete/country	Event(s)/year	Total
1	Merlene Ottey, Jamaica	Overall 1987, 1990 100 meters 1987, 1989, 1991, 1994, 1996 200 meters 1990, 1992	9
2	Sergey Bubka, USSR/Ukraine	Overall 1991, 1993 Pole vault 1985, 1987, 1991, 1993, 1997	7
3 =	Mike Conley, US	Long jump 1985 Triple jump 1986, 1988, 1990, 1992, 1994	6
=	Ana Fidelia Quirot, Cuba	400 meters 1988, 1990 800 meters 1987, 1989, 1991, 1997	6
5 =	Said Aouita, Morocco	Overall 1986, 1988, 1989 5,000 meters 1986 Mile 1988	5
=	Marion Jones, US	Overall 1998 100 meters 1998, 2000 200 meters 1997 Long jump 1998	5
=	Noureddine Morceli, Algeria	Overall 1994 Mile 1990 1,500 meters 1991, 1993, 1994	5
=	Maria Mutola, Mozambique	Overall 1995 800 meters 1993, 1995, 1999, 2001	5
=	Sonia O'Sullivan, Ireland	3,000 meters 1993, 1995, 2000 5,000 meters 1992, 1994	5
=	Jan Zelezny, Czechoslovakia	Javelin 1991, 1993, 1995, 1997, 2001	5

Source: IAAF

The IAAF Grand Prix series was launched in 1985 and is a season-long competition at various venues worldwide. Originally points were given for performances in individual events, with an overall champion at the end of the season being declared. Since 1993, the champion in each event has been decided at the end-of-season Grand Prix final.

Top 10 Medal-winning countries at the World Championships

	Country	Gold medals	Silver medals	Bronze medals	Total
1	US	80	41	47	168
2	USSR/Russia	40	52	53	145
3	Germany/West Germany	21	23	22	66
4	East Germany	21	19	19	59
5	UK	11	22	19	52
6	Kenya	19	16	15	50
7	Jamaica	5	14	23	42
8	Italy	9	13	8	30
9	Cuba	13	10	5	28
10	Spain	6	10	7	23

Source: IAAF

While the United States has won twice as many gold medals as the USSR/Russia, they did not have the first Championship of 1983 all their own way. East Germany dominated the Championship with 10 gold medals, the US and USSR each collecting eight.

The 10 First athletes to win three consecutive individual titles at the World Championships

	Athlete/country	Event	Years
1 =	Sergey Bubka, USSR/Ukraine	Pole vault	1983, 87, 91
=	Greg Foster, US	110-meter hurdles	1983, 87, 91
=	Carl Lewis, US	100 meters	1983, 87, 91
4	Werner Günthör, Switzerland	Shot put	1987, 91, 93
5 =	Moses Kiptanui, Kenya	3,000-meter steeplechase	1991, 93, 95
=	Noureddine Morceli, Algeria	1,500 meters	1991, 93, 95
=	Dan O'Brien, US	Decathlon	1991, 93, 95
=	Lars Riedel, Germany	Discus	1991, 93, 95
9 =	Haile Gebrselassie, Ethiopia	10,000 meters	1993, 95, 97
=	Michael Johnson, USA	400 meters	1993, 95, 97

The first woman to win three consecutive titles was Astrid Kombernuus (Germany), in the shot put, in 1995, 1997, and 1999.

Carl Lewis went on to win an unprecedented 10 World Championship medals—eight gold, one silver, and one bronze. He twice won a record-equaling three golds at one Championship, in 1983 and 1987, each time in the 100 meters, long jump, and sprint relay.

◄ Michael Johnson, winner of the 400-meter title at four consecutive World Championships between 1993 and 1999.

RECORD BREAKERS

- Longest-standing men's world records of all time
- Women's outdoor world records broken most times
- Men's outdoor world records broken most times
- Longest-standing men's outdoor world records
- Longest-standing women's outdoor world records

"It was a lifetime of training for just 10 seconds.

Jesse Owens, Olympic 100-meter record-holder"

Top 10 Longest-standing men's world records of all time*

	Athlete/country#	Event	Date set	Date broken	Duration (y:m:d)		
1	Jesse Owens	Long jump	May 25, 1935	Aug. 12, 1960	25	2	18
2	Patrick Ryan	Hammer	Aug. 17, 1913	Aug. 27, 1938	25	0	10
3	Vince Matthews, Ronald Freeman, Larry James, Lee Evans	4 x 400-meter relay	Oct. 20, 1968	Aug. 8, 1992	23	9	19
4	Bob Beamon	Long jump	Oct. 18, 1968	Aug. 30, 1991	22	10	12
5	Daniel Ahearn	Triple jump	May 30, 1911	Oct. 27, 1931	20	4	28
6	Jesse Owens, Ralph Metcalfe, Foy Draper, Frank Wykoff	4 x 100-meter relay	Aug. 9, 1936	Dec. 1, 1956	20	3	23
7	Jesse Owens	100 meters	June 20, 1936	Aug. 3, 1956	20	1	13
8	Ivan Fuqua, Edgar Ablowich, Karl Warner, Bill Carr	4 x 400-meter relay	Aug. 7, 1932	July 27, 1952	19	11	20
9	Peter O'Connor, UK	Long jump	Aug. 5, 1901	July 23, 1921	19	11	13
10	Lee Evans	400 meters	Oct. 18, 1968	Aug. 17, 1988	19	9	30

* Outdoor world records

\# All US unless otherwise stated

Top 10 Women's outdoor world records broken most times*

	Event	Occasions record broken or equaled
1	Javelin	22
2	Pole vault	19
3	Hammer	14
4 =	5,000 meters	11
=	3,000-meter steeplechase	11
6 =	Heptathlon	9
=	High jump	9
8	Long jump	8
9 =	400-meter hurdles	7
=	10,000 meters	7

* Outdoor world records at recognized Olympic events broken or equaled Jan. 1, 1981–Dec. 31, 2001

The first pole vault world record was not established until 1995. Since then, Emma George of Australia has broken the record 11 times.

One of the main reasons that the javelin record has been broken so often is that new specifications were introduced in 1999–the record has been broken 13 times since the new specifications.

Top 10 Men's outdoor world records broken most times*

	Event	Occasions record broken or equaled
1	Pole vault	20
2	Javelin	11
3 =	5,000 meters	10
=	10,000 meters	10
5 =	Decathlon	9
=	High jump	9
=	100 meters	9
8	4 x 100-meter relay	8
9	1,500 meters	7
10	3,000-meter steeplechase	6

* Outdoor world records at recognized Olympic events broken or equalled Jan. 1, 1981–Dec. 31, 2001

Sergey Bubka (USSR/Ukraine) broke 17 of the 20 pole vault world records.

New marks were set for the javelin in 1986 after a change in specifications. The world record has been broken eight times since the first record was established with the new specifications.

DID YOU KNOW? Jesse Owens set three different world records that each stood for more than 20 years, in the long jump, 100 meters, and 4 x 100-meter relay.

Top 10 Longest-standing men's outdoor world records*

	Athlete/country	Event	Date set
1	Jürgen Schult, East Germany	Discus	June 6, 1986
2	Yuriy Syedikh, USSR	Hammer	Aug. 30, 1986
3	Randy Barnes, US	Shot	May 20, 1990
4	Mike Powell, US	Long jump	Aug. 30, 1991
5	Kevin Young, US	400-meter hurdles	Aug. 6, 1992
6	Michael Marsh, Leroy Burrell, Dennis Mitchell, Carl Lewis, US	4 x 100-meter relay	Aug. 8, 1992
7	Javier Sotomayor, Cuba	High jump	July 27, 1993
8	Colin Jackson, UK	110-meter hurdles	Aug. 20, 1993
9	Jon Drummond, André Cason, Dennis Mitchell, Leroy Burrell, US	4 x 100-meter relay#	Aug. 21, 1993
10	Sergey Bubka, Ukraine	Pole vault	July 3, 1994

* As of January 1, 2002

\# Equaled world record

Top 10 Longest-standing women's outdoor world records*

	Athlete/country	Event	Date set
1	Jarmila Kratochvilova, Czechoslovakia	800 meters	July 26, 1983
2 =	Marita Koch, East Germany	400 meters	Oct. 6, 1985
=	Silke Möller, Sabine Günther, Ingrid Auerswald, Marlies Göhr, East Germany	4 x 100-meter relay	Oct. 6, 1985
4	Natalya Lisovskaya, USSR	Shot put	June 7, 1987
5	Stefka Kostadinova, Bulgaria	High jump	Aug. 30, 1987
6	Galina Chistyakova, USSR	Long jump	June 11, 1988
7	Gabriele Reinsch, East Germany	Discus	July 9, 1988
8	Florence Griffith-Joyner, US	100 meters	July 16, 1988
9	Yordanka Donkova, Bulgaria	100-meter hurdles	Aug. 20, 1988
10	Jackie Joyner-Kersee, US	Heptathlon	Sep. 24, 1988

* As of January 1, 2002

▼ Nazi propaganda had portrayed black people as inferior just before the 1936 Berlin Olympics. Jesse Owens proved them wrong with four gold medals.

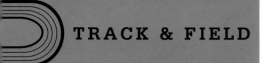

THE WORLD MILE RECORD

- Fastest milers of all time
- Fastest miles ever run
- Fastest miles ever run by a woman
- Fastest miles run in Oslo
- First athletes to run the mile in under four minutes
- Youngest men to set the world mile record
- First US runners to run a sub-four-minute mile

THE FOUR-MINUTE MILE

Within a little over two years of Roger Bannister's shattering the four-minute-mile barrier, the number of athletes to do so had risen to 10, although none had succeeded in taking more than two seconds off the record. The time has been progressively reduced in subsequent years, however, by athletes such as Sebastian Coe, Steve Ovett, and Noureddine Morceli. The current world record is held by Hicham El Guerrouj (Morocco), who, in 1999, brought the time down to 3 minutes 43.13 seconds.

Top 10 Fastest milers of all time*

	Athlete/country	Year	Time (min:sec)
1	Hicham El Guerrouj, Morocco	1999	3:43.13
2	Noah Ngeny, Kenya	1999	3:43.40
3	Noureddine Morceli, Algeria	1993	3:44.39
4	Steve Cram, UK	1985	3:46.32
5	Daniel Komen, Kenya	1997	3:46.38
6	Venuste Niyongabo, Burundi	1997	3:46.70
7	Said Aouita, Morocco	1987	3:46.76
8	Bernard Lagat, Kenya	2001	3:47.28
9	Sebastian Coe, UK	1981	3:47.33
10	Laban Rotich, Kenya	1997	3:47.65

* Outdoor records; based on best time of each athlete

Hicham El Guerrouj took the world mile record off Noureddine Morceli in Rome in 1999. A year earlier, also in Rome, he deprived Morceli of the 1,500-meter world record.

Top 10 Fastest miles ever run

	Athlete/country	Year	Time (min:sec)
1	Hicham El Guerrouj, Morocco	1999	3:43.13
2	Noah Ngeny, Kenya	1999	3:43.40
3	Noureddine Morceli, Algeria	1993	3:44.39
4	Hicham El Guerrouj	1998	3:44.60
5	Hicham El Guerrouj	1997	3:44.90
6	Hicham El Guerrouj	2001	3:44.95
7	Noureddine Morceli	1995	3:45.19
8	Hicham El Guerrouj	1997	3:45.64
9	Hicham El Guerrouj	2000	3:45.96
10	Hicham El Guerrouj	2000	3:46.24

When Hicham El Guerrouj set the new world mile record in 1999, the old world record was also beaten by the second-place finisher, 20-year-old Noah Ngeny of Kenya.

Top 10 Fastest miles ever run by a woman

	Athlete/country	Year	Time (min:sec)
1	Svetlana Masterkova, Russia	1996	4:12.56
2	Paula Ivan, Romania	1989	4:15.61
3	Natalya Artyomova, USSR	1984	4:15.80
4	Mary Slaney, US	1985	4:16.71
5	Natalya Artyomova, Russia	1991	4:17.00
6	Sonia O'Sullivan, Ireland	1994	4:17.25
7	Maricica Puica, Romania	1985	4:17.33
8	Maricica Puica, Romania	1982	4:17.44
9	Zola Pieterse (née Budd), UK	1985	4:17.47
10	Mary Slaney, US	1982	4:18.08

The only two milers on the above list to have won the Olympic title in the 1,500 meters are Paula Ivan in 1988 and Svetlana Masterkova in 1996.

Top 10 Fastest miles run in Oslo*

	Athlete/country	Date	Time (min:sec)
1	Hicham El Guerrouj, Morroco	July 4, 1997	3:44.90
2	Hicham El Guerrouj, Morocco	July 28, 2000	3:46.24
3	Steve Cram, UK	July 27, 1985	3:46.32
4	Laban Rotich, Kenya	July 4, 1997	3:47.65
5	Steve Scott, US	July 7, 1982	3:47.69
6	Noureddine Morceli, Algeria	July 10, 1993	3:47.78
7	José Luis González, Spain	July 27, 1985	3:47.79
8	John Kibowen, Kenya	July 4, 1997	3:47.88
9	William Chirchir, Kenya	July 28, 2000	3:47.94
10	Noureddine Morceli, Algeria	July 5, 1996	3:48.15

* At the Bislet Stadium, venue for many world records

Many world records have been set at the Bislet Stadium, but only three mile records have been set in Oslo, and all were by Britons: Steve Ovett, Sebastian Coe, and Steve Cram.

▶ Roger Bannister crosses the finishing line at Iffley Road Track, Oxford, England, on May 6, 1954, unaware that he had become the first man to run the mile in under four minutes.

◀ Roger Bannister (right) with the world mile record-holder Hicham El Guerrouj.

The 10 First athletes to run the mile in under four minutes

	Athlete/country	Venue	Time (min:sec)	Date
1	Roger Bannister, UK	Oxford, England	3:59.4	May 6, 1954
2	John Landy, Australia	Turku, Finland	3:57.9	June 21, 1954
3	Laszlo Tabori, Hungary	London, England	3:59.0	May 28, 1955
4 =	Chris Chataway, UK	London, England	3:59.8	May 28, 1955
=	Brian Hewson, UK	London, England	3:59.8	May 28, 1955
6	Jim Bailey, Australia	Los Angeles, CA	3:58.6	May 5, 1956
7	Gunnar Nielsen, Denmark	Compton, CA	3:59.1	June 1, 1956
8	Ron Delany, Ireland	Compton, CA	3:59.4	June 1, 1956
9	Derek Ibbotson, UK	London, England	3:59.4	Aug. 6, 1956
10	István Rózsavölgyi, Hungary	Budapest, Hungary	3:59.0	Aug. 26, 1956

Chris Chataway, fourth equal in this list, was runner-up to Roger Bannister when he broke the four-minute barrier. Chataway was also in second place behind John Landy when he became the next man to run the distance in less than four minutes.

The only other occasion on which Bannister ran the mile in under four minutes was at the 1954 Vancouver Commonwealth Games when he beat Landy in what was heralded as the "Race of the Century." It certainly lived up to its billing, with Bannister winning in 3 min 58.8 sec to Landy's 3 min 59.6 sec.

Top 10 Youngest men to set the world mile record*

	Athlete/country	Date record set	Age (y:m:d)		
1	Jim Ryun, US	July 17, 1966	19	2	18
2	Herb Elliott, Australia	Aug. 6, 1958	20	5	9
3	Filbert Bayi, Tanzania	May 17, 1975	21	10	24
4	Sebastian Coe, UK	July 17, 1979	22	8	11
5	Peter Snell, New Zealand	Jan. 27, 1962	23	1	10
6	Noureddine Morceli, Algeria	Sep. 5, 1993	23	6	5
7	John Walker, New Zealand	Aug. 12, 1975	23	7	0
8	John Landy, Australia	June 21, 1954	24	2	9
9	Steve Ovett, UK	July 1, 1980	24	8	23
10	Steve Cram, UK	July 27, 1985	24	9	13

* Men's outdoor world records; based on age when they first set the record

The year before he set the world record in Dublin in 1958, Australia's Herb Elliott held the world junior records for the mile, 1,500 meters, two, and three miles. He ran his first mile at the age of 14 and won, in a race against many older boys, with a time of 5 minutes 35 seconds. On 25 January 1958, a month before his 20th birthday, he became the first teenager to run a mile in under four minutes, when he clocked a time of 3 minutes 59.9 at the Olympic Park in Melbourne.

The 10 First US runners to run a sub-four-minute mile

	Athlete	Time (min:sec)	Date
1	Don Bowden	3:58.7	June 1, 1957
2	Dyrol Burleson	3:58.6	Apr. 23, 1960
3	Jim Beatty	3:58.0	May 28, 1960
4	Jim Grelle	3:59.9	Apr. 28, 1962
5	Keith Forman	3:58.3	May 26, 1962
6	Cary Weisiger	3:59.3	May 26, 1962
7	Bill Dotson	3:59.0	June 23, 1962
8	Bob Seaman	3:58.07	Aug. 18, 1962
9	Tom O'Hara	3:59.2	Feb. 15, 1963
10	Archie San Romani	3:57.6	June 5, 1964

Apart from San Romani, three other United States runners broke the sub-four-minute barrier for the first time at the Compton Invitational Mile on June 5, 1964. One of them, in 8th place with a time of 3 min 59.0 sec, was 17-year-old Jim Ryun, who went on to become the greatest US miler of all time—and, at the age of 19 in 1966, the youngest man ever to hold the world mile record. He remains the only American to hold the record. He went into the Olympics as world record holder at 880 yards, 1,500 meters, and the mile, and was unbeaten over the two longer distances in three years, but illness just before the Games, combined with the effects of the high altitude of Mexico City, meant he had to settle for silver medal in the 1,500 meters.

MARATHONS

- Fastest winning times in the London Marathon
- Closest London Marathons
- Fastest winning times in the Boston Marathon
- Fastest winning times in the New York City Marathon

GOING THE DISTANCE

The now standard distance for the marathon of 26 miles 385 yards was adopted at the 1908 London Olympics. The race was from Windsor to the Olympic Stadium in Shepherd's Bush, London, England and measured 26 miles but to make sure the race concluded in front of the Royal Box, where King Edward VII was sitting, the athletes had to run a further 385 yards.

Top 10 Fastest winning times in the London Marathon

	Athlete/country	Year	Time (hr:min:sec)
1	Khalid Khannouchi, US	2002	2:05:38
2	Antonio Pinto, Portugal	2000	2:06:36
3	Abdelkader El Mouaziz, Morocco	2001	2:07:11
4	Antonio Pinto, Portugal	1997	2:07:55
5 =	Abel Anton, Spain	1998	2:07:57
=	Abdelkader El Mouaziz, Morocco	1999	2:07:57
7	Steve Jones, UK	1985	2:08:16
8	Dionicio Ceron, Mexico	1995	2:08:30
9	Dionicio Ceron, Mexico	1994	2:08:53
10	Douglas Wakiihuri, Kenya	1989	2:09:03

The first London Marathon was run in March 1981. It was the brainchild of former Olympic steeplechaser Chris Brasher after he had competed in the 1979 New York City Marathon. The women's record was set in 2002 when Britain's Paula Radcliffe won in 2 hr 18 min 56 sec.

Top 10 Closest London Marathons

Winning athlete/country	Runner-up athlete/country	Year	Winning margin (sec)
1 Dick Beardsley, US	–		
Inge Simonsen, Norway	–	1981	dead heat
2 Joyce Chepchumba, Kenya*	Liz McColgan, UK	1997	1
3 Antonio Pinto, Portugal	Stefano Baldini, Italy	1997	2
4 = Dionicio Ceron, Mexico	Steve Moneghetti, Australia	1995	3
= Eamonn Martin, UK	Isidro Rico, Mexico	1993	3
= Derartu Tulu, Ethiopia	Svetlana Zakharova, Russia	2001*	3
= Douglas Wakiihuri, Kenya	Steve Moneghetti, Australia	1989	3
8 Antonio Pinto, Portugal	Jan Huruk, Poland	1992	5
9 = Abel Anton, Spain	Abdelkadar El Mouaziz, Morocco	1998	10
= Khalid Khannouchi, US	Paul Tergat, Kenya	2002	10
= Malgorzata Sobanska, Poland	Manuela Machado, Portugal	1995*	10

* Women's race

The biggest winning margin was in the women's race at the inaugural London Marathon in 1981, when Joyce Smith (UK) won by 7 min 15 sec over Gillian Drake (New Zealand).

▶ Just a few of the thousands of runners in the London Marathon, going past the Tower of London.

> If you want to run a mile, then run a mile. If you want to experience another life, run a marathon.
>
> Emil Zatopek

Top 10 Fastest winning times in the Boston Marathon

	Athlete/country	Year	Time (hr:min:sec)
1	Cosmas Ndeti, Kenya	1994	2:07:15
2	Andres Espinosa, Mexico	1994	2:07:19
3	Moses Tanui, Kenya	1998	2:07:34
4	Joseph Chebet, Kenya	1998	2:07:37
5	Rob de Castella, Australia	1986	2:07:51
6	Gert Thys, South Africa	1998	2:07:52
7	Jackson Kipngok, Kenya	1994	2:08:08
8	Hwang Young-Cho, Korea	1994	2:08:09
9	Ibrahim Hussein, Kenya	1992	2:08:14
10	Gelindo Bordin, Italy	1990	2:08:19

The women's record was set in 1994 when Uta Pippig of Germany won in 2 hr 21 min and 45 sec.

Top 10 Fastest winning times in the New York City Marathon

	Athlete/country	Year	Time (hr:min:sec)
1	Tesfaye Jifar, Ethiopia	2001	2:07:43
2	Juma Ikangaa, Tanzania	1989	2:08:01
3	John Kagwe, Kenya	1997	2:08:12
4	Alberto Salazar, US	1981	2:08:13
5	Steve Jones, UK	1988	2:08:20
6	John Kagwe, Kenya	1998	2:08:45
7	Rod Dixon, New Zealand	1983	2:08:59
8	Joseph Chebet, Kenya	1999	2:09:14
9	Salvador Garcia, Mexico	1991	2:09:28
10 =	Willie Mtolo, South Africa	1992	2:09:29
=	Alberto Salazar, US	1982	2:09:29

The women's record was also set in 2001 when Margaret Okayo of Kenya won in 2 hr 24 min and 21 sec.

GOLF

At the Start

It is arguable whether golf originated in the Netherlands, Belgium, or Scotland, but the earliest recorded reference dates from the latter in 1457, when King James II banned "gouf," along with "fute-ball." His successors, however, were golf enthusiasts—Mary, Queen of Scots was the earliest known female golfer. The first international game took place in Leith in 1682, when the Duke of York and a shoemaker beat two English noblemen. The Edinburgh Golfing Society was founded in Leith in 1735. The "Royal & Ancient" St. Andrews Club was founded in 1754, and the Blackheath Club in England in 1766. The first match was played in the United States in 1779, and the South Carolina Golf Club established in 1786. Golf has been played professionally since the 19th century.

THE RYDER CUP

- Most appearances in the Ryder Cup for Europe
- Most appearances in the Ryder Cup for the US
- European players with the most wins in the Ryder Cup
- American players with the most wins in the Ryder Cup
- Biggest winning matches in the Ryder Cup
- Biggest winning margins in the Ryder Cup

THE CUP'S ORIGINS

The Ryder Cup was launched in 1927 by British seed merchant and golf enthusiast Samuel Ryder (1858–1936). It is held every two years (with a break between 1939 and 1945 due to World War II), and the venues alternate between the United States and Europe. The United States originally competed against Great Britain and Ireland, but since 1979 it has competed against Europe.

Top 10 Most appearances in the Ryder Cup for Europe

	Player/country*#	Years	Apps
1	Nick Faldo	1977-97	11
2	Christy O'Connor, Sr.	1955-73	10
3 =	Bernhard Langer, Germany	1981-97	9
=	Dai Rees	1937-61	9
5 =	Peter Alliss	1953-69	8
=	Seve Ballesteros, Spain	1979-85	8
=	Neil Coles	1961-77	8
=	Bernard Gallacher	1969-83	8
=	Bernard Hunt	1953-69	8
=	Sam Torrance	1981-95	8
=	Ian Woosnam	1983-97	8

* Great Britain & Ireland up to 1977

\# All UK unless otherwise stated

Alf Padgham (1933, 1935, 1937), John Panton (1951, 1953, 1961), and Alf Perry (1933, 1935, 1937) all played in three Ryder Cups without winning a match, a feat no US golfer has equaled.

Top 10 Most appearances in the Ryder Cup for the US

	Player	Years	Apps
1 =	Billy Casper	1961-75	8
=	Ray Floyd	1969-93	8
=	Lanny Wadkins	1977-93	8
4 =	Gene Littler	1961-75	7
=	Sam Snead	1937-59	7
6 =	Tom Kite	1979-93	6
=	Jack Nicklaus	1969-81	6
=	Arnold Palmer	1961-73	6
=	Gene Sarazen	1927-37	6
=	Lee Trevino	1969-81	6

Two of Sam Snead's seven appearances were as captain: in 1951 in Pinehurst, North Carolina, and in 1959 at Eldorado Country Club, Palm Springs, California. On both occasions, he led the United States to victory, winning both his matches in 1951 and winning one and halving the other in 1959. He was also the nonplaying captain in 1969.

Top 10 European players with the most wins in the Ryder Cup

	Player/country*#	Wins
1	Nick Faldo	23
2	Seve Ballesteros, Spain	20
3	Bernhard Langer	18
4	José Maria Olázabal, Spain	15
5 =	Peter Oosterhuis	14
=	Ian Woosnam	14
7 =	Bernard Gallacher	13
=	Tony Jacklin	13
9 =	Neil Coles	12
=	Colin Montgomerie	12

* Great Britain & Ireland up to 1977

\# All UK unless otherwise stated

Nick Faldo and Peter Oosterhuis have each won a record six singles matches in the Ryder Cup. Peter Oosterhuis beat Arnold Palmer in the singles in each of his first two Ryder Cup matches. Nick Faldo's first singles win was over Tom Watson in 1977, and both Faldo and Oosterhuis have beaten Johnny Miller in singles matches.

Top 10 American players with the most wins in the Ryder Cup

	Player	Wins
1	Arnold Palmer	22
2 =	Billy Casper	20
=	Lanny Wadkins	20
4 =	Jack Nicklaus	17
=	Lee Trevino	17
6	Tom Kite	15
7	Gene Littler	14
8	Hale Irwin	13
9	Ray Floyd	12
10 =	Sam Snead	10
=	Tom Watson	10

Arnold Palmer, Billy Casper, Sam Snead, and Lee Trevino have each won a record six singles matches for the US. Arnold Palmer's first Ryder Cup match was in the foursomes with Billy Casper in 1961. They beat Dai Rees and Ken Bousfield 2 & 1. Palmer's first singles was the same year when he halved with Peter Alliss. He bowed out by losing 4 & 2 to Peter Oosterhuis in 1973 at Muirfield Golf Course in Scotland.

Top 10 Biggest winning matches in the Ryder Cup

	Match	Year	Margin
1	George Duncan beat Walter Hagen (US)	1929	10 & 8
2 =	Walter Hagen/Denny Shute (US) beat George Duncan/Arthur Havers	1931	10 & 9
=	Ed Oliver/Lew Worsham (US) beat Henry Cotton/Arthur Lees	1947	10 & 9
4	Fred Daly beat Ted Kroll (US)	1953	9 & 7
5 =	Leo Diegel (US) beat Abe Mitchell	1929	9 & 8
=	Abe Mitchell beat Olin Dutra (US)	1933	9 & 8
=	Paul Runyan/Horton Smith (US) beat Bill Cox/Edward Jarman	1935	9 & 8
8 =	Johnny Farrell/Jim Turnesa (US) beat George Duncan/Archie Compston	1927	8 & 6
=	Denny Shute (US) beat Bert Hodson	1931	8 & 6
=	Charles Whitcombe beat Johnny Farrell (US)	1929	8 & 6

The biggest winning margins since 1953 occurred in 1987 when Tom Kite (US) beat Howard Clark 8 & 7, and in 1997 when Fred Couples (US) beat Ian Woosnam 8 & 7. The 1929 Ryder Cup—the first on British soil—was not only notable for the first UK win, but also produced some high-scoring matches. The United States led by one point going into the singles and it was the "Battle of the Captains," George Duncan versus Walter Hagen, that saw the UK skipper win 10 & 8 and set his side on the way to victory. Charles Whitcombe beat Johnny Farrell 10 & 8, Archie Compston beat Gene Sarazen 6 & 4, and victory was secured for the home team when 22-year-old newcomer Henry Cotton beat Al Watrous 4 & 3.

Top 10 Biggest winning margins in the Ryder Cup

	Winners	Score	Year	Winning captain	Margin
1	US	23½–8½	1967	Ben Hogan	15
2	US	23–9	1963	Arnold Palmer	14
3 =	US	11–1	1947	Ben Hogan	10
=	US	21–11	1975	Arnold Palmer	10
5	US	18½–9½	1981	Dave Marr	9
6 =	US	9½–2½	1951	Sam Snead	7
=	US	19½–12½	1965	Byron Nelson	7
8 =	US	9–3	1931	Walter Hagen	6
=	US	9–3	1935	Walter Hagen	6
=	US	19–13	1973	Jack Burke	6
=	US	17–11	1979	Billy Casper	6

The biggest winning margin by either the British or the European team was in 1985 when Europe, captained by Tony Jacklin, won 16½–11½. Five men played in the United States' two biggest wins of 1963 and 1967. They were: Arnold Palmer, Johnny Pott, Billy Casper, Julius Boros, and Gene Littler.

▼ European team captain Seve Ballesteros proudly holds the trophy after victory over the US in the Ryder Cup at the Valderrama Golf Cub in Sotogrande, Spain, in 1997.

TOURNAMENT & MONEY WINNERS

- Players with the most wins on the US Tour in a career
- Most wins on the US Tour in a calendar year
- Career money-winners on the US Seniors Tour
- Career money-winners on the European PGA Tour
- Career money-winners of all time
- Career earnings by women

> It's nice to have the opportunity to play for so much money, but it's nicer to win.
> **Patty Sheenan**

Top 10 Players with the most wins on the US Tour in a career

	Player*	Tour wins
1	Sam Snead	81
2	Jack Nicklaus	70
3	Ben Hogan	63
4	Arnold Palmer	60
5	Byron Nelson	52
6	Billy Casper	51
7 =	Walter Hagen	40
=	Cary Middlecoff	40
9	Gene Sarazen	38
10	Lloyd Mangrum	36

* All US

For many years, Sam Snead's total number of career wins was put at 84. However, the PGA Tour amended this figure in 1990 after discrepancies were found in their previous lists. They deducted 11 wins from his total, but added eight others that should have been included, giving a revised total of 81.

The most successful woman on the US Women's Tour is Kathy Whitworth, with 88 tour wins. The highest-placed overseas player is Gary Player (South Africa) with 22 wins.

Top 10 Most wins on the US Tour in a calendar year

	Player*	Year	Wins
1	Byron Nelson	1945	18
2	Ben Hogan	1946	13
3	Sam Snead	1950	11
4	Ben Hogan	1948	10
5 =	Paul Runyan	1933	9
=	Tiger Woods	2000	9
7 =	Harry Cooper	1937	8
=	Johnny Miller	1974	8
=	Byron Nelson	1944	8
=	Arnold Palmer	1960	8
=	Henry Picard	1939	8
=	Gene Sarazen	1930	8
=	Horton Smith	1929	8
=	Sam Snead	1938	8
=	Tiger Woods	1999	8

* All US

Having won eight Tour events in 1944, Byron Nelson shattered the US record the following year with a stunning 18 wins. His remarkable year included a run of 11 consecutive tournament wins, also a US record.

Top 10 Career money-winners on the US Seniors Tour

	Player/country*	Career winnings ($)#
1	Hale Irwin	13,921,874
2	Jim Colbert	10,553,940
3	Gil Morgan	9,749,317
4	Lee Trevino	9,426,642
5	Dave Stockton	9,140,870
6	Bob Charles, New Zealand	8,564,577
7	Ray Floyd	8,229,505
8	Larry Nelson	8,086,397
9	George Archer	8,000,911
10	Jim Dent	7,832,042

* All US unless otherwise stated
# As of the end of the 2001 season

Hale Irwin joined the Seniors Tour in 1995 after 20 victories on the regular Tour stretching from 1971 to 1994. After joining the Seniors, he won an additional 32 tournaments to the end of the 2001 season.

Top 10 Career money-winners on the European PGA Tour

	Player/country	Career winnings ($)*
1	Colin Montgomerie, Scotland	12,469,070
2	Bernhard Langer, Germany	9,244,335
3	Darren Clarke, Northern Ireland	8,474,129
4	Ian Woosnam, Wales	7,352,102
5	Lee Westwood, England	7,081,672
6	José Maria Olázabal, Spain	6,586,064
7	Ernie Els, South Africa	6,091,128
8	Retief Goosen, South Africa	5,927,409
9	Nick Faldo, England	5,802,977
10	Miguel Angel Jiménez, Spain	5,435,283

* As of the end of the 2001 season

Colin Montgomerie, who turned professional in 1987, first topped the European money list in 1993, and was number one for the following six seasons.

◀ Prior to the arrival of Tiger Woods, the last man to show anything like domination of world golf was Jack Nicklaus.

Top 10 Career money-winners of all time

	Player/country*	Career winnings ($)#
1	Tiger Woods	26,191,227
2	Davis Love III	17,994,690
3	Phil Mickelson	17,837,998
4	David Duval	15,312,553
5	Scott Hoch	14,553,202
6	Vijay Singh, Fiji	14,524,452
7	Nick Price, Zimbabwe	14,477,425
8	Hal Sutton	13,885,946
9	Mark Calcavecchia	13,409,349
10	Greg Norman, Australia	13,344,142

* All US unless otherwise stated

\# As of the end of the 2001 season

Tiger Woods turned professional in August 1996 and won nearly $800,000 in just eight tournaments in his rookie year. The following year he was top money winner with over $2,000,000, and in 2000 won a record $9,188,320.

▶ Not only a top money-winner but also a low scorer—in the 2001 Standard Register Ping tournament at Moon Valley, Phoenix, Annika Sorenstam shot a record 13 under par 59.

Top 10 Career earnings by women

	Player/country*	Career winnings (£)#
1	Annika Sorenstam, Sweden	8,306,464
2	Karrie Webb, Australia	7,698,299
3	Betsy King	7,187,444
4	Dottie Pepper	6,658,613
5	Juli Inkster	6,512,487
6	Beth Daniel	6,433,001
7	Meg Mallon	5,954,573
8	Pat Bradley	5,743,605
9	Laura Davies, UK	5,695,525
10	Rosie Jones	5,683,934

* All US unless otherwise stated

\# As of the end of the 2001 season

Annika Sorenstam won more tournaments on the US LPGA Tour in the 1990s than anyone else—18. She is also one of only two women to win $1,000,000 in a season on three occasions; Karrie Webb is the other.

THE MAJOR RECORDS

- Biggest winning margins in the Majors

- Most frequent runners-up in the Majors

- Players to win the most Majors in a career

- Lowest four-round totals in the Majors

Top 10 Biggest winning margins in the Majors

	Player/country	Year	Tournament	Venue	Winning margin
1	Tiger Woods, US	2000	US Open	Pebble Beach	15
2	Tom Morris, Sr., UK	1862	British Open	Prestwick	13
3 =	Tom Morris, Jr., UK	1870	British Open	Prestwick	12
=	Tiger Woods, US	1997	US Masters	Augusta	12
5	Willie Smith, US	1899	US Open	Baltimore	11
6 =	Jim Barnes, US	1921	US Open	Columbia	9
=	Jack Nicklaus, US	1965	US Masters	Augusta	9
8 =	James Braid, UK	1908	British Open	Prestwick	8
=	Ray Floyd, US	1976	US Masters	Augusta	8
=	J. H. Taylor, UK	1900	British Open	St. Andrews	8
=	J. H. Taylor, UK	1913	British Open	Hoylake	8
=	Tiger Woods, US	2000	British Open	St. Andrews	8

The biggest winning margin in the other Major, the US PGA Championship, was in 1980, when Jack Nicklaus won by seven strokes over Andy Bean at Oak Hill.

THE FOUR MAJORS

The four Majors are the British Open, the US Open, the US Masters, and the US PGA. The oldest is the British Open, first played at Prestwick in 1860 and won by Willie Park. The youngest of the four Majors is the US Masters, played over the beautiful Augusta National course in Georgia. Entry is by invitation only, and the first winner was Horton Smith in 1934.

◄ One of golf's first greats, Tom Morris, Sr. He and his son, "Young Tom," together won eight British Open titles.

Top 10 Most frequent runners-up in the Majors

	Player/country*	British Open	US Open	US PGA	US Masters	Total
1	Jack Nicklaus	7	4	4	4	19
2	Arnold Palmer	1	4	3	2	10
3 =	Greg Norman, Australia	1	2	2	3	8
=	Sam Snead	0	4	2	2	8
5 =	J. H. Taylor, UK	6	1	0	0	7
=	Tom Watson	1	2	1	3	7
7 =	Ben Hogan	0	2	0	4	6
=	Byron Nelson	0	1	3	2	6
=	Gary Player, South Africa	0	2	2	2	6
=	Harry Vardon, UK	4	2	0	0	6

* All US unless otherwise stated

In addition to the four players above, the only other player to finish as runner-up in all four Majors was Craig Wood (US).

Top 10 Players to win the most Majors in a career

	Player/country*	British Open	US Open	US PGA	US Masters	Total
1	Jack Nicklaus	3	4	5	6	18
2	Walter Hagen	4	2	5	0	11
3 =	Ben Hogan	1	4	2	2	9
=	Gary Player, South Africa	3	1	2	3	9
5	Tom Watson	5	1	0	2	8
6 =	Bobby Jones	3	4	0	0	7
=	Arnold Palmer	2	1	0	4	7
=	Gene Sarazen	1	2	3	1	7
=	Sam Snead	1	0	3	3	7
=	Harry Vardon, UK	6	1	0	0	7
=	Tiger Woods, US	1	1	2	3	7

* All US unless otherwise stated

No man has won all four Majors in one year. Ben Hogan, in 1953, won three of the four, but did not compete in the PGA Championship. Bobby Jones achieved a unique Grand Slam in 1930 by winning the British Open and US Open, as well as winning the amateur titles in both countries.

Top 10 Lowest four-round totals in the Majors

	Player/country	Venue	Year	Total
1	David Toms, US	Atlanta	2001*	265
2	Phil Mickelson, US	Atlanta	2001*	266
3 =	Steve Elkington, Australia	Riviera	1995*	267
=	Colin Montgomerie, UK	Riviera	1995*	267
=	Greg Norman, Australia	Royal St. George's, Sandwich	1993#	267
6 =	Steve Lowery, US	Atlanta	2001*	268
=	Nick Price, Zimbabwe	Turnberry	1994#	268
=	Tom Watson, US	Turnberry	1977#	268
9 =	Nick Faldo, UK	Royal St. George's, Sandwich	1993#	269
=	Davis Love III, US	Winged Foot	1997*	269
=	Jack Nicklaus, US	Turnberry	1977#	269
=	Jesper Parnevik, Sweden	Turnberry	1994#	269
=	Nick Price, Zimbabwe	Southern Hills	1994*	269
=	Tiger Woods, US	St. Andrews	1999#	269

* US PGA Championship
# British Open Championship

In the US Masters, the lowest four-round total is 270 by Tiger Woods (US) in Augusta, Georgia, 1997. In the US Open, the lowest four-round total is 272 by Jack Nicklaus (US) at Baltusrol Golf Club, Springfield, New Jersey, 1980, Lee Janzen (US) at Baltusrol, 1993, and Tiger Woods in Pebble Beach, California, 2000.

◄ Jose-Maria Olázabal of Spain at the 18th green, Augusta, 1995. It was not to be back-to-back Masters victories for the Spaniard as he lost his title to American Ben Crenshaw.

THE US MASTERS

- ● Biggest winning margins in the US Masters
- ● First players to hole in one at the US Masters
- ● Lowest winning totals in the US Masters
- ● Finishers in the first US Masters, 1934
- ● Players with the most US Masters titles

THE AUGUSTA COURSE

The US Masters, the brainchild of American amateur golfer Robert Tyre "Bobby" Jones, is the only Major played on the same course each year, in Augusta, Georgia. The course was built on the site of an old nursery, and the abundance of flowers, shrubs, and plants is a reminder of its former days, with each of the 18 holes named after the plants growing adjacent to it.

Top 10 Biggest winning margins in the US Masters

	Player/country*	Year	Score	Runner(s)-up*	Score	Margin
1	Tiger Woods	1997	270	Tom Kite	282	12
2	Jack Nicklaus	1965	271	Arnold Palmer, Gary Player, South Africa	280	9
3	Ray Floyd	1976	271	Ben Crenshaw	279	8
4	Arnold Palmer	1964	276	Dave Marr, Jack Nicklaus	282	6
5 =	Nick Faldo, UK	1996	276	Greg Norman, Australia	281	5
=	Claude Harmon	1948	279	Cary Middlecoff	284	5
=	Ben Hogan	1953	274	Porky Oliver	279	5
8 =	Seve Ballesteros, Spain	1980	275	Gibby Gilbert, Jack Newton, Australia	279	4
=	Seve Ballesteros, Spain	1983	280	Ben Crenshaw, Tom Kite	284	4
=	Jimmy Demaret	1940	280	Lloyd Mangrum	284	4
=	Bernhard Langer, Germany	1993	277	Chip Beck	281	4
=	Sam Snead	1952	286	Jack Burke, Jr.	290	4

* All US unless otherwise stated

Top 10 First players to hole in one at the US Masters

	Player/country*	Hole	Year
1	Ross Somerville#	16	1934
2	Willie Goggin	16	1935
3	Ray Billows#	16	1940
4	Claude Harmon	12	1947
5	John Dawson#	16	1949
6	Leland Gibson	6	1954
7	Billy Joe Patton#	6	1954
8	William Hyndman III#	12	1959
9	Clive Clark, UK	16	1968
10	Charles Coody	6	1972

* All US unless otherwise stated

Amateur

The only other occasion, apart from 1954 above, when two men holed in one at the same US Masters tournament was in 1992 when Jeff Sluman (US) aced the 4th and Corey Pavin (US) aced the 16th.

Top 10 Lowest winning totals in the US Masters

	Player/country*	Year	Score
1	Tiger Woods	1997	270
2 =	Ray Floyd	1976	271
=	Jack Nicklaus	1965	271
4	Tiger Woods	2001	272
5 =	Ben Crenshaw	1995	274
=	Ben Hogan	1953	274
7 =	Seve Ballesteros, Spain	1980	275
=	Fred Couples	1992	275
9 =	Nick Faldo, UK	1996	276
=	Jack Nicklaus	1975	276
=	Arnold Palmer	1964	276
=	Tom Watson	1977	276
=	Tiger Woods	2002	276

* All US unless otherwise stated

There isn't a flaw in his golf or his makeup. He will win more majors than Arnold Palmer and me combined.

Jack Nicklaus on Tiger Woods

Top 10 Finishers in the first US Masters, 1934

	Player	Round 1	Round 2	Round 3	Round 4	Total
1	Horton Smith	70	72	70	72	284
2	Craig Wood	71	74	69	71	285
3 =	Billy Burke	72	71	70	73	286
=	Paul Runyan	74	71	70	71	286
5	Ed Dudley	74	69	71	74	288
6	Willie MacFarlane	74	73	70	74	291
7 =	Al Espinosa	75	70	75	72	292
=	Jimmy Hines	70	74	74	74	292
=	Harold McSpaden	77	74	72	69	292
=	Macdonald Smith	74	70	74	74	292

Horton Smith sank a 20-foot birdie putt at the 17th and then parred the 18th to snatch victory by one stroke.

Top 10 Players with the most US Masters titles

	Player/country*	Years	Wins
1	Jack Nicklaus	1963, 1965–66, 1972, 1975, 1986	6
2	Arnold Palmer	1958, 1960, 1962, 1964	4
3 =	Jimmy Demaret	1940, 1947, 1950	3
=	Nick Faldo, UK	1989–90, 1996	3
=	Gary Player, South Africa	1961, 1974, 1978	3
=	Sam Snead	1949, 1952, 1954	3
=	Tiger Woods	1997, 2001–02	3
8 =	Seve Ballesteros, Spain	1980, 1983	2
=	Ben Crenshaw	1984, 1995	2
=	Ben Hogan	1951, 1953	2
=	Bernhard Langer, Germany	1985, 1993	2
=	Byron Nelson	1937, 1942	2
=	José Maria Olázabal, Spain	1994, 1999	2
=	Horton Smith	1934, 1936	2
=	Tom Watson	1977, 1981	2

* All US unless otherwise stated

◀ Not only did Tiger Woods win the 1997 US Masters with a record winning margin, he was also the youngest-ever winner of the event at 22 years 3 months.

GOLF

- Biggest winning margins in the British Open

- Most British Open titles

- All-time lowest four-round totals in the British Open

- Youngest winners of the British Open

> Any golfer worth his salt has to cross the sea and try to win the British Open.
>
> Jack Nicklaus

THE BRITISH OPEN

Top 10 Biggest winning margins in the British Open

	Player/country*	Year	Score	Runner(s)-up*	Score	Margin
1	Tom Morris, Sr.	1862	163	Willie Park	176	13
2	Tom Morris, Jr.	1870	149	Bob Kirk, David Strath	161	12
3 =	James Braid	1908	291	Tom Ball	299	8
=	J. H. Taylor	1900	309	Harry Vardon	317	8
=	J. H. Taylor	1913	304	Ted Ray	312	8
=	Tiger Woods, US	2000	269	Thomas Bjorn, Denmark Ernie Els, South Africa	277	8
7 =	Walter Hagen, US	1929	292	Johnny Farrell, US	298	6
=	Bobby Jones, US	1927	285	Aubrey Boomer Fred Robson	291	6
=	Johnny Miller, US	1976	279	Seve Ballesteros, Spain Jack Nicklaus, US	285	6
=	Arnold Palmer, US	1962	276	Kel Nagle, Australia	282	6
=	Harry Vardon	1903	300	Tom Vardon	306	6

* All UK unless otherwise stated

◀ J. H. Taylor (left), James Braid (center), and Harry Vardon. In the 21 years between 1894 and 1914, they won 16 British Open titles.

Most British Open titles

	Player/country	Years	Titles
1	Harry Vardon, UK	1896, 1898–99, 1903, 1911, 1914	6
2 =	James Braid, UK	1901, 1905–06, 1908, 1910	5
=	J. H. Taylor, UK	1894–95, 1900, 1909, 1913	5
=	Peter Thomson, Australia	1954–56, 1958, 1965	5
=	Tom Watson, US	1975, 1977, 1980, 1982–83	5
6 =	Walter Hagen, US	1922, 1924, 1928–29	4
=	Bobby Locke, South Africa	1949–50, 1952, 1957	4
=	Tom Morris, Sr., UK	1861–62, 1864, 1867	4
=	Tom Morris, Jr., UK	1868–70, 1872	4
=	Willie Park, Sr., UK	1860, 1863, 1866, 1875	4

The best total by a current tour player is three wins each by Seve Ballesteros (Spain) and Nick Faldo (UK).

▼ Tiger Woods on his way to winning his first British Open at St. Andrews. It was the second of three Majors for Woods in 2000.

All-time lowest four-round totals in the British Open

	Player/country	Venue	Year	Total
1	Greg Norman, Australia	Royal St. George's	1993	267
2 =	Nick Price, Zimbabwe	Turnberry	1994	268
=	Tom Watson, US	Turnberry	1977	268
4 =	Nick Faldo, UK	Royal St. George's	1993	269
=	Jack Nicklaus, US	Turnberry	1977	269
=	Jesper Parnevik, Sweden	Turnberry	1994	269
=	Tiger Woods, US	St. Andrews	2000	269
8 =	Nick Faldo, UK	St. Andrews	1990	270
=	Bernhard Langer, Germany	Royal St. George's	1993	270
10 =	Tom Lehman, US	Lytham	1996	271
=	Tom Watson, US	Muirfield	1980	271
=	Fuzzy Zoeller, US	Turnberry	1994	271

The first time the Open Championship was played over four rounds of 18 holes was at Muirfield in 1892, when the amateur Harold H. Hilton won with a total of 305. The record has kept falling since then and, at Turnberry in 1977, Tom Watson destroyed British Open records, winning with a record 268. This remained unbeaten until 1993, when Australia's Greg Norman became the first champion to shoot four rounds under 70 when he won with 267 at Sandwich. The lowest individual round is 63, which has been achieved by seven golfers: Mark Hayes (US), Turnberry 1977; Isao Aoki (Japan), Muirfield 1980; Greg Norman (Australia), Turnberry 1986; Paul Broadhurst (UK), St. Andrews 1990; Jodie Mudd (US), Royal Birkdale 1991; Nick Faldo (UK), Sandwich 1993; and Payne Stewart (US), Sandwich 1993.

Youngest winners of the British Open

	Player/country	Age (years:months)
1	Tom Morris Jnr., UK	17y 5m
2	Willie Auchterlonie, UK	21y 1m
3	Seve Ballesteros, Spain	22y 3m
4	John H. Taylor, UK	23y 3m
5	Gary Player, South Africa	23y 8m
6	Bobby Jones, US	24y 3m
7	Tiger Woods, US	24y 6m
8	Peter Thomson, Australia	24y 11m
9 =	Arthur Havers, UK	25y 0m
=	Tony Jacklin, UK	25y 0m

The ages of Arthur Havers and Tony Jacklin were an identical 25 years 5 days when they won the Open in 1923 and 1969, respectively. The dates of birth for Tom Kidd and Jack Simpson, the 1873 and 1884 winners, have never been established. Hugh Kirkaldy, the 1891 winner, was born in 1865 and could have been either 25 or 26 when he won the title but, again, his exact date of birth has never been confirmed.

THE US OPEN & THE US PGA

- Lowest winning totals in the US PGA Championship
- Biggest winning margins in the US Open
- Lowest rounds in the US Open
- Most wins in the US PGA Championship
- Best finishes by Sam Snead in the US Open

Top 10 Lowest winning totals in the US PGA Championship*

	Player/country#	Year	Venue	Score
1	David Toms	2001	Atlanta	265
2	Steve Elkington, Australia	1995	Riviera	267
3 =	Davis Love III	1997	Winged Foot	269
=	Nick Price, Zimbabwe	1994	Southern Hills	269
5	Tiger Woods	2000	Valhalla	270
6 =	Bobby Nichols	1964	Columbus	271
=	Vijay Singh, Fiji	1998	Sahalee	271
8 =	Paul Azinger	1993	Inverness Club, Toledo	272
=	Ray Floyd	1982	Southern Hills	272
=	David Graham, Australia	1979	Oakland Hills	272
=	Jeff Sluman	1988	Oak Tree	272

* Since 1958, when it became a stroke-play tournament

\# All US unless otherwise stated

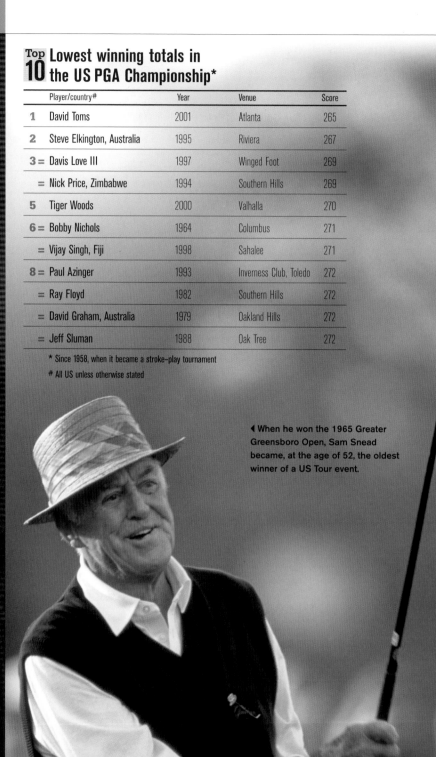

◀ When he won the 1965 Greater Greensboro Open, Sam Snead became, at the age of 52, the oldest winner of a US Tour event.

> Any player can win a US Open, but it takes a helluva player to win two.
> **Walter Hagen**

Top 10 Biggest winning margins in the US Open

	Player/country*	Year	Score	Runner(s)-up*	Score	Margin
1	Tiger Woods	2000	272	Miguel Angel Jimenez, Spain Ernie Els, South Africa	287	15
2	Willie Smith	1899	315	George Low, W. H. Way, Val Fitzjohn	326	11
3	Jim Barnes	1921	289	Walter Hagen, Fred McLeod	298	9
4 =	Fred Herd	1898	328	Alex Smith	335	7
=	Tony Jacklin, UK	1970	281	Dave Hill	288	7
=	Alex Smith	1906	295	Willie Smith	302	7
7 =	Laurie Auchterlonie	1902	307	Stewart Gardner, Walter J. Travis	313	6
=	Ralph Guldhal	1938	284	Dick Metz	290	6
=	Ben Hogan	1953	283	Sam Snead	289	6
10	Willie Anderson	1904	303	Gil Nicholls	308	5

*All US unless otherwise stated

In his record-breaking win, Woods opened with a first round 65 and led by one from Jimenez. One of only three men to break par in round two, Woods went six shots clear of Jimenez and Thomas Bjorn with a 69. He stretched his lead to 10 shots in round three, ahead of Ernie Els, and completed his 15-stroke winning margin with a final round 67.

Top 10 Most wins in the US PGA Championship

	Player/country*	Years	Wins
1 =	Walter Hagen	1921, 1924–27	5
=	Jack Nicklaus	1962, 1971, 1973, 1975, 1980	5
3 =	Gene Sarazen	1922–23, 1933	3
=	Sam Snead	1942, 1949, 1951	3
5 =	Jim Barnes	1916, 1919	2
=	Leo Diegel	1928–29	2
=	Ray Floyd	1969, 1982	2
=	Ben Hogan	1946, 1948	2
=	Byron Nelson	1940, 1945	2
=	Larry Nelson	1981, 1987	2
=	Gary Player, South Africa	1962, 1972	2
=	Nick Price, Zimbabwe	1992, 1994	2
=	Paul Runyan	1934, 1938	2
=	Denny Shute	1936–37	2
=	Dave Stockton	1970, 1976	2
=	Lee Trevino	1974, 1984	2
=	Tiger Woods	1999–2000	2

*All US unless otherwise stated

Top 10 Lowest rounds in the US Open*

	Player#	Years	Score
1 =	Johnny Miller	1973	63
=	Jack Nicklaus	1980	63
=	Tom Weiskopf	1980	63
4 =	Mark Brooks	2001	64
=	Keith Clearwater	1967	64
=	Ben Crenshaw	1981	64
=	Tommy Jacobs	1964	64
=	Peter Jacobsen	1988	64
=	Tom Kite	2001	64
=	Lee Mackey, Jr.	1950	64
=	Rives McBee	1966	64
=	Loren Roberts	1994	64
=	Vijay Singh, Fiji	2001	64
=	Curtis Strange	1989	64

*Over 18 holes, unless otherwise stated

All US unless otherwise stated

When Lee Mackey, Jr. became the first man to shoot a 64, he beat the three-year-old record of 65 set by James McHale, Jr. at St. Louis Country Club in 1947.

Top 10 Best finishes by Sam Snead in the US Open

	Venue	Year	Position
1 =	Oakland Hills	1937	2nd
=	Medinah	1949	Tied 2nd
=	St. Louis	1947	2nd
=	Oakmont	1953	2nd
5	The Olympic Club	1955	Tied 3rd
6 =	Philadelphia	1939	5th
=	Riviera	1948	5th
8 =	Inverness	1957	Tied 8th
=	Winged Foot	1959	Tied 8th
10	Oak Hill	1968	Tied 9th

Snead never won the US Open, despite winning all of the other three Majors. The closest he came to winning the title was in 1947, when he lost in a play-off to Lew Worsham by one shot. Snead had holed an 18-foot putt to earn the right to play off, but he missed from less than three feet on the last hole, costing him his one and only chance at the Open.

MISCELLANEOUS RECORDS

- Longest holes at St. Andrews
- Winners of women's Majors
- Winners of the World Cup
- Winners of the Vardon Trophy
- Winners of the US Women's Open

Top 10 Longest holes at St. Andrews*

	Hole name	Hole no.	Par	Yards
1	Long Hole	14	5	523
2	Hole o'Cross (out)	5	5	514
3	Road Hole	17	4	461
4	Ginger Beer	4	4	419
5	Dyke	2	4	411
6	Cartgate (in)	15	4	401
7	Hole o'Cross (in)	13	4	398
8	Heathery (out)	6	4	374
9	Burn	1	4	370
10	High Hole (out)	7	4	359

* Old (Championship) course

St. Andrews is unquestionably the "home" of golf, and the game was first recorded as being played there in 1552. The Society of St. Andrews Golfers was formed in 1754 and the original course was laid out alongside St. Andrews Bay. It consisted of 22 holes, but with only 12 huge greens. It is now a par-72 course measuring 6,566 yards. There are five 18-hole courses at St. Andrews: the Old Course, New Course, Jubilee, Eden, and Strathtyrum courses. There is also the 9-hole Balgove course. St. Andrews has hosted the Open Championship a record 26 times.

Top 10 Winners of women's Majors

	Player*	Titles
1	Patty Berg	16
2 =	Louise Suggs	13
=	Mickey Wright	13
4	Babe Zaharias	12
5 =	Juli Inkster#	9
=	Betsy Rawls	8
7	JoAnne Carner#	7
8 =	Pat Bradley#	6
=	Betsy King#	6
=	Patty Sheehan#	6
=	Glenna C. Vare	6
=	Kathy Whitworth	6

* All US

\# Current player

The present-day Majors are the US Open, LPGA Championship, Nabisco Championship, British Open, and the amateur championships of both the United States and Great Britain. Also taken into account in this Top 10 list are wins in the former Majors: the Western Open (1937–67), Titleholders Championship (1930–72), and the Du Maurier Classic (1977–2000).

▶ Australia's Karrie Webb during the 2001 US Women's Open at Pine Needles Lodge and Golf Club. Webb went on to win by eight strokes over Se Ri Pak.

> Don't play too much golf. Two rounds a day are plenty.
> Harry Vardon

DID YOU KNOW? Only three men have won both the British Open and the British Amateur Championship: John Ball (UK), Bobby Jones (US), and Harold Hilton (UK).

Top 10 Winners of the World Cup

	Country	Years	Wins
1	United States	1955-56, 1960-64, 1966-67, 1969, 1971, 1973, 1975, 1978-79, 1983, 1988, 1992-95, 1999-2000	23
2 =	Australia	1954, 1959, 1970, 1989	4
=	South Africa	1965, 1974, 1996, 2001	4
=	Spain	1976-77, 1982, 1984	4
5	Canada	1968, 1980, 1985	3
6	Ireland	1958, 1997	2
7 =	Argentina	1953	1
=	England	1998	1
=	Germany	1990	1
=	Japan	1957	1
=	Sweden	1991	1
=	Taiwan	1972	1
=	Wales	1987	1

The first World Cup, then known as the Canada Cup, was contested in 1953 at Beaconfield Golf Club, Montreal, and was won by Argentina. The trophy was the brainchild of Canadian industrialist John Jay Hopkins, who donated the trophy to be contested by two-man teams of professional golfers who represented their country. Its name was changed to the World Cup in 1967, and in 2000 it became the EMC World Cup. There were no tournaments in 1981 and 1986.

Top 10 Winners of the Vardon Trophy

	Player/country*	Years	Wins
1 =	Billy Casper	1960, 1963, 1965-66, 1968	5
=	Lee Trevino	1970-72, 1974, 1980	5
3 =	Arnold Palmer	1961-62, 1964, 1967	4
=	Sam Snead	1938, 1949-50, 1955	4
5 =	Ben Hogan	1940-41, 1948	3
=	Greg Norman, Australia	1989-90, 1994	3
=	Tom Watson	1977-79	3
=	Tiger Woods	1999, 2000-01	3
9 =	Fred Couples	1991-92	2
=	Bruce Crampton, Australia	1973, 1975	2
=	Tom Kite	1981-82	2
=	Lloyd Mangrum	1951, 1953	2
=	Nick Price, Zimbabwe	1993, 1997	2

* All US unless otherwise stated

Inaugurated in 1937, the Vardon Trophy was awarded until 1941 on a point system, but since then has been awarded by the US PGA to the player on the regular tour with the lowest scoring average. The first winner was Harry Cooper. The trophy is named after six-time British Open winner Harry Vardon, who also won the US Open in 1900. The first man to win with an average under 70 was Jimmy Demaret in 1947 (69.90). Greg Norman, in 1994, was the first player to win with less than 69 (68.81), while Tiger Woods won it in 2000 with the first average under 68 (67.79).

Top 10 Winners of the US Women's Open

	Player*	Years	Titles
1 =	Betsy Rawls	1951, 1953, 1957, 1960	4
=	Mickey Wright	1958-59, 1961, 1964	4
3 =	Susie Berning	1968, 1972-73	3
=	Hollis Stacy	1977-78, 1984	3
=	Babe Zaharias	1948, 1950, 1954	3
6 =	Donna Caponi	1969-70	2
=	JoAnne Carner#	1971, 1976	2
=	Betsy King#	1989-90	2
=	Patty Sheehan#	1992, 1994	2
=	Annika Sorenstam, Sweden#	1995-96	2
=	Louise Suggs	1949, 1952	2
=	Karrie Webb#	2000-01	2

* All US unless otherwise stated

\# Current player

At the Start

One of man's most primitive means of attack and defense, fistfighting, developed as a sport some 6,000 years ago. It was added to the Olympic Games in 688 BC, when a fighter called Onomastus of Smyrna emerged as the first champion. As spikes and studs were attached to the hands, the sport became ever more akin to gladiatorial contests and was banned in medieval Europe. Bare-knuckle fighting was revived in England in the 17th century, and the first recorded match in the United Kingdom took place in 1681, when the Duke of Albemarle organized a bout between his butler and his butcher. In 1719, fight expert James Figg set up a boxing academy in London. The transition to gloved fighting and the introduction from 1867 of the Queensberry Rules mark the transition to the modern sport.

HEAVYWEIGHT BOXING

- First boxers to regain the World Heavyweight title
- Heaviest combined weight of boxers at a Championship fight
- Heaviest boxers to contest a World Heavyweight title fight
- Oldest World Heavyweight champions
- World Heavyweight champions with the best undefeated professional records

The 10 First boxers to regain the World Heavyweight title

	Boxer/country*	Lost to	Year	Won back from	Year
1	Floyd Patterson	Ingemar Johansson, Sweden	1959	Ingemar Johansson	1960
2	Muhammad Ali	Joe Frazier	1971	George Foreman	1974
3	Muhammad Ali	Leon Spinks	1978	Leon Spinks	1978
4	Tim Witherspoon	Pinklon Thomas	1984	Tony Tubbs	1986
5	Evander Holyfield	Riddick Bowe	1992	Riddick Bowe	1993
6	George Foreman	Muhammad Ali	1974	Michael Moorer	1994
7	Michael Moorer	George Foreman	1994	Axel Schulz, Germany	1996
8	Mike Tyson	James "Buster" Douglas	1990	Frank Bruno, UK	1996
9	Evander Holyfield	Michael Moorer	1994	Mike Tyson	1996
10	Lennox Lewis, UK	Oliver McCall	1994	Oliver McCall	1997

* All US unless otherwise stated

Floyd Patterson had an interesting career as the world heavyweight champion. He became the youngest-ever champion when he beat Archie Moore for the vacant title in 1956. His opponent in his second defense of the title was Pete Rademacher, who was making his professional debut in the fight. In June 1960, Patterson became the first man to regain the title by beating Sweden's Ingemar Johansson, the man who had taken his title from him a year earlier. He lost his title with a first-round knockout by Sonny Liston in 1962.

Top 10 Heaviest combined weight of boxers at a Championship fight

	Boxers*/weight (lb)	Date	Combined weight (lb)
1	Lennox Lewis (247) vs. Michael Grant (250)	Apr. 29, 2000	497
2	Primo Carnera (259½) vs. Paulino Uzcudun (229¼)	Oct. 22, 1933	488¾
3 =	Lennox Lewis (251) vs. Oliver McCall (237)	July 2, 1997	488
=	Lennox Lewis (244) vs. Andrew Golota (244)	Oct. 14, 1997	488
5	Riddick Bowe (243) vs. Michael Dokes (244)	Feb. 6, 1993	487
6	Lennox Lewis (242) vs. Henry Akinwande (237½)	July 12, 1997	479½
7	George Foreman (256) vs. Axel Schulz (221)	Apr. 22, 1995	477
8	Max Baer (209½) vs. Primo Carnera (263¼)	June 14, 1934	472¾
9	George Foreman (250) vs. Michael Moorer (222)	Nov. 5, 1994	472
10 =	Tim Witherspoon (227) vs. Tony Tubbs (244)	Jan. 17, 1986	471
=	Lennox Lewis (243) vs. Shannon Briggs (228)	Mar. 28, 1998	471

* Winner first; all US except: Lennox Lewis (UK), Primo Carnera (Italy), Paulino Uzcudun (Spain), Henry Akinwande (UK), and Axel Schulz (Germany)

Lennox Lewis, who appears in the list on five occasions, never fought at less than 233 lb, his weight during his first defense of his WBC title in 1993 against Frank Bruno. The heaviest man to have boxed professionally was Jimmy Black (US) who weighed in at around 360 lb in the early 1970s. When he fought Claude McBride on June 1, 1971, the combined weight of the two men was 700 lb.

GOING THE DISTANCE

The last world heavyweight title fight to go 15 rounds was when Michael Spinks beat Larry Holmes to retain his IBF title in Las Vegas on April 19, 1986. The last time a heavyweight contest went beyond 15 rounds was on April 5, 1915 when Jess Willard deprived Jack Johnson of his title amid controversy in Havana, Cuba, over 26 rounds.

> I'm not the greatest. I'm the double greatest. Not only do I knock 'em out, I pick the round.
>
> Muhammad Ali

Top 10 Heaviest boxers to contest a World Heavyweight title fight*

	Boxer/country#	Opponent#	Year	Weight (lb)
1	Primo Carnera†, Italy	Tommy Loughran	1934	270
2	George Foreman	Evander Holyfield†	1991	257
3	Abe Simon	Joe Louis†	1942	255½
4	Leroy Jones	Larry Holmes†	1980	254½
5	Lennox Lewis, UK	Hasim Rahman†	2001	253
6 =	Buddy Baer	Joe Louis†	1942	250
=	Michael Grant	Lennox Lewis†, UK	2000	250
8	Frank Bruno†, UK	Oliver McCall	1995	248
9	Lennox Lewis†, UK	Hasim Rahman	2001	246½
10 =	Riddick Bowe	Evander Holyfield†	1993	246
=	James "Buster" Douglas	Evander Holyfield†	1990	246

* Based on their heaviest weight at which they fought
# All US unless otherwise stated
† Winner

Top 10 Oldest World Heavyweight champions*

	Boxer/country#	Date of win	Age (yr:mth:days)
1	George Foreman†	Nov. 5, 1994	46:9:14
2	Evander Holyfield†	Aug. 12, 2000	37:9:13
3	Jersey Joe Walcott	July 18, 1951	37:6:5
4	Muhammad Ali†	Sept. 15, 1978	36:7:29
5	Lennox Lewis†, UK	Nov. 17, 2001	36:2:15
6	Evander Holyfield†	Nov. 9, 1996	34:0:21
7	Bob Fitzsimmons, UK	Mar. 17, 1897	33:9:24
8	Frank Bruno, UK	Sept. 2, 1995	33:9:16
9	Trevor Berbick, Jamaica	Mar. 22, 1986	33:7:21
10	Jess Willard	Apr. 5, 1915	33:3:7

* Based on age when they first won or regained world title
# All US unless otherwise stated
† Age at time of regaining title

Jersey Joe Walcott is the oldest man to have won the title for the first time.

Top 10 World Heavyweight champions with the best undefeated professional records*

	Boxer/country#	Year of first title	Record W-L-D
1	Rocky Marciano	1952	43-0-0
2	George Foreman	1973	37-0-0
3	Frans Botha†, South Africa	1995	36-0-0
4	Michael Moorer	1994	35-0-0
5	Riddick Bowe	1992	32-0-0
6 =	Larry Holmes	1978	28-0-0
=	Michael Spinks	1985	28-0-0
=	Mike Tyson	1986	28-0-0
9	Michael Dokes	1982	26-0-1
10 =	Joe Frazier§	1970	25-0-0
=	Evander Holyfield	1990	25-0-0

* When they won their first heavyweight title
# All US unless otherwise stated
† Botha was stripped of the IBF title shortly after winning it from Axel Schulz of Germany in December 1995 because of illegal use of steroids
§ When Frazier won the New York version of the title in 1968, his record was 21-0-0

▶ Rocky Marciano, "The Brockton Blockbuster," retired as undefeated world heavyweight champion in 1955 with a record of 49 wins from 49 fights.

BOXING

- Attendances at World Heavyweight title fights
- Last fights of Muhammad Ali
- Shortest World Heavyweight title fights
- Last bare-knuckle champions
- Most wins in World Heavyweight title fights

> Honey, I forgot to duck.
>
> **Jack Dempsey** to his wife, after his 1926 defeat by Gene Tunney

HEAVYWEIGHT CHAMPIONS

Top 10 Attendances at World Heavyweight title fights

	Fight	Venue	Date	Attendance
1	Jack Dempsey vs. Gene Tunney	Philadelphia	Sept. 23, 1926	120,757
2	Jack Dempsey vs. Gene Tunney	Chicago	Sept. 22, 1927	104,943
3	Jack Dempsey vs. Luis Angel Firpo	New York	Sept. 14, 1923	82,000
4	Georges Carpentier vs. Jack Dempsey	Jersey City	July 2, 1921	80,183
5	Max Schmeling vs. Jack Sharkey	New York	June 12, 1930	79,222
6	Joe Louis vs. Max Schmeling	New York	June 22, 1938	70,043
7	Muhammad Ali vs. George Foreman	Kinshasa, Zaïre	Oct. 30, 1974	65,000
8	Muhammad Ali vs. Leon Spinks	New Orleans	Sept. 15, 1978	63,350
9	Primo Carnera vs. Joe Louis	New York	June 25, 1935	62,000
10	Max Schmeling vs. Jack Sharkey	Long Island	June 21, 1932	61,863

The Jack Dempsey–Gene Tunney contest at Soldier Field, Chicago, in 1927 was notable for the famous "Battle of the Long Count" in which Tunney was floored in the seventh round. Dempsey stood over him while the timekeeper commenced the count, but the referee would not start until Dempsey had moved to a neutral corner. When he did so, the referee started counting. Tunney got up on the count of nine–a full 14 seconds after the timekeeper had started the count.

The 10 Last fights of Muhammad Ali

	Opponent	Venue	Decision	Title(s)	Date
1	Trevor Berbick	Nassau, Bahamas	Lost points 10	None	Dec. 11, 1981
2	Larry Holmes	Las Vegas	Lost TKO 11	WBC	Oct. 2, 1980
3	Leon Spinks	New Orleans	Won points 15	WBA	Sept. 15, 1978
4	Leon Spinks	Las Vegas	Lost points 15	WBA/WBC	Feb. 15, 1978
5	Earnie Shavers	New York	Won points 15	WBA/WBC	Sept. 29, 1977
6	Alfredo Evangelista	Landover, Maryland	Won points 15	WBA/WBC	May 16, 1977
7	Ken Norton	New York	Won points 15	WBA/WBC	Sept. 28, 1976
8	Richard Dunn	Munich, Germany	Won TKO 5	WBA/WBC	May 24, 1976
9	Jimmy Young	Landover, Maryland	Won points 15	WBA/WBC	Apr. 30, 1976
10	Jean-Pierre Coopman	San Juan, Puerto Rico	Won KO 5	WBA/WBC	Feb. 20, 1976

Ali's fight with Earnie Shavers at Madison Square Garden in 1977 made history as the first championship bout to have a female judge, Eva Shain.

Ali's last opponent, Jamaican-born Trevor Berbick, had a brief spell as World Heavyweight champion. Having lost to Larry Holmes on points in Las Vegas in 1981, he captured the WBC version of the title five years later by beating Pinklon Thomas on points over 12 rounds. He held the title for just eight months before losing it to Mike Tyson in just two rounds.

◀ Lennox Lewis, the UK's first World Heavyweight champion of the 20th century and the first since Bob Fitzsimmons in 1899.

The 10 Shortest World Heavyweight title fights

	Winner/country*	Loser/country*	Date	Duration (secs)
1	Mike Dokes	Mike Weaver	Dec. 10, 1982	63
2	Tommy Burns, Canada	Jem Roche, Ireland	Mar. 17, 1908	88
3	Mike Tyson	Michael Spinks	June 27, 1988	91
4	Mike Tyson	Carl Williams	July 21, 1989	93
5	Lennox Lewis, UK	Andrew Golota	Oct. 4, 1997	95
6	Joe Frazier	Dave Zyglewicz	Apr. 22, 1969	96
7	Mike Tyson	Bruce Seldon	Nov. 9, 1996	109
8	Muhammad Ali	Sonny Liston	May 25, 1965	112
9	George Foreman	Joe Roman, Puerto Rico	Sept. 1, 1973	120
10	Riddick Bowe	Michael Dokes	Feb. 6, 1993	139

* All US unless otherwise stated

▼ He claimed he was "The Greatest" and the rest of the world never argued with him. Muhammad Ali, formerly Cassius Clay.

The 10 Last bare-knuckle champions*

	Boxer/country	Nickname	Reign begins	Reign ends
1	John L. Sullivan, US	Boston Strong Boy	1882	1889
2	Paddy Ryan, US	–	1880	1882
3	Joe Goss, UK	–	1876	1880
4	Tom Allen, UK	–	1873	1876
5	Jem Mace, UK	The Gypsy	1870	1873
6	Mike McCoole, Ireland	The Deck Hand Champion	1869	1870
7	Tom King,* UK	–	1863	1869
8	Joe Coburn, Ireland	–	1863	1865
9	John Camel Heenan, US	The Benica Boy	1860	1863
10	John Morrissey, Ireland	Old Smoke	1853	1859

* To 1863 as Champions of America, since then as Champions of the World

Tom King beat John Heenan for the first world title in Wadhurst, England, on December 10, 1863, while Joe Coburn remained as the American champion. The last bare-knuckle contest for the world title was between John L. Sullivan and Jake Kilrain in Richburg, Mississippi, on July 8,1889.

Top 10 Most wins in World Heavyweight title fights

	Boxer/country*	Bouts	Wins
1	Joe Louis	27	26
2	Muhammad Ali/Cassius Clay	25	22
3	Larry Holmes	25	21
4	Lennox Lewis, UK	15	14
5 =	Tommy Burns, Canada	13	12
=	Mike Tyson	15	12
7 =	Joe Frazier	11	10
=	Evander Holyfield	15	10
=	Jack Johnson	11	10
10	Ezzard Charles	13	9

* All US unless otherwise stated

This list also represents the Top 10 most World Heavyweight title bouts, with the exception of Floyd Patterson (US) who would be in at 9th with 12 fights. James J. Jeffries, with eight wins from eight fights, represents the best record of boxers undefeated in World Heavyweight Championship fights.

- Boxing World Champions with the most consecutive successful defenses

- Most winners of the International Boxing Hall of Fame's Fighter of the Year award

- First Olympic champions to win professional world titles

- World Champions with the longest professional careers

BOXING GREATS

Top 10 Boxing World Champions with the most consecutive successful defenses*

	Boxer/country	Weight division	Years	Defenses
1	Joe Louis, US	Heavyweight#	1937–49	25
2	Ricardo Lopez, Mexico	WBC/WBA Strawweight	1990–98	22
3 =	Henry Armstrong, US	Welterweight#	1938–40	19
=	Khaosai Galaxy, Thailand	WBA Junior Bantamweight	1984–91	19
=	Eusebio Pedroza, Panama	WBA Featherweight	1978–85	19
6 =	Wilfredo Gomez, Puerto Rico	WBC Junior Featherweight	1977–83	17
=	Myung Woo Yuh, South Korea	WBA Junior Flyweight	1985–91	17
8	Orlando Canizares, US	IBF Bantamweight	1988–94	16
9	Bernard Hopkins, US	IBF/WBC/WBA Middleweight	1995–2002	15
10 =	Miguel Canto, Mexico	WBC Flyweight	1975–79	14
=	Bob Foster, US	Light Heavyweight#	1968–74	14

* One champion per division listed

\# Undisputed champion

"THE RING"

Boxing's "Bible," *The Ring*, was founded by Nat Fleischer in 1922. From 1928, the magazine presented its annual Fighter of the Year Award. The first winner was Gene Tunney. Since 1945, there has also been an award for the Fight of the Year, in which Muhammad Ali featured a record six times.

DID YOU KNOW? The UK's Bob Fitzsimmons is the lightest man to have held the World Heavyweight title. He weighed in at just 167 lb when he won the title in 1897.

Top 10 Most winners of the International Boxing Hall of Fame's Fighter of the Year award*

	Boxer/country#	Years	Wins
1	Muhammad Ali	1963†, 1972§, 1974–75, 1978	5
2	Joe Louis	1936, 1938–39, 1941	4
3 =	Joe Frazier	1967, 1970–71	3
=	Evander Holyfield	1987, 1996–97	3
=	Rocky Marciano	1952, 1954–55	3
6 =	Ezzard Charles	1949–50	2
=	George Foreman	1973, 1976	2
=	Marvin Hagler	1983, 1985§	2
=	Thomas Hearns	1980, 1984	2
=	Ingemar Johansson, Sweden	1958–59	2
=	Sugar Ray Leonard	1979, 1981§	2
=	Tommy Loughran	1929, 1931	2
=	Floyd Patterson	1956, 1960	2
=	Barney Ross	1934§–35	2
=	Dick Tiger, Nigeria	1962, 1965	2
=	Mike Tyson	1986, 1988	2

* Formerly The Ring Fighter of the Year award

\# All US unless otherwise stated

† As Cassius Clay

§ Shared award

Top 10 First Olympic champions to win professional world titles

	Boxer/country	Olympic title/year	First pro. title/year
1	Fidel la Barba, US	Flyweight 1924	Flyweight 1925
2	Frankie Genaro, US	Flyweight 1920	Flyweight 1927
3	Jackie Fields, US	Featherweight 1924	Welterweight 1929
4	Pascual Perez, Argentina	Flyweight 1948	Flyweight 1954
5	Floyd Patterson, US	Middleweight 1952	Heavyweight 1956
6	Cassius Clay, US	Light Heavyweight 1960	Heavyweight 1964
7	Nino Benvenuti, Italy	Light Middleweight 1960	Junior Middleweight 1965
8	Joe Frazier, US	Heavyweight 1964	Heavyweight 1968
9	George Foreman, US	Heavyweight 1968	Heavyweight 1973
10	Mate Parlov, Yugoslavia	Light Heavyweight 1972	Light Heavyweight 1978

Willie Smith (US) took the Olympic Bantamweight title in 1924 and three years later won the British version of the world title. However, he is not universally acknowledged as the world champion. Joe Frazier, 1964, George Foreman, 1968, and Lennox Lewis, 1988, are the only Olympic heavyweight/super-heavyweight champions to go on to win the professional World Heavyweight title. Ray Mercer won the Heavyweight title in 1988 and later went on to win the WBO version of the title.

◀ Two of the best-known fighters in the 1980s, Sugar Ray Leonard (left) and Marvin Hagler. Their World title fight at Caesar's Palace in 1987 was staged before a full house.

Top 10 World Champions with the longest professional careers

	Boxer/country	Fought professionally	Years
1 =	Bob Fitzsimmons, UK	1883–1914	31
=	Jack Johnson, US	1897–1928	31
3 =	George Foreman, US	1969–97	28
=	Archie Moore, US	1935–63	28*
5	Joe Brown, US	1943–70	27
6 =	Billy Murphy, New Zealand	1881–1907	26
=	Willie Pep, US	1940–66	26
8 =	Jack Britton, US	1905–30	25
=	Young Griffo, Australia	1886–1911	25
=	Harold Johnson, US	1946–71	25
=	Charles "Kid" McCoy, US	1891–1916	25
=	Sugar Ray Robinson, US	1940–65	25

* Archie Moore engaged in an exhibition bout in 1965, which, if counted, increases his career span to 30 years

Dates of many fights in the last century are not recorded, so it is impossible to establish the exact length of some careers. The longest career of any professional boxer is believed to be that of Bobby Dobbs, who fought for 39 years between 1875 and 1914. His last fight is alleged to have been when he was 56.

BOXING

- First countries to produce World Champions
- First World Champions under Queensberry Rules
- First men to regain world titles
- First American-born World Champions
- First men to win world titles at three different weights

QUEENSBERRY RULES

The original Queensberry Rules, as drawn up in 1867 by John Sholto Douglas, the 8th Marquess of Queensberry, contained 12 rules. The three most significant, which are still adhered to today, were: (a) boxers should wear gloves, (b) all rounds should last three minutes (previously a round ended when a fighter was knocked down), and (c) wrestling (as permitted under the London Rules) was outlawed.

BOXING FIRSTS

The 10 First countries to produce World Champions*

	Country#	Boxer	Weight	Year
1	Ireland	Jack "Nonpareil" Dempsey	Middleweight	1884
2	US	Paddy Duffy	Welterweight	1888
3	UK	Ike Weir	Featherweight	1889
4	Canada	George LaBlanche	Middleweight	1889
5	New Zealand	Billy Murphy	Featherweight	1890
6	Australia	Young Griffo	Featherweight	1890
7	Switzerland	Frank Erne	Lightweight	1899
8	Barbados	Joe Walcott	Welterweight	1901
9	Austria	Jack Root	Light Heavyweight	1903
10	Denmark	Battling Nelson	Lightweight	1908

* Under Queensberry Rules
\# Of birth

Despite producing many of the early world champions, Ireland did not stage its first world title fight until 1908 when Canada's Tommy Burns made the seventh defense of his World Heavyweight title against local hero Jem Roche from Wexford, in Dublin. He did not remain a hero for long—Burns knocked him out in the first round.

The 10 First World Champions under Queensberry Rules*

	Boxer/country	Weight	Year
1	Jack Dempsey, Ireland	Middleweight	1884
2	Jack McAuliffe, Ireland	Lightweight	1887
3	Paddy Duffy, US	Welterweight	1888
4	Ike Weir, UK	Featherweight	1889
5	George Dixon, Canada	Bantamweight	1890
6	James J. Corbett, US	Heavyweight	1892
7	Jack Root, Austria	Light Heavyweight	1903
8	Jimmy Wilde, UK	Flyweight	1916
9	Johnny Dundee, Italy	Junior Lightweight	1921
10	Mushy Callahan, US	Junior Welterweight	1926

* First champion per division listed

Jack "Nonpareil" Dempsey, not to be confused with the heavyweight champion of the same name, was the sport's first world champion with gloves. Born in County Kildare, Ireland, in 1862, Dempsey won the world middleweight title at the age of 21. He lost it to Bob Fitzsimmons in 1891. Four years later, he attempted to win the welterweight title but was thwarted by Tommy Ryan.

The 10 First men to regain world titles

	Boxer/country*	Weight	Year
1	Mysterious Billy Smith	Welterweight	1898
2	George Dixon, Canada	Featherweight	1898
3	Rube Ferns	Welterweight	1901
4	Stanley Ketchel	Middleweight	1908
5	Billy Papke	Middleweight	1910
6	Ted "Kid" Lewis, UK	Welterweight	1917
7	Jack Britton	Welterweight	1919
8	Peter Herman	Bantamweight	1921
9	Joe Lynch	Bantamweight	1922
10	Johnny Dundee, Italy	Junior Lightweight	1923

* All US-born unless otherwise stated

Billy Papke was the first man to regain a world title on two occasions. Having lost the middleweight crown to Stanley Ketchel in 1909, he regained it with a third-round knockout of Willie Lewis eight months later. He lost it again to Johnny Thompson in February 1911, but beat Jim Sullivan four months later to regain it.

▶ Thomas Hearns on his way to beating Nate Miller in April 1999 and capturing the vacant IBO Cruiserweight title.

◀ Ghanaian world champion Azumah Nelson won the WBC Super Featherweight title in 1995 at the age of 37.

The 10 First American-born World Champions*

	Boxer	Birth place	Weight	Date of first title
1	Paddy Duffy	Boston, Massachusetts	Welterweight	Oct. 30, 1888
2	James J. Corbett	San Francisco	Heavyweight	Sept. 7, 1892
3	Tommy Ryan	Redwood, New York	Welterweight	July 26, 1894
4	Charles "Kid" McCoy	Rush County, Indiana	Welterweight	Mar. 2, 1896
5	George "Kid" Lavigne	Bay City, Michigan	Lightweight	June 1, 1896
6	Solly Smith	Los Angeles	Featherweight	Oct. 4, 1897
7	Jimmy Barry	Chicago	Bantamweight	Dec. 6, 1897
8	James J. Jeffries	Carroll, Ohio	Heavyweight	June 9, 1899
9	Terry McGovern	Johnstown, Pennsylvania	Bantamweight	Sept. 12, 1899
10	Rube Ferns	Pittsburgh, Kansas	Welterweight	Jan. 15, 1900

* Under Queensberry Rules

The first recognized world champion under Queensberry Rules was middleweight Jack "Nonpareil" Dempsey, who captured the title in 1884. However, although he represented the United States, Dempsey was in fact born in County Kildare in the Republic of Ireland.

The 10 First men to win world titles at three different weights

	Boxer/country	Weights/years of first titles
1	Bob Fitzsimmons, UK	Middle 1891, Heavy 1897, Light Heavy 1903
2	Tony Canzoneri, US	Feather* 1927, Light 1930, Junior Welter 1931
3	Barney Ross, US	Light 1933, Junior Welter 1933, Welter 1934
4	Henry Armstrong, US	Feather 1937, Welter 1938, Light 1938
5	Wilfred Benitez, US	Junior Welter 1976, Welter 1979, Junior Middle 1981
6	Alexis Arguello, Nicaragua	Feather 1974, Junior Light 1978, Light 1981
7	Roberto Duran, Panama	Light 1972, Welter 1980, Junior Middle 1983
8	Wilfredo Gomez, Puerto Rico	Junior Feather 1977, Feather 1984, Junior Light 1985
9	Thomas Hearns, US	Welter 1980, Junior Middle 1982, Light Heavy 1987
10	Sugar Ray Leonard, US	Welter 1979, Junior Middle 1981, Middle 1987

* New York version of the title

BOXING

- Longest World Championship boxing contests
- Longest reigns as World Champion
- Most knockouts in a career
- Most fights in a career

THE GREAT JOE LOUIS

Joe Louis' reign as World Heavyweight champion started with an 8th-round knockout of James J. Braddock in Chicago in 1937. Louis remained undefeated until he announced his retirement on March 1, 1949. He made 25 defenses of his titles, including a remarkable seven in 1941. Louis came out of retirement in 1950, but his bid to regain the title ended in defeat by Ezzard Charles on points over 15 rounds.

TITLES & RECORDS

Top 10 Longest World Championship boxing contests

	Boxers	Weight	Date	Rounds
1	Ike Weir vs. Frank Murphy	Featherweight	Mar. 31, 1889	80
2	Jack McAuliffe vs. Jem Carney	Lightweight	Nov. 16, 1887	74
3	Paddy Duffy vs. Tom Meadows	Welterweight	Mar. 29, 1889	45
4	Joe Gans vs. Battling Nelson	Lightweight	Sept. 3, 1906	42
5 =	George Dixon vs. Johnny Murphy	Bantamweight	Oct. 23, 1890	40
=	Ad Wolgast vs. Battling Nelson	Lightweight	Feb. 22, 1910	40
7 =	George LaBlanche vs. Jack Dempsey	Middleweight	Aug. 27, 1889	32
=	Stanley Ketchel vs. Joe Thomas	Middleweight	Sept. 2, 1907	32
9	Jack Dempsey vs. Billy McCarthy	Middleweight	Feb. 18, 1890	28
10	Jack Dempsey vs. Jack Fogarty	Middleweight	Feb. 3, 1886	27

All these were World Championship contests under the Marquess of Queensberry Rules (first published in 1867), which set the length of a round at three minutes. Prior to the rules, a round ended when a fighter was knocked down, and consequently many fights in the bare-knuckle days consisted of many rounds, the longest being the 276-round contest between Jack Jones and Patsy Tunney in Cheshire, in 1825. The fight lasted 4 hours 30 minutes. The longest heavyweight contest under Queensberry rules was the Jess Willard vs. Jack Johnson contest on April 5, 1915, which lasted 26 rounds.

Top 10 Longest reigns as World Champion*

	Boxer/country	Weight	Years	Reign (yrs:mths)
1	Joe Louis, US	Heavyweight	1937–49	11:7
2	Johnny Kilbane, US	Featherweight	1912–23	11:4
3	Archie Moore, US	Light Heavyweight	1952–62	9:2
4	Ricardo Lopez, Mexico	Strawweight	1990–99	8:11
5	Benny Leonard, US	Lightweight	1917–25	7:8
6	Jimmy Wilde, UK	Flyweight	1916–23	7:4
7	Flash Elorde, Philippines	Junior Lightweight	1960–67	7:3
8	Khaosai Galaxy, Thailand	Junior Bantamweight	1984–91	7:1
9	Carlos Monzon, Argentina#	Middleweight	1970–77	6:8
10	Felix Trinidad, Puerto Rico#	Welterweight	1993–99	6:8

   * Based on longest uninterrupted reign in each weight division

   # Carlos Monzon's reign beats that of Felix Trinidad by a matter of 8 days

Boxing history was made on May 9, 1988 when Kaokar Galaxy won the WBA Bantamweight title while his twin brother Khaosai was the holder of the WBA Junior Bantamweight title at the time—the first time twins had held world titles.

▶ Archie Moore (left) retains his World Light Heavyweight title with a 10-round points win over Yolande Pompey in London in June 1956.

> Joe Louis was my inspiration. I idolize him. I just give lip service to being the greatest. He was the greatest.
>
> **Muhammad Ali** on the death of Joe Louis, April 12, 1981

Top 10 Most knockouts in a career

	Boxer/country	Weight	Years	KOs
1	Archie Moore, US	Light Heavyweight	1936–63	130
2	Young Stribling, US	Heavyweight	1921–33	126
3	Billy Bird, US	Welterweight	1920–48	125
4	George Odwell, US	Welterweight	1930–45	114
5	Sugar Ray Robinson, US	Middleweight	1940–65	110
6	Sandy Saddler, US	Featherweight	1944–56	103
7	Sam Langford, Canada	Middleweight	1902–26	102
8	Henry Armstrong, US	Welterweight	1931–45	100
9	Jimmy Wilde, UK	Flyweight	1911–23	98
10	Len Wickwar, US	Light Heavyweight	1928–47	93

Top 10 Most fights in a career

	Boxer/country	Years	Fights
1	Len Wickwar, US	1928–47	466
2	Wildcat Monte, US	1923–37	406
3	Jack Britton, US	1904–30	357
4	Johnny Dundee, Italy	1910–32	340
5	Billy Bird, US	1920–48	318
6	George Marsden, US	1928–46	311
7	Duke Tramel, US	1922–36	305
8	Maxie Rosenbloom, US	1923–39	300
9	Harry Greb, US	1913–26	299
10	Sam Langford, Canada	1902–26	298

The most professional bouts by a World Heavyweight Champion is 122 by Ezzard Charles (US), between 1940 and 1959. Hal Bagwell (UK) had 180 contests (175 wins and five draws) in the period 1938–48, the most contests without defeat.

TENNIS

At the Start

Tennis has its roots in a game played in France in an indoor court. As "real," or royal, tennis, it was played in England from the medieval period, and as "field tennis" during the late 18th and early 19th centuries. In 1874, Major Walter Clopton Wingfield patented *sphairistiké* (Greek for "ball games"), or lawn tennis, as a more vigorous version of badminton (which developed from the ancient children's game of battledore and shuttlecock). The Marylebone Cricket Club revised Wingfield's original rules and, in 1877, the game came under the aegis of the Wimbledon-based All England Croquet Club, which added the name Lawn Tennis to its own, holding the first championships in 1877. The world's first national governing body for tennis was the United States Lawn Tennis Association, which was formed at the Fifth Avenue Hotel, New York on 21 May 1881.

GRAND SLAM CHAMPIONS

- Most Grand Slam men's singles titles
- Most Grand Slam women's singles titles
- Most Grand Slam men's titles
- First players to perform the Grand Slam
- Most Grand Slam women's titles

LOSING STREAK

Despite reaching four US Open finals, Bjorn Borg was a runner-up on each occasion, something that happened to him only once in a Wimbledon final and not at all in six French Open finals.

Top 10 Most Grand Slam men's singles titles

	Player/country	A	F	W	US	Total
1	Pete Sampras, US	2	0	7	4	13
2	Roy Emerson, Australia	6	2	2	2	12
3 =	Bjorn Borg, Sweden	0	6	5	0	11
=	Rod Laver, Australia	3	2	4	2	11
5	Bill Tilden, US	0	0	3	7	10
6 =	Jimmy Connors, US	1	0	2	5	8
=	Ivan Lendl, Czechoslovakia	2	3	0	3	8
=	Fred Perry, UK	1	1	3	3	8
=	Ken Rosewall, Australia	4	2	0	2	8
10 =	Andre Agassi, US	3	1	1	2	7
=	Henri Cochet, France	0	4	2	1	7
=	René Lacoste, France	0	3	2	2	7
=	William Larned, US	0	0	0	7	7
=	John McEnroe, US	0	0	3	4	7
=	John Newcombe, Australia	2	0	3	2	7
=	Bill Renshaw, UK	0	0	7	0	7
=	Richard Sears, US	0	0	0	7	7
=	Mats Wilander, Sweden	3	3	0	1	7

A – Australian Open; F – French Open; W – Wimbledon; US – US Open

Top 10 Most Grand Slam women's singles titles

	Player/country	A	F	W	US	Total
1	Margaret Court* (née Smith), Australia	11	5	3	7	26
2	Steffi Graf, West Germany/Germany	4	6	7	5	22
3	Helen Wills-Moody, US	0	4	8	7	19
4 =	Chris Evert-Lloyd, US	2	7	3	6	18
=	Martina Navratilova, Czechoslovakia/US	3	2	9	4	18
6	Billie Jean King (née Moffitt), US	1	1	6	4	12
7 =	Maureen Connolly, US	1	2	3	3	9
=	Monica Seles, Yugoslavia/US	4	3	0	2	9
9 =	Suzanne Lenglen,# France	0	2	6	0	8
=	Molla Mallory (née Bjurstedt), US	0	0	0	8	8

A – Australian Open; F – French Open; W – Wimbledon; US – US Open

* Includes two wins in Amateur Championships in 1968 and 1969, which were held alongside the Open Championship

Lenglen also won four French singles titles pre-1925 when the tournament was a "closed" event

◀ Billie Jean King, winner of more Wimbledon titles than any other player.

Top 10 Most Grand Slam men's titles

	Player/country	Singles	Doubles	Mixed	Total
1	Roy Emerson, Australia	12	16	0	28
2	John Newcombe, Australia	7	17	1	25
3	Frank Sedgman, Australia	5	9	8	22
4	Bill Tilden, US	10	6	5	21
5	Rod Laver, Australia	11	6	3	20
6 =	John Browmwich, Australia	2	13	4	19
=	Neale Fraser, Australia	3	11	5	19
8 =	Jean Borotra, France	4	9	5	18
=	Ken Rosewall, Australia	8	9	1	18
=	Fred Stolle, Australia	2	10	6	18
=	Todd Woodbridge, Australia	0	12	6	18

Top 10 First players to perform the Grand Slam*

	Player/country	Event	Year
1	Donald Budge, US	Singles	1938
2 =	Ken McGregor, Australia	Doubles	1951
=	Frank Sedgman, Australia	Doubles	1951
4	Maureen Connolly, US	Singles	1953
5	Maria Bueno,# Brazil	Doubles	1960
6	Rod Laver, Australia	Singles	1962
7 =	Ken Fletcher, Australia	Mixed	1963
=	Margaret Smith, Australia	Mixed	1963
9	Owen Davidson,† Australia	Mixed	1967
10	Rod Laver, Australia	Singles	1969

* Winning singles, doubles, or mixed doubles at all four Grand Slam events in one year

\# Bueno completed the doubles Grand Slam in 1960 with two different partners: Christine Truman (UK) and Darlene Hard (US)

† Davidson completed the mixed doubles Grand Slam in 1967 with two different partners: Lesley Turner (Australia) and Billie Jean King (US)

Apart from Budge, Connolly, and Laver, the only other players to have performed the singles Grand Slam are: Margaret Court (Australia) in 1970 and Steffi Graf (West Germany) in 1988. Graf also won the Olympic title in the same year. The last player to perform the Grand Slam was Martina Hingis (Switzerland), who won the Ladies' Doubles at all four events in 1998.

◀ "Pistol Pete" Sampras, one of the world's greatest tennis players, and a dominant force in the men's game in the 1990s.

Top 10 Most Grand Slam women's titles

	Player/country	Singles	Doubles	Mixed	Total
1	Margaret Court (née Smith), Australia	24	19	19	62
2	Martina Navratilova, Czechoslovakia/US	18	31	7	56
3	Bille Jean King (née Moffitt), US	12	16	11	39
4	Margaret Du Pont, US	6	21	10	37
5 =	Louise Brough, US	6	21	8	35
=	Doris Hart, US	6	14	15	35
7	Helen Wills-Moody, US	19	9	3	31
8	Elizabeth Ryan, US	0	17	9	26
9	Suzanne Lenglen, France	12	8	5	25
10	Steffi Graf, West Germany/Germany	22	1	0	23

Steffi Graf's only doubles title was at Wimbledon in 1988 when she partnered Gabriela Sabatini (Argentina) to victory.

- ● Most US Open men's titles
- ● Most US Open women's titles
- ● Most US Open women's singles titles
- ● Most US Open men's singles titles
- ● Most singles matches won in a US Open career

DID YOU KNOW?

Organized lawn tennis started in the United States following the formation of the US Lawn Tennis Association on May 21, 1881, and on August 31 that year the first national championships got underway on the courts of the Newport [Rhode Island] Casino. The men's singles and doubles were the only events contested, with competitors playing in a wide variety of attire, including colored blazers and cravats. The first winner of the singles title was Richard Sears, who dominated the event in its early years, winning the first seven titles, until deposed by Henry Slocum in 1888.

US OPEN RECORDS

Top 10 Most US Open men's titles

	Player/country*	Years	Singles	Doubles	Mixed	Total titles
1	Bill Tilden	1913–29	7	5	4	16
2	Richard Sears	1881–87	7	6	0	13
3 =	Neale Fraser, Australia	1957–60	2	3	3	8
=	George M. Lott, Jr.	1928–34	0	5	3	8
=	John McEnroe	1979–89	4	4	0	8
=	Billy Talbert	1942–48	0	4	4	8
7 =	Jack Kramer	1940–47	2	4	1	7
=	Bill Larned	1901–11	7	0	0	7
=	Vincent Richards	1918–26	0	5	2	7
=	Holcombe Ward	1899–1906	1	6	0	7

* All US unless otherwise stated

Jack Kramer turned professional shortly after winning the US Open and Wimbledon in 1947. He made his professional debut on December 26, 1947 against Bobby Riggs at Madison Square Garden. Despite a heavy snowfall and the cancellation of public transportation, over 15,000 fans turned out—some arriving on skis.

Top 10 Most US Open women's titles

	Player/country*	Years	Singles	Doubles	Mixed	Total titles
1	Margaret Du Pont (née Osborne)	1941–60	3	13	9	25
2	Margaret Court# (née Smith), Australia	1961–75	7	5	8	20
3	Louise Brough	1942–57	1	12	4	17
4	Hazel Wightman (née Hotchkiss)	1909–28	4	6	6	16
5 =	Sarah Cooke (née Palfrey)	1930–45	2	9	4	15
=	Martina Navratilova, Czechoslovakia/US	1977–90	4	9	2	15
7 =	Juliette Atkinson	1894–1902	3	7	3	13
=	Billie Jean King (née Moffitt)	1964–80	4	5	4	13
=	Molla Mallory (née Bjurstedt)	1915–26	8	2	3	13
=	Helen Wills-Moody	1922–31	7	4	2	13

* All US unless otherwise stated

\# Includes two wins in Amateur Championships of 1968 and 1969, which were held alongside the Open Championship

Margaret Du Pont was one of the leading exponents of the doubles game, winning 21 doubles titles at Grand Slam events. She enjoyed a long career, first entering the US Top 10 rankings in 1938. Twenty years later she was still ranked number five.

▶ Chris Evert-Lloyd, the only player to win 100 matches in the US Open.

Top 10 Most US Open women's singles titles

	Player/country*	Years	Titles
1	Molla Mallory (née Bjurstedt)	1915–26	8
2 =	Margaret Court# (née Smith), Australia	1962–70	7
=	Helen Wills-Moody	1923–31	7
4	Chris Evert-Lloyd	1975–82	6
5	Steffi Graf, West Germany/Germany	1988–96	5
6 =	Pauline Betz	1942–46	4
=	Maria Bueno, Brazil	1959–66	4
=	Helen Jacobs	1932–35	4
=	Billie Jean King (née Moffitt)	1967–74	4
=	Alice Marble	1936–40	4
=	Elizabeth Moore	1896–1905	4
=	Martina Navratilova	1983–87	4
=	Hazel Wightman (née Hotchkiss)	1909–19	4

* All US unless otherwise stated

\# Includes two wins in Amateur Championships of 1968 and 1969, which were held alongside the Open Championship

Top 10 Most US Open men's singles titles

	Player/country*	Years	Titles
1 =	William Larned	1901–11	7
=	Richard Sears	1881–87	7
=	Bill Tilden	1920–29	7
4	Jimmy Connors	1974–83	5
5 =	John McEnroe	1979–84	4
=	Pete Sampras	1990–96	4
=	Robert Wrenn	1893–97	4
8 =	Oliver Campbell	1890–92	3
=	Ivan Lendl, Czechoslovakia	1985–87	3
=	Fred Perry, UK	1933–36	3
=	Malcolm Whitman	1898–1900	3

* All US unless otherwise stated

Top 10 Most singles matches won in a US Open career

	Player/country*	Years	Total wins
1	Chris Evert-Lloyd	1971–89	101
2	Jimmy Connors	1970–92	98
3	Martina Navratilova, Czechoslovakia/US	1973–93	89
4	Vic Seixas	1940–69	75
5 =	Steffi Graf, West Germany/Germany	1984–2000	73
=	Ivan Lendl, Czechoslovakia	1979–94	73
7	Bill Tilden	1916–30	71
8	R. Norris Williams	1912–35	69
9 =	John McEnroe	1977–92	65
=	Molla Mallory (née Bjurstedt)	1915–29	65

* All US unless otherwise stated

WIMBLEDON RECORDS

- Most Wimbledon men's titles
- First players to win three Wimbledon titles in one year
- Lowest-seeded Wimbledon men's champions
- Most Wimbledon women's titles
- Most Wimbledon men's singles titles
- Most Wimbledon women's singles titles

THE LADIES' PLATE

The Wimbledon women's singles plate is known as the Venus Rosewater Dish and is a copy of a pewter original exhibited in the Louvre, Paris.

Top 10 Most Wimbledon men's titles

	Player/country	Years	Singles	Doubles	Mixed	Total titles
1	William Renshaw, UK	1880–89	7	7	0	14
2	Lawrence Doherty, UK	1897–1905	5	8	0	13
3	Reginald Doherty, UK	1897–1905	4	8	0	12
4	John Newcombe, Australia	1965–74	3	6	0	9
5 =	Ernest Renshaw, UK	1880–89	1	7	0	8
=	Tony Wilding, New Zealand	1907–14	4	4	0	8
7 =	Wilfred Baddeley, UK	1891–96	3	4	0	7
=	Bob Hewitt, Australia/South Africa	1962–79	0	5	2	7
=	Rod Laver, Australia	1959–69	4	1	2	7
=	John McEnroe, US	1979–84	3	4	0	7
=	Pete Sampras, US	1993–2000	7	0	0	7
=	Todd Woodbridge, Australia	1993–2000	0	6	1	7
=	Mark Woodforde, Australia	1993–2000	0	6	1	7

Top 10 First players to win three Wimbledon titles in one year*

	Player/country	Year
1	Suzanne Lenglen, France	1920
2	Suzanne Lenglen, France	1922
3	Suzanne Lenglen, France	1925
4	Donald Budge, US	1937
5	Donald Budge, US	1938
6 =	Alice Marble, US	1939
=	Bobby Riggs, US	1939
8	Louise Brough, US	1948
9	Louise Brough, US	1950
10	Doris Hart, US	1951

* Singles, doubles, and mixed doubles

The last person to win all three titles in one year was Billie Jean King (USA) in 1973. The last man to perform the feat was Frank Sedgman (Australia) in 1952.

Top 10 Lowest-seeded Wimbledon men's champions

	Player/country	Year	Seed
1 =	Boris Becker, Germany	1985	U*
=	Goran Ivanisevic, Croatia	2001	U*
=	Richard Krajicek, Netherlands	1996	U*
4	Andre Agassi, US	1992	12
5 =	Pat Cash, Australia	1987	11
=	Jaroslav Drobny, Egypt	1954	11
7 =	Bob Falkenburg, US	1948	7
=	Sidney Wood, UK	1931	7
9 =	Arthur Ashe, US	1975	6
=	Dick Savitt, US	1951	6
=	Michael Stich, Germany	1991	6

* Unseeded

The 1927 Championship was the first with seeding, and that year's final was between the fourth seed, Henry Cochet (France), and his fellow countryman and number one seed Jean Borotra. The first time the number one seed won the men's title was in 1929 when Cochet beat Borotra. The 1996 final between Krajicek (Netherlands) and MalVai Washington (US) is the only singles final, men's or women's, to be contested by two unseeded players.

◀ An aerial view of Wimbledon's center and outside courts.

Top 10 Most Wimbledon women's titles

	Player/country	Years	Singles	Doubles	Mixed	Total titles
1	Billie Jean King (née Moffitt), US	1961–79	6	10	4	20
2 =	Martina Navratilova, Czechoslovakia/US	1976–95	9	7	3	19
=	Elizabeth Ryan, US	1914–34	0	12	7	19
4	Suzanne Lenglen, France	1919–25	6	6	3	15
5	Louise Brough, US	1946–55	4	5	4	13
6	Helen Wills-Moody, US	1927–38	8	3	1	12
7 =	Margaret Court (née Smith), Australia	1953–75	3	2	5	10
=	Doris Hart, US	1947–55	1	4	5	10
9 =	Maria Bueno, Brazil	1958–66	3	5	0	8
=	Steffi Graf, West Germany/Germany	1988–98	7	1	0	8

Top 10 Most Wimbledon men's singles titles

	Player/country	Years	Titles
1 =	William Renshaw, UK	1881–89	7
=	Pete Sampras, US	1993–2000	7
3 =	Bjorn Borg, Sweden	1976–80	5
=	Laurence Doherty, UK	1902–06	5
5 =	Reginald Doherty, UK	1897–1900	4
=	Rod Laver, Australia	1961–69	4
=	Tony Wilding, New Zealand	1910–13	4
8 =	Wilfred Baddeley, UK	1891–95	3
=	Boris Becker, West Germany	1985–89	3
=	Arthur Gore, UK	1901–09	3
=	John McEnroe, US	1981–84	3
=	John Newcombe, Australia	1967–71	3
=	Fred Perry, UK	1934–36	3
=	Bill Tilden, US	1920–30	3

Top 10 Most Wimbledon women's singles titles

	Player/country	Years	Titles
1	Martina Navratilova, Czechoslovakia/US	1978–90	9
2	Helen Wills-Moody, US	1927–38	8
3 =	Dorothea Chambers (née Douglass), UK	1903–14	7
=	Steffi Graf, West Germany/Germany	1988–1996	7
5 =	Blanche Hillyward, (née Bingley), UK	1886–1900	6
=	Billie Jean King, US	1966–75	6
=	Suzanne Lenglen, France	1919–25	6
8 =	Lottie Dodd, UK	1887–93	5
=	Charlotte Sterry (née Cooper), UK	1895–1908	5
10	Louise Brough, US	1948–55	4

◀ Martina Navratilova holding up the Wimbledon Ladies' Championship plate, which she won a record nine times.

AUSTRALIAN & FRENCH OPEN RECORDS

- Most French Open men's singles titles
- Most French Open women's singles titles
- Most French Open titles
- Most Australian Open singles titles
- Most Australian Open titles

FIRST AND LAST

Bjorn Borg's sixth and last French Open win was in 1981, when he beat Ivan Lendl in the final. It was Lendl's first appearance in a Grand Slam final.

Top 10 Most French Open men's singles titles

	Player/country	Years	Titles
1	Bjorn Borg, Sweden	1974-81	6
2	Henri Cochet, France	1926-32	4
3 =	Gustavo Kuerten, Brazil	1997-2001	3
=	René Lacoste, France	1925-29	3
=	Ivan Lendl, Czechoslovakia	1986-87	3
=	Mats Wilander, Sweden	1985-88	3
7 =	Sergi Bruguera, Spain	1993-94	2
=	Jim Courier, US	1991-92	2
=	Jaroslav Drobny, Egypt	1951-52	2
=	Roy Emerson, Australia	1963-67	2
=	Jan Kodes, Czechoslovakia	1970-71	2
=	Rod Laver, Australia	1962-69	2
=	Frank Parker, US	1948-49	2
=	Nicola Pietrangeli, Italy	1959-60	2
=	Ken Rosewall, Australia	1953-68	2
=	Manuel Santana, Spain	1961-64	2
=	Tony Trabert, US	1954-55	2
=	Gottfried von Cramm, Germany	1934-36	2

Max Decugis (France) won a record eight titles in the pre-1925 championships.

Top 10 Most French Open women's singles titles

	Player/country	Years	Titles
1	Chris Evert-Lloyd, US	1974-86	7
2	Steffi Graf, West Germany/ Germany	1987-99	6
3	Margaret Court (née Smith), Australia	1962-73	5
4	Helen Wills-Moody, US	1928-32	4
5 =	Arantxa Sanchez Vicario, Spain	1989-98	3
=	Monica Seles, Yugoslavia	1990-93	3
=	Hilde Sperling, Germany	1935-37	3
8 =	Maureen Connolly, US	1953-54	2
=	Margaret Du Pont (née Osborne), US	1946-49	2
=	Doris Hart, US	1950-52	2
=	Ann Jones (née Haydon), UK	1961-66	2
=	Suzanne Lenglen*, France	1925-26	2
=	Simone Mathieu, France	1938-39	2
=	Martina Navratilova, US	1982-84	2
=	Margaret Scriven, UK	1933-34	2
=	Lesley Turner, Australia	1963-65	2

* Lenglen also won four French titles pre-1925 when the tournament was a "closed" event

Top 10 Most French Open titles*

	Player/country	Singles	Doubles	Mixed	Total titles
1	Margaret Court (née Smith), Australia	5	4	4	13
2 =	Doris Hart, US	2	5	4	11
=	Martina Navratilova, Czechoslovakia/US	2	7	2	11
4	Simone Mathieu, France	2	6	2	10
5 =	Françoise Durr, France	1	5	3	9
=	Chris Evert-Lloyd, US	7	2	0	9
7 =	Jean Borotra, France	1	5	2	8
=	Henri Cochet, France	4	3	1	8
=	Roy Emerson, Australia	2	6	0	8
10 =	Bjorn Borg, Sweden	6	0	0	6
=	Gigi Fernandez, US	0	6	0	6
=	Steffi Graf, West Germany/Germany	6	0	0	6
=	Helen Wills-Moody, US	4	2	0	6
=	Natasha Zvereva, Belarus	0	6	0	6

* Men and women

◄ Margaret Court, winner of 36 French and Australian titles.

Top 10 Most Australian Open singles titles*

	Player/country#	Years	Titles
1	Margaret Court (née Smith)	1960–73	11
2 =	Nancye Bolton (née Wynne)	1937–51	6
=	Roy Emerson	1961–67	6
4	Daphne Akhurst	1925–30	5
5 =	Evonne Cawley (née Goolagong)	1974–77	4
=	Jack Crawford	1931–35	4
=	Steffi Graf, West Germany/ Germany	1988–94	4
=	Ken Rosewall	1953–72	4
=	Monica Seles, Yugoslavia/US	1991–96	4
10 =	Andre Agassi, US	1995–2001	3
=	James Anderson	1922–25	3
=	Joan Hartigan	1933–36	3
=	Martina Hingis, Switzerland	1997–99	3
=	Rod Laver	1960–69	3
=	Martina Navratilova, Czechoslovakia/US	1981–85	3
=	Adrian Quist	1936–48	3
=	Mats Wilander, Sweden	1983–88	3

* Men and women
\# All Australia unless otherwise stated

Top 10 Most Australian Open titles*

	Player/country#	Years	Singles	Doubles	Mixed	Total titles
1	Margaret Court (née Smith)	1960–73	11	8	4	23
2	Nancye Bolton (née Wynne)	1926–51	6	10	4	20
3	Thelma Long	1936–58	2	12	4	18
4 =	Daphne Akhurst	1924–30	5	4	4	13
=	Adrian Quist	1936–50	3	10	0	13
6 =	John Bromwich	1938–50	2	8	1	11
=	Jack Crawford	1929–35	4	4	3	11
=	Martina Navratilova, Czechoslovakia/US	1975–89	3	8	0	11
9 =	Evonne Cawley (née Goolagong)	1971–83	4	5	0	9
=	Roy Emerson	1961–69	6	3	0	9

* Men and women
\# All Australia unless otherwise stated

▼ Although he won six French singles titles, Sweden's Bjorn Borg never played in the Australian Open.

THE DAVIS CUP

- Davis Cup teams
- Most appearances in Davis Cup finals
- Most Davis Cup wins
- Davis Cup-winning captains
- Highest-scoring sets in Davis Cup finals

Top 10 Davis Cup teams

	Country	Points*
1	Sweden	69
2	US	62
3	Australia	59
4	France	47
5	Germany/West Germany	46
6	Czechoslovakia/Czech Republic	40
7	Italy	36
8	Spain	29
9	USSR/Russia	24
10 =	Argentina	18
=	India	18
=	Switzerland	18

* Based on five points for winning the tournament, four for runner-up, three for losing semifinalist, and so on

This is for matches played since 1981, when the World Group, featuring the top 16 nations, was introduced. They play a straight knockout tournament during the course of the year, with the final played each December.

Top 10 Most appearances in Davis Cup finals

	Country	Finals
1	US	59
2	Australasia/Australia	46
3	British Isles/UK	17
4	France	14
5	Sweden	12
6	Italy	7
7	West Germany/Germany	5
8 =	Romania	3
=	Spain	3
9 =	Czechoslovakia	2
=	India*	2
=	Russia	2

* India also qualified for the 1974 final against South Africa but refused to play because of the South African government's apartheid policies

Top 10 Most Davis Cup wins

	Country	Years	Wins
1	US	1900–95	31
2	Australasia/Australia	1907–99	27
3 =	British Isles/UK	1903–36	9
=	France	1927–2001	9
5	Sweden	1975–98	7
6	West Germany/Germany	1988–93	3
7 =	Czechoslovakia	1980	1
=	Italy	1976	1
=	South Africa	1974	1
=	Spain	2000	1

> I guess I was the first Englishman to bring the American attitude to the game of lawn tennis.
>
> Fred Perry

Top 10 Davis Cup-winning captains

	Captain	Country	Years	Wins
1	Harry Hopman	Australia	1939–67	16
2 =	Norman Brookes	Australasia/Australia	1907–19	6
=	Norris Williams	US	1921–26	6
4 =	William Collins	Britain	1903–06	4
=	Neale Fraser	Australia	1973–86	4
=	Pierre Gillou	France	1927–30	4
=	Herbert Roper-Barrett	Great Britain	1933–36	4
8 =	Walter Pate	US	1937–46	3
=	Niki Pilic	Germany	1988–93	3
=	Hans Olsson	Sweden	1984–87	3

(Richard) Norris Williams II has the unique distinction of being the only Davis Cup captain to survive the *Titanic* sinking of 1912. He was in a first-class cabin, with ticket number PC 17597. Williams dived off the ship and clung to a half-submerged lifeboat for six hours before being rescued. Sadly, his father went down with the ship.

Top 10 Highest-scoring sets in Davis Cup finals

	Match	Year	Score
1 =	Maurice McLoughlin, US vs. Norman Brookes, Australia	1914	17–15
=	Bill Tilden/Richard Williams, US vs. James Anderson/John Hawkes, Australia	1923	17–15
3	Alex Olmedo/Ham Richardson, US vs. Mal Anderson/Neale Fraser, Australia	1958	16–14
4 =	Fred Perry, UK vs. Francis Shields, US	1934	15–13
=	Donald Budge, US vs. Charles Hare, UK	1937	15–13
=	Manuel Santana, Spain vs. Roy Emerson, Australia	1965	15–13
=	Arthur Ashe, US vs. Ilie Nastase, Romania	1969	15–13
8 =	Vic Seixas/Tony Trabert, US vs. Rex Hartwig/Lew Hoad, Australia	1955	14–12
9 =	Arthur Gore/Herbert Roper-Barrett, UK vs. Norman Brookes/Anthony Wilding, Australia	1907	13–11
=	James Anderson/John Hawkes, Australia vs. Bill Tilden/Richard Williams, US	1923	13–11
=	Jacques Brugnon/Henri Cochet, France vs. Wilmer Allison/John Van Ryn, US	1932	13–11
=	Ken McGregor, Australia vs. Ted Schroeder, US	1950	13–11
=	Ted Schroeder, US vs. Mervyn Rose, Australia	1951	13–11
=	Lew Hoad, Australia vs. Tony Trabert, Australia	1953	13–11
=	Vic Seixas, US vs. Mal Anderson, Australia	1957	13–11
=	Mal Anderson, Australia vs. Barry MacKay, US	1958	13–11
=	Arthur Ashe, US vs. Christian Kuhnke, West Germany	1970	13–11
=	Henrik Sundstrom, Sweden vs. John McEnroe, US	1984	13–11
=	Pat Cash, Australia vs. Stefan Edberg, Sweden	1986	13–11*
=	Pat Cash, Australia vs. Stefan Edberg, Sweden	1986	13–11#

* First set

\# Second set

The fifth and final game of the 1977 final between Tony Roche (Australia) and Corrado Barazzutti (Italy) was unfinished at 12–12 in the first set.

◀ Jim Courier, Andre Agassi, coach Tom Gullikson, and Pete Sampras of the US team pose with the Davis Cup Trophy after beating Russia 3–2 to win the title in 1995.

ATP & WTA RECORD BREAKERS

- Men with most tournament wins
- Women with most tournament wins
- Women with most career wins
- Women spending most weeks at top of ATP world rankings
- Men spending most weeks at top of ATP world rankings
- Career earnings by men
- Career earnings by women

> Nobody reminds me of me, I'm an original.
>
> **Jimmy Connors**

Top 10 Men with most tournament wins*

	Player/country	Wins
1	Jimmy Connors, US	109
2	Ivan Lendl, Czechoslovakia/US	94
3	John McEnroe, US	77
4	Pete Sampras, US	63
5 =	Bjorn Borg, Sweden	62
=	Guillermo Vilas, Argentina	62
7	Ilie Nastase, Romania	57
8 =	Andre Agassi, US	49
=	Boris Becker, Germany	49
10	Rod Laver, Australia	47

* In singles events in the Open era, 1968–January 1, 2002

Top 10 Women with most tournament wins*

	Player/country	Wins
1	Martina Navratilova, Czechoslovakia/US	167
2	Chris Evert-Lloyd, US	157
3	Steffi Graff, West Germany/Germany	107
4	Evonne Cawley (née Goolagong), Australia	88
5	Margaret Court (née Smith), Australia	79
6	Billie Jean King (née Moffitt), US	67
7	Virginia Wade, UK	55
8	Monica Seles, Yugoslavia/US	51
9 =	Lindsay Davenport, US	38
=	Martina Hingis, Switzerland	38

* In singles events in the Open era, 1968–January 1, 2002

Top 10 Women with most career wins*

	Player/country	Wins
1	Chris Evert-Lloyd, US	1,304
2	Steffi Graf, West Germany/Germany	900
3	Martina Navratilova, Czechoslovakia/US	773
4	Arantxa Sanchez Vicario, Spain	734
5	Conchita Martinez, Spain	635
6	Gabriela Sabatini, Argentina	632
7	Pam Shriver, US	625
8	Helena Sukova, Czechoslovakia	614
9	Zina Jackson (née Garrison), US	587
10	Wendy Turnbull, Australia	577

* Singles only in the Open era since 1968–February 11, 2002
Source: WTA

Chris Evert-Lloyd also has the best ratio of wins with 1,304 wins and just 144 losses from 75 tournaments, representing a win ratio of .901

Top 10 Women spending most weeks at top of WTA world rankings*

	Player/country	Weeks
1	Steffi Graf, West Germany/Germany	377
2	Martina Navratilova, Czechoslovakia/US	331
3	Chris Evert-Lloyd, US	262
4	Martina Hingis, Switzerland	209
5	Monica Seles, Yugoslavia/US	178
6	Lindsay Davenport, US	38
7	Tracy Austin, US	22
8	Arantxa Sanchez Vicario, Spain	11
9	Jennifer Capriati, US	6
10	Venus Williams, US	1

* As of March 1, 2002
Source: WTA

The Sanex WTA Rankings are computer rankings based on a player's performance over the year and take into account their best 17 results at singles and best 11 at doubles. Points are awarded based on performance at each event played.

◄ Jimmy Connors was ranked world number one five years in a row, from 1974 to 1978.

Top 10 Men spending most weeks at top of ATP world rankings*

Player/country	Weeks
1 Pete Sampras, US	286
2 Ivan Lendl, Czechoslovakia/US	270
3 Jimmy Connors, US	268
4 John McEnroe, US	170
5 Bjorn Borg, Sweden	109
6 Andre Agassi, US	87
7 Stefan Edberg, Sweden	72
8 Jim Courier, US	58
9 Gustavo Kuerten, Brazil	43
10 Ilie Nastase, Romania	40

* As of January 1, 2002

Source: ATP

Top 10 Career earnings by men*

Player/country	Winnings ($)
1 Pete Sampras, US	42,057,490
2 Boris Becker, West Germany/Germany	25,079,186
3 Andre Agassi, US	23,482,490
4 Yevgeny Kafelnikov, Russia	21,423,535
5 Ivan Lendl, Czechoslovakia/US	21,262,417
6 Stefan Edberg, Sweden	20,630,941
7 Goran Ivanisevic, Croatia	19,682,620
8 Michael Chang, US	18,904,768
9 Jim Courier, US	13,978,963
10 Gustavo Kuerten, Brazil	13,014,235

* As of January 1, 2002

Top 10 Career earnings by women*

Player/country	Winnings ($)*
1 Steffi Graff, West Germany/Germany	21,895,277
2 Martina Navratilova, Czechoslovakia/US	20,344,061
3 Martina Hingis, Switzerland	16,845,441
4 Arantxa Sanchez Vicario, Spain	16,472,594
5 Lindsay Davenport, US	14,036,870
6 Monica Seles, Yugoslavia/US	13,518,919
7 Jana Novotna, Czechoslovakia	11,249,134
8 Conchita Martinez, Spain	9,779,780
9 Venus Williams, US	9,319,337
10 Chris Evert-Lloyd, US	8,896,195

* As of January 1, 2002

◄ Steffi Graf ended Martina Navratilova's five-year reign as number one by deposing her in 1986.

FOOTBALL

At the Start

American football shares its early history with the English games of football and rugby. American football and rugby both use an oval ball, H-shaped goalposts, and a similar-sized field. In the first half of the 19th century, American school and college football rules varied, with some teams handling the ball and others not, and the game was banned by Harvard and other universities. Princeton introduced the first set of rules in 1867 for a variation of soccer (played with teams of 25), but, in 1876 switched to rugby. The first match, played under "Rutgers Rules," was on November 6, 1869, when Rutgers beat Princeton 6–4. Two weeks later Princeton won 8–0 under Princeton Rules. The professional game started in 1895, with a match between Latrobe and Jeanette, Pennsylvania. Latrobe won 12–0.

SUPER BOWL RECORDS

- Most points in a Super Bowl career
- Largest-winning margins in the Super Bowl
- Most receptions in a Super Bowl career
- Most Super Bowl appearances
- Most yards gained passing in a single game

> I don't see any way in the world the 49ers won't win this football game. This sucker could be as bad as 55–3.
> **Terry Bradshaw,** prior to the 49ers 55–10 win against the Denver Broncos in Super Bowl XXIV

Top 10 Most points in a Super Bowl career

	Player/team	Games	Touchdowns	Field goals	PAT*	Points
1	Jerry Rice, San Francisco 49ers	3	7	0	0	42
2	Emmitt Smith, Dallas Cowboys	3	5	0	0	30
3 =	Roger Craig, San Francisco 49ers	3	4	0	0	24
=	John Elway, Denver Broncos	5	4	0	0	24
=	Franco Harris, Pittsburgh Steelers	4	4	0	0	24
=	Thurman Thomas, Buffalo Bills	4	4	0	0	24
7	Ray Wersching, San Francisco 49ers	2	0	5	7	22
8	Don Chandler, Green Bay Packers	2	0	4	8	20
9 =	Cliff Branch, Los Angeles Raiders	3	3	0	0	18
=	Terrell Davis, Denver Broncos	2	3	0	0	18
=	Antonio Freeman, Green Bay Packers	2	3	0	0	18
=	John Stallworth, Pittsburgh Steelers	4	3	0	0	18
=	Lynn Swann, Pittsburgh Steelers	4	3	0	0	18
=	Ricky Watters, San Francisco 49ers	1	3	0	0	18

* Point after touchdown

This list also represents all the players who have scored three or more touchdowns in a Super Bowl career.

Top 10 Largest-winning margins in the Super Bowl

	Winners	Runners-up	Year	Score	Margin
1	San Francisco 49ers	Denver Broncos	1990	55-10	45
2	Chicago Bears	New England Patriots	1986	46-10	36
3	Dallas Cowboys	Buffalo Bills	1993	52-17	35
4	Washington Redskins	Denver Broncos	1988	42-10	32
5	Los Angeles Raiders	Washington Redskins	1984	38-9	29
6	Baltimore Ravens	New York Giants	2001	34-7	27
7	Green Bay Packers	Kansas City Chiefs	1967	35-10	25
8	San Francisco 49ers	San Diego Chargers	1995	49-26	23
9	San Francisco 49ers	Miami Dolphins	1985	38-16	22
10	Dallas Cowboys	Miami Dolphins	1972	24-3	21

Source: National Football League

When they beat Denver 55–10 in Super Bowl XXIV at the Louisiana Superdome in 1990, the 49ers joined Pittsburgh as the most successful team in Super Bowl history with their fourth win. They have since gone on to win the coveted title a fifth time.

◄ In 1998, Minnesota Vikings kicker Gary Anderson became the first player in 15 years to score 150 points in a season in the NFL.

Top 10 Most receptions in a Super Bowl career

	Player/team	Games	Receptions
1	Jerry Rice, San Francisco 49ers	3	28
2	Andre Reed, Buffalo Bills	4	27
3 =	Roger Craig, San Francisco 49ers	3	20
=	Thurman Thomas, Buffalo Bills	4	20
5	Jay Novacek, Dallas Cowboys	3	17
6 =	Michael Irvin, Dallas Cowboys	3	16
=	Lynn Swann, Pittsburgh Steelers	4	16
8	Chuck Foreman, Minnesota Vikings	3	15
9	Cliff Branch, Los Angeles Raiders	3	14
10 =	Don Beebe, Buffalo Bills	3	12
=	Kenneth Davis, Buffalo Bills	4	12
=	Antonio Freeman, Green Bay Packers	2	12
=	Preston Pearson, Baltimore Colts/ Pittsburgh Steelers/Dallas Cowboys	5	12

San Francisco wide receiver Jerry Rice won the MVP at Super Bowl XXIII in 1989 after catching 11 passes for a Super Bowl record 215 yards in the 49ers' nail-biting win over the Cincinnati Bengals.

Top 10 Most Super Bowl appearances

	Team	Wins	Losses	Apps
1	Dallas Cowboys	5	3	8
2	Denver Broncos	2	4	6
3 =	Miami Dolphins	2	3	5
=	Pittsburgh Steelers	4	1	5
=	San Francisco 49ers	5	0	5
=	Washington Redskins	3	2	5
7 =	Buffalo Bills	0	4	4
=	Green Bay Packers	3	1	4
=	Minnesota Vikings	0	4	4
=	Oakland/Los Angeles Raiders	3	1	4

Top 10 Most yards gained passing in a single Super Bowl

	Player	Match	Year	Yards
1	Kurt Warner	St. Louis Rams vs. Tennessee Titans	2000	414
2	Kurt Warner	St. Louis Rams vs. New England Patriots	2002	365
3	Joe Montana	San Francisco 49ers vs. Cincinnati Bengals	1989	357
4	Doug Williams	Washington Redskins vs. Denver Broncos	1988	340
5	John Elway	Denver Broncos vs. Atlanta Falcons	1999	336
6	Joe Montana	San Francisco 49ers vs. Miami Dolphins	1985	331
7	Steve Young	San Francisco 49ers vs. San Diego Chargers	1995	325
8 =	Terry Bradshaw	Pittsburgh Steelers vs. Dallas Cowboys	1979	318
=	Dan Marino	Miami Dolphins vs. San Francisco 49ers	1985	318
10	Terry Bradshaw	Pittsburgh Steelers vs. Los Angeles Rams	1980	309

► After 16 successful seasons with the 49ers, Super Bowl hero Jerry Rice moved to the Oakland Raiders for the 2001 season.

CHAMPIONSHIP & POST-SEASON GAMES

- Highest scoring AFL-AFC Championship games
- Highest scoring NFL-NFC Championship games
- Best records in post-season games
- Most AFL-AFC Championships
- Most NFL-NFC Championships

CLEVELAND BROWNS

Cleveland Browns is the only present-day AFC team to have won the NFL (now NFC) title, winning it four times between 1950 and 1964.

Top 10 Highest-scoring AFL-AFC Championship games*

	Winners/losers	Year	Score
1 =	Buffalo Bills vs. Los Angeles Raiders	1990	51–3
=	San Diego Chargers vs. Boston Patriots	1963	51–10
3	Miami Dolphins vs. Pittsburgh Steelers	1984	45–28
4	Oakland Raiders vs. Houston Oilers	1967	40–7
5	Denver Broncos vs. Cleveland Browns	1987	38–33
6	Denver Broncos vs. Cleveland Browns	1989	37–21
7 =	Oakland Raiders vs. San Diego Chargers	1980	34–27
=	Pittsburgh Steelers vs. Houston Oilers	1978	34–5
9	Tennessee Titans vs. Jacksonville Jaguars	1999	33–14
10 =	Kansas City Chiefs vs. Buffalo Bills	1966	31–7
=	New England Patriots vs. Miami Dolphins	1985	31–14

* Based on score of winning team

The Miami vs. Pittsburgh game of 1984 was the highest-scoring Championship game, with a total of 73 points scored, equaling the NFL-NFC record set when Chicago beat Washington 73-0 in the 1940 Championship.

◄ The Green Bay Packers discussing tactics. The Packers have won more NFL-NFC Championships than any other team.

Top 10 Highest-scoring NFL-NFC Championship games*

	Winners/losers	Year	Score
1	Chicago Bears vs. Washington Redskins	1940	73-0
2	Detroit Lions vs. Cleveland Browns	1957	59-14
3	Cleveland Browns vs. Detroit Lions	1954	56-10
4	New York Giants vs. Chicago Bears	1956	47-7
5 =	Chicago Bears vs. Washington Redskins	1943	41-21
=	New York Giants vs. Minnesota Vikings	2000	41-0
=	Washington Redskins vs. Detroit Lions	1991	41-10
8 =	Cleveland Browns vs. Los Angeles Rams	1955	38-14
=	Dallas Cowboys vs. San Francisco 49ers	1993	38-21
=	Dallas Cowboys vs. Green Bay Packers	1995	38-27
=	San Francisco 49ers vs. Dallas Cowboys	1994	38-28

* Based on score of winning team

The Bears' rout of the Redskins started when Bill Osmanski ran in from 68 yards, and their famous "T" formation carried them on to the Championship in convincing style. It was the first Championship game to be broadcast on national network radio.

Top 10 Best records in post-season games*

	Team	Played	Won	Lost	Percentages
1	Baltimore Ravens	6	5	1	.833
2	Green Bay Packers	34	23	11	.676
3	Dallas Cowboys	53	32	21	.604
4	San Francisco 49ers	40	24	16	.600
5	Boston/Washington Redskins	37	22	15	.595
6	Pittsburgh Steelers	38	22	16	.579
7	Oakland/Los Angeles Raiders	40	23	17	.575
8	Denver Broncos	28	16	12	.571
9	Miami Dolphins	39	20	19	.513
10 =	Boston/New England Patriots	20	10	10	.500
=	Carolina Panthers	2	1	1	.500
=	Jacksonville Jaguars	8	4	4	.500

* Based on percentage wins in all post-season playoff games 1933–2001

Green Bay's first post-season game was in the 1936 Championship game at the New York Polo Grounds. They beat the Boston Redskins 21–6.

Top 10 Most AFL-AFC Championships*

	Team	Years	Titles
1 =	Buffalo Bills	1964-92	6
=	Denver Broncos	1977-98	6
3 =	Miami Dolphins	1971-84	5
=	Pittsburgh Steelers	1974-95	5
5	Los Angeles/Oakland Raiders	1967-83	4
6 =	Dallas Texans/Kansas City Chiefs	1962-69	3
=	Houston Oilers#	1960-61	3
=	New England Patriots	1985-2001	3
9 =	Cincinnati Bengals	1981-88	2
=	San Diego Chargers	1963-94	2

* 1960–69 for the AFL Championship and since 1970 for the AFC Championship following the merger of the NFL and the AFL at the end of the 1969 season

\# Now the Tennessee Titans

Top 10 Most NFL-NFC Championships*

	Team	Years	Titles
1	Green Bay Packers	1936-97	10
2	Dallas Cowboys	1970-95	8
3 =	Chicago Bears	1933-85	7
=	Washington Redskins	1937-91	7
5	New York Giants	1934-2000	6
6 =	Cleveland/Los Angeles/St. Louis Rams	1946-2001	5
=	San Francisco 49ers	1981-94	5
8 =	Cleveland Browns	1950-64	4
=	Detroit Lions	1935-57	4
=	Minnesota Vikings	1969-76	4
=	Philadelphia Eagles	1948-80	4

* 1933–69 for the NFL Championship and since 1970 for the NFC Championship following the merger of the NFL and the AFL at the end of the 1969 season

The New York Giants have appeared in a record 17 NFL-NFC Championship games.

◄ At 45 pounds lighter than Baltimore Ravens linebacker Ray Lewis, Giants running back Tiki Barber uses the weight difference to attempt to escape a tackle.

RECORD-BREAKERS

- Most touchdowns in a career
- Most touchdown passes in a career
- Most yards gained passing in a career
- Most receptions in a career
- Most yards gained rushing in a career
- Most passes intercepted in a career
- Most points in a career

Top 10 Most touchdowns in a career

Player	Points
1 Jerry Rice*	196
2 Emmitt Smith*	158
3 Marcus Allen	145
4 Cris Carter*	130
5 Jim Brown	126
6 Walter Payton	125
7 John Riggins	116
8 Lenny Moore	113
9 Barry Sanders	109
10 Don Hutson	105

* Active during 2001 season

Top 10 Most touchdown passes in a career

Player	Total
1 Dan Marino	420
2 Fran Tarkenton	342
3 John Elway	300
4 Warren Moon	291
5 Johnny Unitas	290
6 Brett Favre*	287
7 Joe Montana	273
8 Dave Krieg	261
9 Sonny Jurgensen	255
10 Dan Fouts	254

* Active during 2001 season

" Marino will break all the passing records.

Don Shula's prophetic comment after Dan Marino passed the 30,000-yard mark on November 26, 1990 "

Top 10 Most yards gained passing in a career

	Player	Attempted	Completed	Perecentage	Yards
1	Dan Marino	8,358	4,967	59.4	61,361
2	John Elway	7,250	4,123	56.9	51,475
3	Warren Moon	6,823	3,988	58.5	49,325
4	Fran Tarkenton	6,467	3,686	57.0	47,003
5	Dan Fouts	5,604	3,297	58.8	43,040
6	Joe Montana	5,391	3,409	63.2	40,551
7	Johnny Unitas	5,186	2,830	54.6	40,239
8	Vinny Testaverde*	5,644	3,157	55.9	39,059
9	Brett Favre*	5,442	3,311	60.8	38,627
10	Dave Krieg	5,311	3,105	58.5	38,147

* Active during 2001 season

Top 10 Most receptions in a career

	Player	Yards	Average	Touchdowns	Receptions
1	Jerry Rice*	20,386	14.9	185	1,364
2	Cris Carter*	13,833	12.7	129	1,093
3	Andre Reed	13,198	13.9	87	951
4	Art Monk	12,721	13.5	68	940
5	Tim Brown*	13,237	14.1	95	937
6	Irving Fryar	12,785	15.0	84	851
7	Steve Largent	13,089	16.0	100	819
8	Henry Ellard	13,777	16.9	65	814
9	James Lofton	14,004	18.3	75	764
10 =	Michael Irvin	11,904	15.9	65	750
=	Charlie Joiner	12,146	16.2	65	750

* Active during 2001 season

Top 10 Most yards gained rushing in a career

	Player	Yards
1	Walter Payton	16,726
2	Emmitt Smith*	16,187
3	Barry Sanders	15,269
4	Eric Dickerson	13,259
5	Tony Dorsett	12,739
6	Jim Brown	12,312
7	Marcus Allen	12,243
8	Franco Harris	12,120
9	Thurman Thomas	12,074
10	John Riggins	11,352

* Active during 2001 season

Born in Columbia, Missouri, Walter Payton graduated from Jackson State and spent his entire professional career with the Chicago Bears. He held 28 Bears and eight NFL records at the time of his retirement in 1987. He died at the age of 45 in 1999.

Top 10 Most passes intercepted in a career

	Player	Total
1	George Blanda	277
2	John Hadl	268
3	Fran Tarkenton	266
4	Norm Snead	257
5	Johnny Unitas	253
6	Dan Marino	252
7	Jim Hart	247
8	Bobby Layne	245
9	Dan Fouts	242
10	Warren Moon	233

George Blanda is the only man to have played pro football for 25 years. He led the NFL eight times as scoring leader and he was, until 2000, the all-time top scorer in the NFL. He entered the Hall of Fame in 1981, his first year of eligibility.

Top 10 Most points in a career

	Player	Points
1	Gary Anderson*	2,133
2	Morten Andersen*	2,036
3	George Blanda	2,002
4	Norm Johnson	1,736
5	Nick Lowery	1,711
6	Jan Stenerud	1,699
7	Eddie Murray	1,594
8	Al Del Greco	1,584
9	Pat Leahy	1,470
10	Jim Turner	1,439

* Active during 2001 season

Gary Anderson's career points have come with the following teams: Pittsburgh, Philadelphia, San Francisco, and Minnesota. His 164 points in 1998 is an NFL record for most points in a season without a touchdown in the points tally.

◀ In 1998 Minnesota Vikings kicker Gary Anderson became the first player in 15 years to score 150 points in a season in the NFL.

- Most yards gained passing in a season
- Most touchdowns rushing in a season
- Most receptions in a season
- Most touchdowns in a season
- Most points in a season

" When I watch myself on film, sometimes I don't even believe some of the things I do.

Walter Payton "

SEASON RECORDS

Top 10 Most yards gained passing in a season

Player/team	Season	Yards
1 Dan Marino, Miami Dolphins	1984	5,084
2 Kurt Warner, St. Louis Rams	2001	4,830
3 Dan Fouts, San Diego Chargers	1981	4,802
4 Dan Marino, Miami Dolphins	1986	4,746
5 Dan Fouts, San Diego Chargers	1980	4,715
6 Warren Moon, Houston Oilers	1991	4,690
7 Warren Moon, Houston Oilers	1990	4,689
8 Neil Lomax, St. Louis Cardinals	1984	4,614
9 Drew Bledsoe, New England Patriots	1994	4,555
10 Lynn Dickey, Green Bay Packers	1983	4,458

Thanks to Dan Marino's efforts in 1984, the Dolphins topped the AFC Eastern Division with a 14–2–0 record. They went on to play the 49ers in the Super Bowl in a game that was watched by nearly 116 million people in the United States and a further six million in the United Kingdom.

◀ Dan Marino completed nine out of ten passes for 103 yards in the first quarter of Super Bowl XIX but was still on the losing side as the Dolphins lost to the 49ers.

Top 10 Most touchdowns rushing in a season

	Player/team	Season	Touchdowns
1	Emmitt Smith, Dallas Cowboys	1995	25
2	John Riggins, Washington Redskins	1983	24
3 =	Terry Allen, Washington Redskins	1996	21
=	Terrell Davis, Denver Broncos	1998	21
=	Joe Morris, New York Giants	1985	21
=	Emmitt Smith, Dallas Cowboys	1994	21
7 =	Earl Campbell, Houston Oilers	1979	19
=	Chuck Muncie, San Diego Chargers	1981	19
=	Jim Taylor, Green Bay Packers	1962	19
10 =	Eric Dickerson, Los Angeles Rams	1983	18
=	Marshall Faulk, St. Louis Rams	2000	18
=	George Rogers, Washington Redskins	1986	18
=	Emmitt Smith, Dallas Cowboys	1992	18

Top 10 Most receptions in a season

	Player/team	Season	Yards	Receptions
1	Herman Moore, Detroit Lions	1995	1,686	123
2 =	Cris Carter, Minnesota Vikings	1995	1,371	122
=	Cris Carter, Minnesota Vikings	1994	1,256	122
=	Jerry Rice, San Francisco 49ers	1995	1,848	122
5	Isaac Bruce, St. Louis Rams	1995	1,781	119
6	Jimmy Smith, Jacksonville Jaguars	1999	1,636	116
7	Marvin Harrison, Indianapolis Colts	1999	1,663	115
8	Rod Smith, Denver Broncos	2001	1,343	113
9 =	Jerry Rice, San Francisco 49ers	1994	1,499	112
=	Sterling Sharpe, Green Bay Packers	1993	1,274	112
=	Jimmy Smith, Jacksonville Jaguars	2001	1,373	112

During his record-breaking season, Herman Moore had 14 receptions in the game against the Chicago Bears on December 4, 1995. This is an NFL record for the most receptions in a Monday night game.

Top 10 Most touchdowns in a season

	Player/team	Season	Touchdowns
1	Marshall Faulk, St. Louis Rams	2000	26
2	Emmitt Smith, Dallas Cowboys	1995	25
3	John Riggins, Washington Redskins	1983	24
4 =	Terrell Davis, Denver Broncos	1998	23
=	Jerry Rice, San Francisco 49ers	1987	23
=	O. J. Simpson, Buffalo Bills	1975	23
7 =	Chuck Foreman, Minnesota Vikings	1975	22
=	Gale Sayers, Chicago Bears	1966	22
=	Emmitt Smith, Dallas Cowboys	1994	22
10 =	Terry Allen, Washington Redskins	1996	21
=	Jim Brown, Cleveland Browns	1965	21
=	Marsall Faulk, St. Louis Rams	2001	21
=	Joe Morris, New York Giants	1985	21

Top 10 Most points in a season

	Player/team	Season	Points
1	Paul Hornung, Green Bay Packers	1960	176
2	Gary Anderson, Minnnesota Vikings	1998	164
3	Mark Moseley, Washington Redskins	1983	161
4	Marshall Faulk, St. Louis Rams	2000	160
5	Gino Cappelletti, Boston Patriots	1964	155
6	Emmitt Smith, Dallas Cowboys	1995	150
7	Chip Lohmiller, Washington Redskins	1991	149
8	Gino Cappen, Green Bay Packers	1961	146
9 =	John Kasay, Carolina Panthers	1996	145
=	Jim Turner, New York Jets	1968	145
=	Mike Vanderjagt, Indianapolis Colts	1999	145

A former Heisman trophy winner, Paul Hornung went on to become a star of the Green Bay Packers in the 1960s. He led the NFL three times in scoring and was voted MVP in 1960 and 1961.

◀ Dallas Cowboys running back Emmitt Smith, who headed the NFC rushing list four times in five years (1991–95).

COACHES, DRAFTS & MOST VALUABLE PLAYERS

- Annual most valuable player awards
- NFL coaches
- Coaches with the most NFL titles
- Teams with the most number one draft picks
- First Heisman Trophy winners to be number one draft pick

THE INAUGURAL DRAFT

The first number one choice in the inaugural draft in 1936 was Jay Berwanger from Chicago, who was picked by the Philadelphia Eagles. However, they traded him to the Bears and Berwanger never went on to play professional football, choosing a business career instead. He refereed the 1949 Rose Bowl between Northwestern and California.

Top 10 Annual most valuable player awards

	Player	Team(s)	Years	Wins
1	Jim Brown	Cleveland Browns	1957–58, 1963, 1965	4
2 =	Randall Cunningham	Philadelphia Eagles/Minnesota Vikings	1988, 1990, 1998	3
=	Brett Favre	Green Bay Packers	1995–97	3
=	Johnny Unitas	Baltimore Colts	1959, 1964, 1967	3
=	Y. A. Tittle	San Francisco 49ers/New York Giants	1957, 1962–63	3
6 =	Earl Campbell	Houston Oilers	1978–79	2
=	Otto Graham	Cleveland Browns	1953–55	2
=	Don Hutson	Green Bay Packers	1941–42	2
=	Joe Montana	San Francisco 49ers	1989–90	2
=	Walter Payton	Chicago Bears	1977, 1985	2
=	Barry Sanders	Detroit Lions	1991, 1997	2
=	Ken Stabler	Oakland Raiders	1974, 1976	2
=	Joe Thiesmann	Washington Redskins	1982–83	2
=	Steve Young	San Francisco 49ers	1993–94	2

The prestigious annual MVP trophy goes to the Player of the Year. There are three MVP Awards each year, one by the Pro Football Writers' Association (since 1976), one by the Associated Press (since 1957), and one by the Maxwell Club of Philadelphia for the Bert Bell Trophy (since 1959). The last player to win all three in the same year was Kurt Warner of the St. Louis Rams in 1999.

Top 10 NFL coaches*

	Coach	Team(s)	Years	Wins
1	Don Shula	Baltimore Colts, Miami Dolphins	1963-95	347
2	George Halas	Chicago Bears	1920-67	324
3	Tom Landry	Dallas Cowboys	1960-88	270
4	Curly Lambeau	Green Bay Packers, Chicago Cardinals, Washington Redskins	1921-53	229
5	Chuck Noll	Pittsburgh Steelers	1969-91	209
6	Chuck Knox	Los Angeles Rams, Buffalo Bills, Seattle Seahawks	1973-91	193
7	Dan Reeves	Denver Broncos, New York Giants, Atlanta Falcons	1981-2001	188
8	Paul Brown	Cleveland Browns, Cincinnati Bengals	1950-75	170
9	Bud Grant	Minnesota Vikings	1967-85	168
10	Marty Schottenheimer	Cleveland Browns, Kansas City Chiefs, Washington Redskins	1984-2001	158

* Based on most wins in regular and post-season games

When the Chicago Bears were formed, originally by Decatur businessman A. E. Staley, he called his team the Decatur Staleys and appointed one of his employees as coach. That coach was George Halas, one of the legends of the game. Halas was to spend 40 years with the Bears as head coach. He stepped down for three years 1930–32 and was away serving with the Navy in 1942–45. He eventually retired in 1967 with a record 324 wins to his credit.

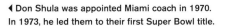

◀ Don Shula was appointed Miami coach in 1970.
In 1973, he led them to their first Super Bowl title.

Top 10 Coaches with the most NFL titles*

	Coach	Super Bowls	NFL-NFC	AFL-AFC	Total
1 =	Chuck Noll	4	0	4	8
=	Don Shula	2	1	5	8
3 =	Joe Gibbs	3	4	0	7
=	Tom Landry	2	5	0	7
=	Vince Lombardi	2	5	0	7
6	Bill Walsh	3	3	0	6
7 =	George Halas	0	5	0	5
=	Bill Parcells	2	2	1	5
9 =	Weeb Ewbank	1	2	1	4
=	Tom Flores	2	0	2	4
=	Bud Grant	0	4	0	4
=	Jimmy Johnson	2	2	0	4
=	Marv Levy	0	0	4	4
=	Dan Reeves	0	1	3	4
=	Mike Shanahan	2	0	2	4
=	Hank Stram	1	0	3	4

* Based on NFL-NFC Championship wins 1933-2002, AFL-AFC Championship wins 1960-2002, and Super Bowl wins 1967-2002

Top 10 Teams with the most number one draft picks

	Team	Years	Picks
1	Baltimore/Indianapolis Colts	1955, 1967, 1983, 1990, 1992, 1998	6
2 =	Boston/New England Patriots	1964, 1971, 1982, 1984, 1993	5
=	Buffalo Bills	1961, 1969, 1972, 1979,1985	5
4 =	Atlanta Falcons	1966, 1975, 1988, 2001	4
=	Chicago Cardinals	1939-40, 1945, 1958	4
=	Cleveland/Los Angeles/St. Louis Rams	1938, 1952, 1960, 1997	4
=	Houston Oilers	1965, 1973, 1978, 2002	4
=	Tampa Bay Buccaneers	1976-77, 1986-97	4
9 =	Cleveland Browns	1954, 1999-2000	3
=	Dallas Cowboys	1975, 1989, 1991	3
=	Detroit Lions	1943, 1950, 1980	3
=	Philadelphia Eagles	1936-37, 1949	3
=	Pittsburgh Steelers	1942, 1956, 1970	3

The draft was introduced in 1936 following a suggestion by Bert Bell, the League's second commissioner and co-owner of the Philadelphia Eagles, who wanted to see an end to the dominance of the Chicago Bears and New York Giants in the 1930s. His suggestion was to allow the worst team each year to have the pick of the top college players for the forthcoming season, the second-worst team having the next pick and so on.

The 10 First Heisman Trophy winners to be the number one draft pick

	Player	College	Picked by	Year
1	Jay Berwanger	Chicago	Philadelphia Eagles	1936
2	Tom Harman	Michigan	Chicago Bears	1941
3	Frank Sinkwich	Georgia	Detroit Lions	1943
4	Angelo Bertelli	Notre Dame	Boston Yanks	1944
5	Leon Hart	Notre Dame	Detroit Lions	1950
6	Paul Hornung	Notre Dame	Green Bay Packers	1957
7	Billy Cannon	Louisiana State	Los Angeles Rams	1960
8	Ernie Davis	Syracuse	Washington Redskins	1962
9	Terry Baker	Oregon State	Los Angeles Rams	1963
10	O. J. Simpson	USC	Buffalo Bills	1969

The Heisman Trophy has been awarded since 1935 and goes to the top college player, as determined by a poll of journalists. It is presented by the Downtown Athletic Club of New York and the trophy (formally called the John W. Heisman Memorial Trophy) is named after a former director of the club.

▶ Jim Brown retired in 1966 at the age of 30 while still at the top. In nine seasons with the Cleveland Browns, he headed the NFL in rushing eight times.

TEAMS, FRANCHISES & STADIUMS

- Most points in NFL history
- Most wins in NFL history
- Newest current NFL teams
- Biggest NFL stadiums
- Oldest NFL stadiums
- Oldest current NFL teams

> I wouldn't ever set out to hurt anyone deliberately unless it was, you know, important—like a league game or something.
>
> **Dick Butkus,** former Chicago Bears linebacker

The 10 Most points in NFL history*

	Team	Points
1	Green Bay Packers	19,725
2	Chicago Bears	19,512
3	Washington Redskins	19,414
4	St. Louis Rams	18,554
5	New York Giants	18,443
6	Detroit Lions	18,316
7	San Francisco 49ers	17,934
8	Philadelphia Eagles	17,804
9	Pittsburgh Steelers	17,681
10	Arizona Cardinals	16,764

* In a regular season, from 1933–2001

Top 10 Most wins in NFL history*

	Team	Wins
1	Chicago Bears	536
2	Green Bay Packers	509
3 =	New York Giants	505
=	Washington Redskins	505
5	Pittsburgh Steelers	469
6	Detroit Lions	444
7	San Francisco 49ers	439
8	St. Louis Rams	438
9	Cleveland Browns	432
10	Philadelphia Eagles	423

* In a regular season, from 1933–2001

The 10 Newest current NFL teams*

	Team	First season
1	Baltimore Ravens	1996
2 =	Carolina Panthers	1995
=	Jacksonville Jaguars	1995
4 =	Seattle Seahawks	1976
=	Tampa Bay Buccaneers	1976
6	Cincinnati Bengals	1968
7	New Orleans Saints	1967
8 =	Atlanta Falcons	1966
=	Miami Dolphins	1966
10	Minnesota Vikings	1961

* Based on first season in the League and excluding name and franchise changes

◄ The Pontiac Silverdome, home of the Detroit Lions, was completed in 1975.

Top 10 Biggest NFL stadiums*

	Team	Stadium	Capacity
1	Detroit Lions	Pontiac Silverdome	80,311
2	Washington Redskins	FedEx Field	80,166
3	New York Giants/Jets	Giants Stadium#	79,469
4	Kansas City Chiefs	Arrowhead Stadium	78,451
5	Denver Broncos	INVESCO Field at Mile High	76,125
6	Miami Dolphins	Pro Player Stadium	74,916
7	Buffalo Bills	Ralph Wilson Stadium	73,967
8	Arizona Cardinals	Sun Devil Stadium	73,273
9	Cleveland Browns	Cleveland Browns Stadium	73,200
10	Jacksonville Jaguars	ALLTEL Stadium	73,000

* By capacity at the start of the 2002 season

\# The capacity of the Giants Stadium is reduced slightly for Jets home games

The smallest capacity is at the RCA Dome, home of the Indianapolis Colts, with a capacity of 56,127.

Top 10 Oldest NFL stadiums

	Team	Stadium	Year opened
1	Seattle Seahawks	Husky Stadium	1920
2	Chicago Bears	Soldier Field	1924
3	Green Bay Packers	Lambeau Fueld	1957
4	Arizona Cardinals	Sun Devil Stadium	1958
5	San Francisco 49ers	3Com Park	1960
6	Oakland Raiders	Network Associates Coliseum	1966
7	San Diego Chargers	Qualcomm Stadium	1967
8	Philadelphia Eagles	Veterans Stadium	Apr. 1971
9	New England Patriots	Foxboro Stadium	Aug. 1971
10	Dallas Cowboys	Texas Stadium	Oct. 1971

The 10 Oldest current NFL teams*

	Team – present name/name during first season	First season
1 =	Arizona Cardinals/Chicago Cardinals	1920
=	Chicago Bears/Decatur Staleys	1920
3	Green Bay Packers/Green Bay Packers	1921
4	New York Giants/New York Giants	1925
5	Detroit Lions/Portsmouth Spartans	1930
6	Washington Redskins/Boston Braves	1932
7 =	Philadelphia Eagles/Philadelphia Eagles	1933
=	Pittsburgh Steelers/Pittsburgh Pirates	1933
9	St. Louis Rams/Cleveland Rams	1937
10 =	Cleveland Browns/Cleveland Browns	1946
=	San Francisco 49ers/San Francisco 49ers	1946

* Based on first season in the League

▼ Soldier Field, venue for the biggest-ever football crowd, when 123,000 fans saw Notre Dame beat Southern California 7–6 on November 26, 1927.

COLLEGE FOOTBALL

- Most Cotton Bowls
- Most Rose Bowls
- Most "Big Five" Bowl wins
- Most Sugar Bowls
- Most Orange Bowls
- Most college football National Championships

INDOOR HOME

When the Sugar Bowl moved to its new home at the Louisiana Superdome in 1975 it became the first, and so far only, major bowl game to be played on an indoor field.

Top 10 Most Cotton Bowls

	College	Bowls
1	Texas	10
2	Notre Dame	5
3	Texas A & M	4
4 =	Arkansas	3
=	Rice	3
6 =	Alabama	2
=	Georgia	2
=	Houston	2
=	LSU	2
=	Penn State	2
=	SMU	2
=	Tennessee	2
=	TCU	2
=	UCLA	2

Originally a post-season game between two high school teams, the Cotton Bowl was first played on New Year's Day 1936. College teams replaced the high school teams the following year and it has been played on January 1 ever since, with the exception of 1966, when it was played on December 31. Originally held at the Fair Park Stadium in Dallas, it now takes place in the Cotton Bowl.

Top 10 Most Rose Bowls

	College	Bowls
1	Southern California	20
2	Michigan	8
3	Washington	7
4	Ohio State	6
5 =	Stanford	5
=	UCLA	5
7	Alabama	4
8 =	Illinois	3
=	Michigan State	3
=	Wisconsin	3

The first-ever Rose Tournament game was held on New Year's Day 1902, at Tournament Park, Pasadena, as part of the annual Tournament of Roses celebration. In this first game, the University of Michigan beat Stanford University 49–0. So great was the defeat that the event's organizers decided not to stage the event again, replacing it the following year with a Roman-style chariot race. It was not until 1916 that football returned to the festivities. As the game grew in popularity, a new 57,000-seat stadium was built, and the first game was held in Pasadena on January 1, 1923. The stadium, and the annual game played there, were named the "Rose Bowl" by Harlan "Dusty" Hall, the Rose Tournament's press agent. The stadium has since been enlarged several times, and for the game on January 1, 1973 held a record crowd of 106,869.

Top 10 Most "Big Five" Bowl wins

	College	Rose Bowl	Orange Bowl	Sugar Bowl	Cotton Bowl	Fiesta Bowl	Total
1	Southern California	20	0	0	1	0	21
2 =	Alabama	4	4	8	2	0	18
=	Oklahoma	0	12	4	1	1	18
4 =	Nebraska	0	8	3	0	2	13
=	Penn State	1	3	1	2	6	13
=	Texas	0	2	1	10	0	13
7 =	Florida State	0	3	4	1	2	10
=	Michigan	8	1	0	0	1	10
=	Notre Dame	0	2	2	5	1	10
10 =	Georgia Tech.	1	3	4	1	0	9
=	Miami	1	5	2	1	0	9
=	Ohio State	6	1	1	1	0	9

> College football today is one of the last great strongholds of genuine old-fashioned American hypocrisy.
>
> Paul Gallico

Top 10 Most Sugar Bowls

	College	Bowls
1	Alabama	8
2	Mississippi	5
3 =	Florida State	4
=	Georgia Tech.	4
=	LSU	4
=	Oklahoma	4
=	Tennessee	4
8	Nebraska	3
9 =	Florida	2
=	Georgia	2
=	Miami	2
=	Notre Dame	2
=	Pittsburgh	2
=	Santa Clara	2
=	TCU	2

First played at the Tulane Stadium on New Year's Day 1935, the Sugar Bowl moved to its present home at the Louisiana Superdome in 1975.

Top 10 Most Orange Bowls

	College	Bowls
1	Oklahoma	12
2	Nebraska	8
3	Miami	5
4	Alabama	4
5 =	Florida	3
=	Florida State	3
=	Georgia Tech.	3
=	Penn State	3
9 =	Clemson	2
=	Colorado	2
=	Georgia	2
=	LSU	2
=	Notre Dame	2
=	Texas	2

The Orange Bowl is the second-oldest bowl game after the Rose Bowl. It was first played in 1935 as part of the Miami Palm Festival. Previously played at the Miami Field Stadium and the Orange Bowl, it is now held at the Pro Player Stadium in Fort Lauderdale.

Top 10 Most college football National Championships

	College	Years	Titles
1 =	Princeton	1869–1935	18
=	Yale	1874–1927	18
3	Notre Dame	1919–88	13
4	Alabama	1925–92	11
5	Harvard	1875–1919	9
6 =	Michigan	1901–97	8
=	Nebraska	1970–87	8
=	Southern California	1928–78	8
9 =	Ohio State	1933–70	7
=	Oklahoma	1950–2000	7

The first National Champions were Princeton in 1869. Between that date and 1935, the champions were decided by polls, mathematical formulas, or historical records. Since 1936, however, the champions have been decided by either media or coaches' polls.

▼ Running back Clinton Portis of Miami carries the ball while eluding the Nebraska defense during the 2002 Rose Bowl Championship.

BASEBALL

At the Start

Medieval manuscripts show ball games with bats, while a game called "base-ball" appears in a picture published in London in 1744, and is mentioned in Jane Austen's novel, *Northanger Abbey*, which she began in 1798. The game of rounders was first described 30 years later, and this or a similar game was known among British settlers in North America. Abner Doubleday is sometimes credited as the game's originator in 1839, but Alexander Joy Cartwright, Jr. drew up baseball's first rules in 1845, founding the first team, the Knickerbocker Base Ball Club of New York. The first game played according to Cartwright rules took place at the Elysian Fields, Hoboken, New Jersey, on June 19, 1846, when his team, the Knickerbockers, was defeated 23–1 by the New York Nine. Professional baseball was introduced in 1871.

BASEBALL

WORLD SERIES RECORDS

- Most home runs in the World Series
- Most games played in the World Series
- Most runs in a World Series career
- Strikeouts in the World Series
- Most World Series wins
- Pitchers with the most strikeouts in a single World Series game
- Biggest single-game wins in the World Series

THE ORIGINS

Major League baseball started with the National League in 1876. The rival American League was started in 1901, and two years later Pittsburgh, champions of the National League, invited American League champions Boston to take part in a best-of-nine games series to establish the "real" champions. Boston won 5–3. It has been a best-of-seven games series since 1905, apart from 1919–21, when it reverted to a nine-game series.

Top 10 Most home runs in the World Series

	Player	Home runs
1	Mickey Mantle	18
2	Babe Ruth	15
3	Yogi Berra	12
4	Duke Snider	11
5 =	Lou Gehrig	10
=	Reggie Jackson	10
7 =	Joe DiMaggio	8
=	Frank Robinson	8
=	Bill Skowron	8
10 =	Hank Bauer	7
=	Leon Goslin	7
=	Gil McDougald	7

Five of Reggie Jackson's total came in the 1977 World Series against the Los Angeles Dodgers, a record for one series.

Top 10 Most games played in the World Series

	Player	Games
1	Yogi Berra	75
2	Mickey Mantle	65
3	Elston Howard	54
4 =	Hank Bauer	53
=	Gil McDougald	53
6	Phil Rizzuto	52
7	Joe DiMaggio	51
8	Frankie Frisch	50
9	Pee Wee Reese	44
10 =	Roger Maris	41
=	Babe Ruth	41

In a career spanning 18 seasons, Yogi Berra appeared in a record 75 World Series games and hit 12 homers. He was widely regarded as one of the game's greatest catchers.

Top 10 Most runs in a World Series career

	Player	Runs
1	Mickey Mantle	42
2	Yogi Berra	41
3	Babe Ruth	37
4	Lou Gehrig	30
5	Joe DiMaggio	27
6	Roger Maris	26
7	Elston Howard	25
8	Gil McDougald	23
9 =	Derek Jeter*	22
=	Jackie Robinson	22

* Active 2001

Babe Ruth, also known as "The Sultan of Swat," was a pitcher with the Red Sox before joining the Yankees in 1920, but his move to the outfield paid dividends because he led the New Yorkers to seven American League pennants and four World Series titles.

Top 10 Strikeouts in the World Series

	Pitcher	Strikeouts
1	Whitey Ford	94
2	Bob Gibson	92
3	Allie Reynolds	62
4 =	Sandy Koufax	61
=	Red Ruffing	61
6	Chief Bender	59
7	George Earnshaw	56
8	John Smoltz	52
9	Waite Hoyt	49
10	Christy Mathewson	48

◀ The greatest name in baseball – Babe Ruth scored his first homer for the Yankees against his former team, the Boston Red Sox, on May 1, 1920.

Top 10 Most World Series wins

	Team	First win	Last win	Total wins
1	New York Yankees	1923	2000	26
2 =	Philadelphia/ Oakland Athletics	1910	1989	9
=	St. Louis Cardinals	1926	1982	9
4	Brooklyn/ Los Angeles Dodgers	1955	1988	6
5 =	Boston Red Sox	1903	1918	5
=	Cincinnati Reds	1919	1990	5
=	New York Giants	1905	1954	5
=	Pittsburgh Pirates	1909	1979	5
9	Detroit Tigers	1935	1984	4
10 =	Baltimore Orioles	1966	1983	3
=	Boston/ Milwaukee/ Atlanta Braves	1914	1995	3
=	Washington Senators/ Minnesota Twins	1924	1991	3

The game's most successful team, the Yankees, started life as the Highlanders and played at Hilltop Park, Manhattan, an all-wood park at 168th Street and Broadway. Their first game was a 3–1 loss at Washington in 1903. The famous pinstripe shirts were first seen in 1912, and the following year, after moving to the Polo grounds, they became known as the Yankees.

Top 10 Pitchers with the most strikeouts in a single World Series game

	Pitcher/match	Game/year	Strikeouts
1	Bob Gibson, Cardinals vs. Tigers	Game 1, 1968	17
2	Sandy Koufax, Dodgers vs. Yankees	Game 1, 1963	15
3	Carl Erskine, Dodgers vs. Yankees	Game 3, 1953	14
4 =	Howard Ehmke, Athletics vs. Cubs	Game 1, 1929	13
=	Bob Gibson, Cardinals vs. Yankees	Game 5, 1964	13
6 =	Mort Cooper, Cardinals vs. Browns	Game 5, 1944	12
=	Bill Donovan, Tigers vs. Cubs	Game 1, 1907	12
=	Orlando Hernandez, Yankees vs. Mets	Game 3, 2000	12
=	Walter Johnson, Senators vs. Giants	Game 1, 1924	12
=	Tom Seaver, Mets vs. Athletics	Game 3, 1973	12
=	Ed Walsh, White Sox vs. Cubs	Game 3, 1906	12

Former Harlem Globetrotter Bob Gibson spent over 17 seasons with the Cardinals and won 20 games fives times. His 1968 season saw him not only register 17 strikeouts in a single World Series game, but also pitch a season ERA of 1.22, the lowest in the League since 1914.

▼ The New York Yankees celebrate winning the 2000 World Series after clinching it in Game 5 against the Mets.

Top 10 Biggest single-game wins in the World Series

	Teams (winners first)/game	Date	Score
1	New York Yankees vs. New York Giants (Game 2)	Oct. 2, 1936	18–4
2 =	Arizona Diamondbacks vs. New York Yankees (Game 6)	Nov. 3, 2001	15–2
=	New York Yankees vs. Pittsburgh Pirates (Game 2)	Oct. 6, 1960	16–3
4 =	Detroit Tigers vs. St. Louis Cardinals (Game 6)	Oct. 9, 1968	13–1
=	New York Yankees vs. Milwaukee Brewers (Game 6)	Oct. 19, 1982	13–1
=	New York Yankees vs. New York Giants (Game 5)	Oct. 9, 1951	13–1
=	New York Yankees vs. Pittsburgh Pirates (Game 6)	Oct. 12, 1960	12–0
8 =	Atlanta Braves vs. New York Yankees (Game 1)	Oct. 20, 1996	12–1
=	Chicago White Sox vs. Los Angeles Dodgers (Game 1)	Oct. 1, 1959	11–0
=	Kansas City Royals vs. St. Louis Cardinals (Game 7)	Oct. 27, 1985	11–0
=	New York Yankees vs. Philadelphia Athletics (Game 6)	Oct. 26, 1911	13–2
=	St. Louis Cardinals vs. Detroit Tigers (Game 7)	Oct. 9, 1934	11–0

Source: Major League Baseball

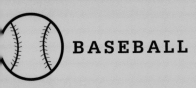
CHAMPIONSHIP SERIES & DIVISIONAL WINNERS

- Best post-season batting averages in a career
- Pitchers with the best post-season ERA in a career
- Teams winning the most American League season and Division titles
- Teams winning the most National League season and Division titles
- Most appearances in post-season games
- Pitchers with the most post-season wins in a career
- Most League Championship Series Pennants

Top 10 Best post-season batting averages in a career

	Player	ERA
1	Bobby Brown	.439
2	Jose Offerman	.429
3	Ichiro Suzuki	.421
4	Pepper Martin	.418
5	Fred Lynn	.407
6	Billy Hatcher	.404
7	Lou Brock	.391
8	Ryne Sandberg	.385
9	Nomar Garciaparra	.383
10	Willie Aikens	.375

Top 10 Pitchers with the best post-season ERA in a career

	Player	ERA
1 =	Joe Niekro	0.00
=	John Rocker	0.00
3	Dave Dravecky	0.35
4	Ken Dayley	0.44
5	Harry Brecheen	0.83
6	Claude Osteen	0.86
7	Babe Ruth	0.87
8	Sherry Smith	0.89
9	Mariano Rivera	0.91
10	Sandy Koufax	0.95

"Some kids dream of joining the circus, others of becoming a major league baseball player. I have been doubly blessed. As a member of the New York Yankees, I have gotten to do both.
Graig Nettles"

Top 10 Teams winning the most American League season and Division titles

	Team	First title	Last title	Total
1	New York Yankees	1921	2001	38
2	Oakland Athletics	1905	1990	14
3 =	Boston Red Sox	1903	1986	9
=	Detroit Tigers	1907	1984	9
5	Baltimore Orioles	1944	1983	7
6	Minnesota Twins	1924	1991	6
7	Cleveland Indians	1920	1997	5
8	Chicago White Sox	1906	1959	4
9 =	Kansas City Royals	1980	1985	2
=	Toronto Blue Jays	1992	1993	2

The Anaheim Angels, Seattle Mariners, Tampa Bay Devil Rays, and Texas Rangers are the only four American League teams never to have won a title.

Top 10 Teams winning the most National League season and Division titles

	Team	First title	Last title	Total
1	Los Angeles Dodgers	1916	1988	18
2	San Francisco Giants	1905	1989	16
3	St. Louis Cardinals	1926	1987	15
4	Chicago Cubs	1906	1945	10
5 =	Atlanta Braves	1914	1999	9
=	Cincinnati Reds	1919	1990	9
7	Pittsburgh Pirates	1903	1979	7
8	Philadelphia Phillies	1915	1993	5
9	New York Mets	1969	2000	4
10	San Diego Padres	1984	1998	2

The Colorado Rockies and the Montreal Expos are the only National League teams never to have won a title.

Top 10 Most appearances in post-season games

	Player	Games
1	David Justice	107
2	Tino Martinez	88
3	Paul O'Neill	85
4	Bernie Williams	83
5	Derek Jeter	78
6	Reggie Jackson	77
7	Yogi Berra	75
8	Chipper Jones	73
9	Pete Rose	67
10 =	Chuck Knoblauch	66
=	Terry Pendleton	66

David Justice's 107 post-season games have come in 20 series with Atlanta, Cleveland, and the New York Yankees. He has gone on to appear in six World Series, winning on two occasions, with the Braves in 1995 and the Yankees in 2001, and has scored 53 post-season runs.

Top 10 Pitchers with the most post-season wins in a career

	Player	Wins
1 =	Tom Glavine	12
=	John Smoltz	12
3 =	Whitey Ford	10
=	Greg Maddux	10
=	Andy Pettitte	10
=	Dave Stewart	10
7 =	Orlando Hernandez	9
=	Catfish Hunter	9
9 =	David Cone	8
=	Orel Hershiser	8
=	Jim Palmer	8
=	David Wells	8

Glavine and Smoltz both had their wins with Atlanta between 1991 and 2001. Glavine played in 21 post-season series, while Smoltz played in only 19, missing the 2000 Championship Series and World Series. Glavine's record stands at 12 wins and 13 losses and Smoltz's 12 wins and just four losses.

Top 10 Most League Championship Series Pennants

	Team	League	Pennants
1	New York Yankees	AL	9
2	Oakland Athletics	AL	6
3 =	Atlanta Braves	NL	5
=	Baltimore Orioles	AL	5
=	Cincinnati Reds	NL	5
=	Los Angeles Dodgers	NL	5
7	New York Mets	NL	4
8 =	Philadelphia Phillies	NL	3
=	St. Louis Cardinals	NL	3
10 =	Boston Red Sox	AL	2
=	Cleveland Indians	AL	2
=	Kansas City Royals	AL	2
=	Minnesota Twins	AL	2
=	Pittsburgh Pirates	NL	2
=	San Diego Padres	NL	2
=	Toronto Blue Jays	AL	2

The League Championship Series started in 1969 after the National League and American League expanded to 12 teams, split into East and West divisions. The divisional winners met for the title of each respective league. Three divisional leagues were introduced in 1994. Each year the three divisional winners, plus a wild-card entrant, take part in each league's playoff.

◄ Luke Prokopec pitching for the Dodgers against the Texas Rangers during their interleague game at the Dodgers Stadium on June 11, 2001.

BATTING HEROES

- Players who took part in the most consecutive games
- Players most at bat in a career
- Players with the highest career batting averages
- Players with the most home runs in an MLB career
- Players with the most hits in a career
- Players who played the most games in a career
- Players with the most runs in a career

> Cobb's the meanest, toughest [so-and-so] who ever walked onto a field. He gave everybody hell, me included, because he couldn't stand to lose. All he wanted was to beat you on Saturday and twice on Sunday. Otherwise he was miserable.
> **Babe Ruth**

Top 10 Players who took part in the most consecutive games

	Player	From	To	Games
1	Cal Ripken, Jr.*	May 30, 1982	Sept. 19, 1998	2,632
2	Lou Gehrig	June 1, 1925	Apr. 20, 1939	2,130
3	Everett Scott	June 20, 1916	May 5, 1925	1,307
4	Steve Garvey	Sept. 3, 1975	July 29, 1983	1,207
5	Billy Williams	Sept. 22, 1963	Sept. 2, 1970	1,117
6	Joe Sewell	Sept. 13, 1922	Apr. 30, 1930	1,103
7	Stan Musial	Apr. 15, 1952	Aug. 23, 1957	895
8	Eddie Yost	Apr. 30, 1949	May 11, 1955	829
9	Gus Suhr	Sept. 11, 1931	June 4, 1937	822
10	Nellie Fox	Aug. 8, 1955	Sept. 3, 1960	798

* Active in 2001

Source: Major League Baseball

Cal Ripken took himself out of the starting line up on September 21, 1998, in a game between the Orioles and the Yankees, having played in every game since May 30, 1982.

Top 10 Players most at bat in a career

	Player	At bat
1	Pete Rose	14,053
2	Hank Aaron	12,364
3	Carl Yastrzemski	11,988
4	Cal Ripken, Jr.*	11,551
5	Ty Cobb	11,434
6	Eddie Murray	11,336
7	Robin Yount	11,008
8	Dave Winfield	11,003
9	Stan Musial	10,972
10	Willie Mays	10,881

* Active in 2001

Source: Major League Baseball

▶ Ty Cobb of the Detroit Tigers was the first batter to hit more than .400 in consecutive years. He hit .420 in 1911 and .410 in 1912.

◀ Pete Rose beat Ty Cobb's 57-year-old record for most career hits on September 11, 1985, when he hit a single for the Cincinnati Reds against San Diego.

Top 10 Players with the highest career batting averages

	Player	At bat	Hits	Average*
1	Ty Cobb	11,434	4,189	.366
2	Rogers Hornsby	8,173	2,930	.358
3	Joe Jackson	4,981	1,772	.356
4	Ed Delahanty	7,505	2,597	.346
5	Tris Speaker	10,195	3,514	.345
6 =	Billy Hamilton	6,268	2,158	.344
=	Ted Williams	7,706	2,654	.344
8 =	Dan Brouthers	6,711	2,296	.342
=	Harry Heilmann	7,787	2,660	.342
=	Babe Ruth	8,399	2,873	.342

* Calculated by dividing the number of hits by the number of times a batter was at bat

Source: Major League Baseball

Second only to the legendary Ty Cobb, Rogers Hornsby stands as the best second-hitting baseman of all time. Perhaps the most consistent right-handed hitter in the game, he won seven batting titles, including six in a row, and averaged more than .400 three times. His .424 in 1924 is a 20th-century record in the National League. He slugged 20-plus homers in a season on seven occasions, ending his career with an average of .358. Known as "The Rajah," he was the player-manager of the first Cardinals team to win the World Series in 1926.

Top 10 Players with the most home runs in an MLB career

	Player	Home runs
1	Hank Aaron	755
2	Babe Ruth	714
3	Willie Mays	660
4	Frank Robinson	586
5	Mark McGwire*	583
6	Harmon Killebrew	573
7	Barry Bonds*	567
8	Reggie Jackson	563
9	Mike Schmidt	548
10	Mickey Mantle	536

* Active in 2001

Source: Major League Baseball

George Herman "Babe" Ruth set a home run record in 1919 by hitting 29, breaking it the next season hitting 54. His career (1914–35) total of 714 came from 8,399 at bats, which represents an average of 8.5 percent—considerably better than the next man in the averages, Harmon Killebrew, with 7.0 percent.

Top 10 Players with the most hits in a career

	Player	Hits
1	Pete Rose	4,256
2	Ty Cobb	4,189
3	Hank Aaron	3,771
4	Stan Musial	3,630
5	Tris Speaker	3,514
6	Carl Yastrzemski	3,419
7	Honus Wagner	3,418
8	Paul Molitor	3,319
9	Eddie Collins	3,313
10	Willie Mays	3,283

Though he is only fifth on this list, Tris Speaker is the all-time leader in outfield assists (449) and doubles (792). He became player-manager of the Cleveland Indians in 1919 and, in his second season in charge, guided them to their first World Championship. He started his Major League career with the Red Sox, who bought him from Houston in the Texas League for $750 in 1907. Speaker's record of 50 steals and 50 doubles in a year (1912) was not equaled until 1998, by Craig Biggio of the Houston Astros.

Top 10 Players who played the most games in a career

	Player	Games
1	Pete Rose	3,562
2	Carl Yastrzemski	3,308
3	Hank Aaron	3,298
4	Ty Cobb	3,034
5 =	Eddie Murray	3,026
=	Stan Musial	3,026
7	Cal Ripken, Jr.*	3,001
8	Willie Mays	2,992
9	Rickey Henderson*	2,979
10	Dave Winfield	2,973

* Active in 2001

Source: Major League Baseball

When Carl Yastrzemski ended his 23-year career with the Red Sox (his only team) in 1983, he had played a record 3,308 games and had more than 3,000 hits and 400 home runs. He was the club leader in eight categories: games played, runs, hit at-bats, doubles, RBI, total bases, and extra base hits. He was, in 1967, the last player to win the American League Triple Crown for best batting average, most home runs, and best RBI.

Top 10 Players with the most runs in a career

	Player	Runs
1	Rickey Henderson*	2,248
2	Ty Cobb	2,245
3 =	Hank Aaron	2,174
=	Babe Ruth	2,174
5	Pete Rose	2,165
6	Willie Mays	2,062
7	Stan Musial	1,949
8	Lou Gehrig	1,888
9	Tris Speaker	1,881
10	Mel Ott	1,859

* Active in 2001

Source: Major League Baseball

Ty Cobb's 73-year-old record of 2,245 runs was eventually beaten by Rickey Henderson of the San Diego Padres on October 4, 2001.

BASEBALL

PITCHING GREATS

- Pitchers with the most career wins
- Lowest ERA in a career
- First pitchers to throw perfect games
- Most innings pitched
- Most games by a pitcher
- Pitchers with the most career strikeouts
- First pitchers to complete the "Triple Crown"

> Ruth made a grave mistake when he gave up pitching. Working once a week, he might have lasted a long time and become a great star.
>
> **Tris Speaker, 1921,** on Babe Ruth's future (how wrong he was!)

Top 10 Pitchers with the most career wins

	Player	Wins
1	Cy Young	511
2	Walter Johnson	417
3 =	Grover Alexander	373
=	Christy Mathewson	373
5	Warren Spahn	363
6 =	Pud Galvin	361
=	Kid Nichols	361
8	Tim Keefe	344
9	Steve Carlton	329
10 =	John Clarkson	326
=	Eddie Plank	326

Source: Major League Baseball

Denton True "Cy" Young won almost 100 games more than the sport's next best pitcher. He topped 30 game wins five times and 20 game wins an amazing 15 times. He was a member of the Boston team that played in the first World Series in 1903, winning two games in a 5–3 series win.

Top 10 Lowest ERA in a career*

	Player	ERA
1	Ed Walsh	1.82
2	Addie Joss	1.89
3	Mordecai Brown	2.06
4	John Ward	2.10
5	Christy Mathewson	2.13
6	Rube Waddell	2.16
7	Walter Johnson	2.17
8	Orval Overall	2.23
9	Tommy Bond	2.25
10 =	Ed Reulbach	2.28
=	Will White	2.28

* Minimum of 1,500 innings pitched

Source: Major League Baseball

Hall-of-Famer Ed Walsh spent 13 seasons with the White Sox between 1904 and 1916 before ending his career with a season for Boston. In the period 1906–12, he averaged over 24 wins a season, and when he retired he had a 195–126 career record.

The 10 First pitchers to throw perfect games

	Player	Match	Date
1	Lee Richmond	Worcester vs. Cleveland	June 12, 1880
2	Monte Ward	Providence vs. Buffalo	June 17, 1880
3	Cy Young	Boston vs. Philadelphia	May 5, 1904
4	Addie Joss	Cleveland vs. Chicago	Oct. 2, 1908
5	Charlie Robertson	Chicago vs. Detroit	Apr. 30, 1922
6	Don Larsen*	New York vs. Brooklyn	Oct. 8, 1956
7 =	Jim Bunning	Philadelphia vs. New York	June 21, 1964
=	Sandy Koufax	Los Angeles vs. Chicago	Sep. 9, 1965
9	Catfish Hunter	Oakland vs. Minnesota	May 8, 1968
10	Len Barker	Cleveland vs. Toronto	May 15, 1981

* Larsen's perfect game was, uniquely, in the World Series

A total of 17 pitchers have thrown perfect games, that is, they have pitched in all nine innings, dismissing 27 opposing batters, and without conceding a run. The last player to pitch a perfect innings was David Cone, for the Yankees against the Montreal Expos, on July 18, 1999. On October 8, 1956, Don Larsen made baseball history by not only pitching a perfect game but also throwing a no-hitter. This remarkable feat was in the fifth game for the Yankees against the Brooklyn Dodgers. However, this was a case of one brief moment of notoriety for a man who left the League in 1967 with a mediocre career average of 81–91 and just 55–68 as a starting pitcher.

▶ In a 22-year career, Jesse Orosco has played with six pro teams: the New York Mets, Los Angeles Dodgers (two spells), Cleveland Indians, Milwaukee Brewers, Baltimore Orioles, and St. Louis Cardinals.

DID YOU KNOW? Although he was one of the game's winningest pitchers, Pud Galvin never pitched for a club that finished better than third in the League.

Top 10 Most innings pitched

Player	Innings pitched
1 Cy Young	7,356.0
2 Pud Galvin	5,941.1
3 Walter Johnson	5,923.2
4 Phil Niekro	5,404.1
5 Nolan Ryan	5,386.0
6 Gaylord Perry	5,350.1
7 Don Sutton	5,282.1
8 Warren Spahn	5,243.2
9 Steve Carlton	5,217.1
10 Grover Alexander	5,189.2

Top 10 Most games by a pitcher

Player	Apps
1 Jesse Orosco*	1,131
2 Dennis Eckersley	1,071
3 Hoyt Wilhelm	1,070
4 Kent Tekulve	1,050
5 Lee Smith	1,022
6 Rich Gossage	1,002
7 John Franco*	998
8 Lindy McDaniel	987
9 Dan Plesac*	946
10 Rollie Fingers	944

* Active in 2001

Top 10 Pitchers with the most career strikeouts

Player	Strikeouts
1 Nolan Ryan	5,714
2 Steve Carlton	4,136
3 Roger Clemens*	3,717
4 Bert Blyleven	3,701
5 Tom Seaver	3,640
6 Don Sutton	3,574
7 Gaylord Perry	3,534
8 Walter Johnson	3,508
9 Randy Johnson*	3,412
10 Phil Niekro	3,342

* Active in 2001

Source: Major League Baseball

Nolan Ryan was known as the "Babe Ruth of strikeout pitchers," pitching faster (a record 101 mph) and longer (27 seasons–1966 and 1968–93) than any previous player. As well as his 5,714 strikeouts, including 383 in one season, he walked 2,795 batters and allowed the fewest hits (6.55) per nine innings.

The 10 First pitchers to complete the "Triple Crown"*

	Player/team	AL/NL	Year
1	Tommy Bond, Boston	NL	1877
2	Hoss Radbourne, Providence	NL	1884
3	Tim Keefe, New York	NL	1888
4	John Clarkson, Boston	NL	1889
5	Amos Rusie, New York	NL	1894
6	Cy Young, Boston	AL	1901
7 =	Christy Mathewson, New York	NL	1905
=	Rube Waddell, Philadelphia	AL	1905
9	Christy Mathewson, New York	NL	1908
10	Walter Johnson, Washington	AL	1913

* The Triple Crown is when a pitcher tops the ERA, Wins, and Strikeouts lists in one season

Apart from 1905, the only years in which National and American League pitchers took the Triple Crown in the same season were 1918 and 1924. The only men to perform the Triple Crown three times are Walter Johnson (Washington) 1913, 1918, 1924, Grover Alexander (Philadelphia) 1915, 1916, 1917, and Sandy Koufax (Los Angeles) 1963, 1965, 1966, Alexander uniquely doing so in consecutive seasons.

BASEBALL

SINGLE-SEASON RECORDS

- Best batting averages in a season
- Most runs in a season
- Most hits in a season
- Most strikeouts in a season
- First players to hit four home runs in one game
- Pitchers with the most wins in a season
- Most home runs in a season

HOMER MARKS

Babe Ruth's 60-homer mark set in the 1927 season was unbroken for 34 years until Roger Maris hit 61 home runs in 1961. Maris' record stood for 37 years, but the 70 scored by Mark McGwire in 1998, establishing a new record, stood for only three years before it was beaten by Barry Bonds in 2001.

Top 10 Best batting averages in a season

	Player	Year	Average
1	Hugh Duffy	1894	.4397
2	Tip O'Neill	1887	.4352
3	Ross Barnes	1876	.4286
4	Nap Lajoie	1901	.4265
5	Willie Keeler	1897	.4238
6	Rogers Hornsby	1924	.4235
7	George Sisler	1922	.4198
8	Ty Cobb	1911	.4196
9	Tuck Turner	1894	.4159
10	Fred Dunlap	1884	.4120

The best batting average by an active 2001 player occurred in 1994, when Tony Gwynn returned an average of .3937 to put him 37th on the all-time list.

Top 10 Most hits in a season

	Player	Year	Hits
1	George Sisler	1920	257
2 =	Lefty O'Doul	1929	254
=	Bill Terry	1930	254
4	Al Simmons	1925	253
5 =	Rogers Hornsby	1922	250
=	Chuck Klein	1930	250
7	Ty Cobb	1911	248
8	George Sisler	1922	246
9	Ichiro Suzuki*	2001	242
10 =	Babe Herman	1930	241
=	Heinie Manush	1928	241

* Active in 2001

By 1922 George Sisler was the best first baseman in the American League and the second best batter in the League behind Babe Ruth. However, injury forced him to miss the 1923 season, and when he returned to the game he wasn't quite the same player. He retired in 1930.

Top 10 Most runs in a season

	Player	Year	Runs
1	Billy Hamilton	1894	192
2 =	Tom Brown	1891	177
=	Babe Ruth	1921	177
4 =	Lou Gehrig	1936	167
=	Tip O'Neill	1887	167
6	Billy Hamilton	1895	166
7 =	Willie Keeler	1894	165
=	Joe Kelley	1894	165
9 =	Lou Gehrig	1931	163
=	Arlie Latham	1887	163
=	Babe Ruth	1928	163

Top 10 Most strikeouts in a season

	Player	Year	Strikeouts
1	Matt Kilroy	1886	513
2	Toad Ramsey	1886	419
3	Hugh Daily	1884	483
4	Dupee Shaw	1884	451
5	Charley Radbourn	1884	441
6	Charlie Buffinton	1884	417
7	Guy Hecker	1884	385
8	Nolan Ryan	1973	383
9	Sandy Koufax	1965	382
10	Bill Sweeney	1884	374

Randy Johnson of Arizona just missed out on making the Top 10 in 2001 with 372 strikeouts.

> Every hitter works on the theory that the pitcher is more afraid of him than he is of the pitcher.
>
> Ty Cobb

The 10 First players to hit four home runs in one game

	Player	Club	Date
1	Bobby Lowe	Boston	May 30, 1884
2	Ed Delahanty	Philadelphia	July 13, 1896
3	Lou Gehrig	New York	June 3, 1932
4	Chuck Klein	Philadelphia	July 10, 1936
5	Pat Seerey	Chicago	July 18, 1948
6	Gil Hodges	Brooklyn	Aug. 31, 1950
7	Joe Adcock	Milwaukee	July 31, 1954
8	Rocky Colavito	Cleveland	June 10, 1959
9	Willie Mays	San Francisco	Apr. 30, 1961
10	Mike Schmidt	Philadelphia	Apr. 17, 1976

The only other players to score four homers in one game are Bob Horner, for Atlanta on July 6, 1986, and Mark Whiten, for St. Louis on September 7, 1993.

Top 10 Pitchers with the most wins in a season

	Pitcher	Year	Wins
1	Charley Radbourn	1884	59
2	John Clarkson	1885	53
3	Guy Hecker	1884	52
4	John Clarkson	1889	49
5 =	Charlie Buffinton	1884	48
=	Charley Radbourn	1883	48
7 =	Al Spalding	1876	47
=	John Ward	1879	47
9 =	Pud Galvin	1883	46
=	Pud Galvin	1884	46
=	Matt Kilroy	1887	46

▼ Barry Bonds of the San Francisco Giants beat Mark McGwire's three-year-old record for most home runs in a season by hitting number 71, and then 72, against the Los Angeles Dodgers at Pacific Bell Park in San Francisco.

Top 10 Most home runs in a season

	Player	Year	Home runs
1	Barry Bonds*	2001	73
2	Mark McGwire*	1998	70
3	Sammy Sosa*	1998	66
4	Mark McGwire*	1999	65
5	Sammy Sosa*	2001	64
6	Sammy Sosa*	1999	63
7	Roger Maris	1961	61
8	Babe Ruth	1927	60
9	Babe Ruth	1921	59
10 =	Jimmie Foxx	1932	58
=	Hank Greenberg	1938	58
=	Mark McGwire*	1997	58

* Active in 2001

Barry Bonds equaled Mark McGwire's three-year-old record on October 4, 2001 when he hit a homer off rookie Wilfredo Rodriguez at Houston. He broke the record the next day when he hit off Chan Ho Park of the Dodgers for a homer and immediately followed that with home run number 72 off the same pitcher. He ended his season on October 7, with homer number 93, also against Los Angeles, this time off the pitching of Dennis Springer.

BASEBALL

MANAGERS, AWARDS & OTHER RECORDS

- Most Little League World Series wins
- Most College World Series titles
- Managers with best win percentage
- Managers with most wins in a career
- Countries of birth of Major League players
- Managers with the most World Series titles

NOT PLAYING BALL

"Professionalism" has crept into Little League Baseball, with the 1992 World Series awarded to Long Beach after it was discovered that the Zamboanga City team from the Philippines had used several players from outside the city limits. They had originally won the match 15–4, but this was later amended to a 6–0 Long Beach victory.

Top 10 Most Little League World Series wins

	Team	Wins
1	Taiwan	16
2 =	California	5
=	Japan	5
4 =	Connecticut	4
=	New Jersey	4
=	Pennsylvania	4
7	Mexico	3
8 =	New York	2
=	South Korea	2
=	Texas	2
=	Venezuela	2

First contested in 1947, the Little League World Series was held at Original Field, Williamsport, Pennsylvania, until 1959, when it moved to the Howard J. Lamade Stadium. In 2001, it moved again, this time to the new Volunteer Stadium (also in Pennsylvania). The biggest winning margin occurred in 1987, when Hua Lian (Taiwan) beat Irvine (California) 21–1. Little League baseball now has over two-and-a-half million boys and girls, between ages five and 18, playing in over 7,000 baseball and softball leagues in more than 80 countries.

Top 10 Most College World Series titles

	Team	Wins
1	USC	12
2 =	Arizona State	5
=	LSU	5
4 =	Miami–FL	4
=	Texas	4
6 =	Arizona	3
=	CS–Fullerton	3
=	Minnesota	3
9 =	California	2
=	Michigan	2
=	Oklahoma	2
=	Stanford	2

The NCAA Division I College World Series was first held in Kalamazoo, Michigan, in 1948. Since 1950, it has been played in Omaha, Nebraska.
The biggest winning margin occurred in 1956, when Minnesota beat Arizona 12–1.

Top 10 Managers with best win percentage*

	Manager	Wins	Losses	Percentage
1	Joe McCarthy	2,125	1,333	61.5
2	Jim Mutrie	658	419	61.1
3	Charlie Comiskey	839	542	60.8
4	Frank Selee	1,284	862	59.8
5	Billy Southworth	1,044	704	59.7
6	Frank Chance	946	648	59.3
7	John McGraw	2,763	1,948	58.6
8	Al Lopez	1,410	1,004	58.4
9	Earl Weaver	1,480	1,060	58.3
10	Harry Wright	1,225	885	58.1

* In a regular season career

During his 24-year career from 1924–50, Joe McCarthy managed the Cubs, the Yankees, and the Red Sox, but it was with the Yankees that he enjoyed his greatest successes, guiding them to eight pennants and seven World Series titles in 15 years.

> Being a manager is simple. All you have to do is keep the five players who hate your guts away from the five who are undecided.
>
> **Casey Stengel,** former New York Yankees and Mets manager, 1974

Top 10 Managers with most wins in a career

	Manager	Year	Wins
1	Connie Mack	53	3,755
2	John McGraw	33	2,866
3	Sparky Anderson	26	2,228
4	Bucky Harris	29	2,168
5	Joe McCarthy	24	2,155
6	Walter Alston	23	2,063
7	Leo Durocher	24	2,015
8	Casey Stengel	25	1,942
9	Gene Mauch	26	1,907
10	Bill McKechnie	25	1,904

Connie Mack (Cornelius Alexander McGillicuddy) was the owner and manager of the Philadelphia Athletics from the club's inception in 1901 until 1950. He continued to own and manage the club until the age of 88 and was in charge for 7,878 games. The highest-placed 2001 active coach was Tony La Russa, at number 11, with 1,859 wins during his 23-year career.

Top 10 Countries of birth of Major League players

	Country	No of players
1	United States	13,797
2	Dominican Republic	314
3	Puerto Rico	199
4	Canada	191
5	Cuba	143
6	Venezuela	135
7	Mexico	86
8	Panama	39
9	Ireland	38
10	Germany	36

The above figures are taken from data available. The birthplaces of some early players are not available. England would finish in 11th place with 31 players; two Welsh-born and ten Scottish-born players have played Major League Baseball. The state providing the most players is California with 1,651, while Alaska has supplied just eight.

Top 10 Managers with the most World Series titles

	Manager	Years	Titles
1 =	Joe McCarthy	1932, 1936–39, 1941	7
=	Casey Stengel	1949–53, 1956, 1958	7
3	Connie Mack	1910–11, 1913, 1929–30	5
4 =	Walter Alston	1955, 1959, 1963, 1965	4
=	Joe Torre*	1996, 1998–2000	4
6 =	Sparky Anderson	1975–76, 1984	3
=	Miller Huggins	1923, 1927–28	3
=	John McGraw	1905, 1921–22	3
9 =	Bill Carrigan	1915–16	2
=	Frank Chance	1907–08	2
=	Cito Gaston	1992–93	2
=	Bucky Harris	1924, 1947	2
=	Ralph Houk	1961–62	2
=	Tom Kelly*	1987, 1991	2
=	Tommy Lasorda	1981, 1988	2
=	Bill McKechnie	1925, 1940	2
=	Danny Murtaugh	1960, 1971	2
=	Billy Southworth	1942, 1944	2
=	Dick Williams	1972–73	2

* Active in 2001

The first manager of a World Series winning team was Jimmy Collins (Boston Red Sox) in 1903. The first man to manage two winning teams was Frank Chance (Chicago Cubs) 1907–08; the first to manage three winning teams was Connie Mack (Philadelphia A's) 1910–11, 1913; Mack was also the first to manage four and five winning teams. Joe McCarthy (New York Yankees) was the first to reach the milestone of managing six and then a record seven winning World Series teams.

◀ Veteran coach Connie Mack. His amazing career stretched from 1894 to 1950. He managed Pittsburgh in the National League from 1894–96 and Philadelphia in the American League 1901–50.

TEAMS & BALLPARKS

- Teams playing the most matches in MLB history
- Teams with most wins in Major League baseball
- Largest Major League ballparks
- Current teams with the most former names
- First players to hit a home run in the all-star game in their home stadium

> I'm just a ball player with one ambition, and that is to give all I've got to help my ball club win. I've never played any other way.
>
> Joe DiMaggio

Top 10 Teams playing the most matches in MLB history

	Team	Played
1	Atlanta Braves	18,712
2	Chicago Cubs	18,539
3	Philadelphia Phillies	18,065
4	San Francisco Giants	17,901
5	Pittsburgh Pirates	17,442
6	Los Angeles Dodgers	17,110
7	Cincinnati Reds	17,063
8	St. Louis Cardinals	16,836
9	New York Yankees	15,868
10	Oakland Athletics	15,695

Known as the Boston Braves until 1953 and then the Milwaukee Braves until 1965, the Atlanta Braves were originally set up in 1871 and are the only franchise to have fielded a team every season since the start of organized professional baseball. They actually started life as the Boston Red Caps, and were also known as the Beaneaters, Doves and Rustlers, before adopting the Braves name in 1912.

Top 10 Teams with most wins in Major League baseball

	Team	Wins
1	San Francisco Giants	9,657
2	Chicago Cubs	9,538
3	Atlanta Braves	9,356
4	New York Yankees	8,975
5	Los Angeles Dodgers	8,942
6	Pittsburgh Pirates	8,934
7	Cincinnati Reds	8,651
8	St. Louis Cardinals	8,513
9	Philadelphia Phillies	8,361
10	Cleveland Indians	8,025

The Giants came into being as the New York Giants in 1883 when tobacco merchant John Day acquired players from the defunct Troy Haymakers. Day also owned the New York Metropolitans, and when he realized the new National league was a more profitable League, he shifted the top players from the Mets to the Giants. The Giants switched their franchise to San Francisco in 1958.

Top 10 Largest Major League ballparks*

	Stadium	Home team	Capacity
1	Qualcomm Stadium	San Diego Padres	66,307
2	Veterans Stadium	Philadelphia Phillies	62,418
3	Yankee Stadium	New York Yankees	57,746
4	Shea Stadium	New York Mets	56,516
5	Dodger Stadium	Los Angeles Dodgers	56,000
6	SkyDome	Toronto Blue Jays	50,516
7	Coors Field	Colorado Rockies	50,449
8	Turner Field	Atlanta Braves	50,062
9	Busch Stadium	St. Louis Cardinals	49,738
10	The Ballpark in Arlington	Texas Rangers	49,115

* By capacity

Source: Major League Baseball

Stadium capacities vary constantly, some being adjusted according to the event: Veterans Stadium, for example, holds fewer for baseball games (62,418) than for football games (65,356). The Colorado Rockies formerly played at the Mile High Stadium, Denver, Colorado, which holds 76,125, but now play at Coors Field, which has a capacity of only 50,449. Had it not been for Babe Ruth, there probably would not have been a Yankees Stadium. It was Ruth who put the Yankees on the baseball map, and the money generated by his presence alone helped build the new and innovative stadium. Consequently, the Yankees Stadium is known as "The House that Ruth Built." When it first opened in 1923, the stadium was capable of seating over 70,000 and was the first purpose-built baseball stadium. Even the right field fence was only 294 feet away, so Ruth's homers wouldn't have far to travel out of the ballpark!

◀ When the Padres moved into the Qualcomm Stadium in 1960 its capacity was 47,634. It is now the biggest-capacity stadium in Major League Baseball.

<table>
<tr><td colspan="2">Top 10 Current teams with the most former names</td></tr>
</table>

Top 10 Current teams with the most former names

Team/former names	No of former names
1 = Atlanta Braves	7
Milwaukee Braves, Boston Braves, Boston Bees, Boston Rustlers, Boston Doves, Boston Beaneaters, and Boston Red Caps	
= Los Angeles Dodgers	7
Brooklyn Dodgers, Brooklyn Robins, Brooklyn Superbas, Brooklyn Bridegrooms, Brooklyn Grooms, Brooklyn Grays, and Brooklyn Atlantics	
3 = Boston Red Sox	3
Boston Pilgrims, Boston Somersets, and Boston Americans	
= Chicago Cubs	3
Chicago Orphans, Chicago Colts, and Chicago White Stockings	
= Cleveland Indians	3
Cleveland Naps, Cleveland Broncos, and Cleveland Blues	
= St. Louis Cardinals	3
St. Louis Perfectos, St. Louis Browns, and St. Louis Brown Stockings	
7 = Anaheim Angels	2
California Angels and Los Angeles Angels	
= Baltimore Orioles	2
St. Louis Browns and Milwaukee Brewers	
= New York Yankees	2
New York Highlanders and Baltimore Orioles	
= Oakland Athletics	2
Kansas City Athletics and Philadelphia Athletics	
= Philadelphia Phillies	2
Philadelphia Blue Jays and Philadelphia Quakers	
= San Francisco Giants	2
New York Giants and New York Gothams	

The 10 First players to hit a home run in the all-star game in their home stadium

	Player	Team	Stadium	Year
1	Joe DiMaggio	New York Yankees	Yankee Stadium	1939
2	Ted Williams	Boston Red Sox	Fenway Park	1946
3	Stan Musial	St. Louis Cardinals	Sportsman's Park	1948
4	Vic Wertz	Detroit Tigers	Briggs Stadium	1951
5	George Kell	Detroit Tigers	Briggs Stadium	1951
6	Al Rosen	Cleveland Indians	Municipal Stadium	1954
7	Larry Doby	Cleveland Indians	Municipal Stadium	1954
8	Jim Gilliam	Los Angeles Dodgers	Memorial Coliseum	1959
9	Harmon Killebrew	Minnesota Twins	Metropolitan Stadium	1965
10	Frank Howard	Washington Senators	RFK Stadium	1969

The Dodgers, along with the Yankees and the Giants, are among the "Big Three" of baseball. Their previous names are among some of the most amusing in the sport; they were known as the Bridesmaids in the 1890s after several of their players got married during the close-season. They were once called the Superbas after a local circus act, and they became known as the Robins in honor of their manager and team president, Wilbert Robinson. Even the name Brooklyn Dodgers comes from the shortened version of the name "Trolley Dodgers," which is what other New Yorkers called Brooklyn residents. Despite their early beginnings, it was not until 1955 that the Dodgers won their first World Series, led by Walter Alston. The Dodgers moved their franchise to Los Angeles after the 1957 season.

▶ Joe DiMaggio was a member of the outstanding Yankees team that dominated the game in the 1940s and '50s. He was equally well known as a former husband of actress Marilyn Monroe.

BASKETBALL

At the Start

The Aztec game of *ollamalitzli* and similar ball and hoop games among other Central and South American peoples may have influenced the modern game of basketball. However, it was actually invented at the International YMCA College in Springfield, Massachusetts, in December 1891 by a Canadian physical education teacher, Dr. James A. Naismith, who set out to devise a game that could be played indoors during the winter. The first public game was played in 1892, and the team size was limited to five in 1895. The National Basketball League (NBL), founded in 1898, was the world's first professional league. In 1949, the NBL merged with the Basketball Association of America to create the National Basketball Association (NBA).

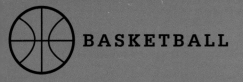

BASKETBALL

NBA FINALS & PLAYOFFS

- Most appearances in playoff games
- Most field goals in playoff games
- Most free throws in playoff games
- Point scorers in playoff games
- Most NBA final appearances
- Scoring averages in playoff games

GREAT RIVALS

Magic Johnson won the 1978–79 NCAA Championship with Michigan State, beating Indiana State 75–64 in the final. Playing for Indiana that day was Larry Bird. Johnson joined the Lakers and Bird went to the Boston Celtics. Throughout the 1980s, the two men vied for the position of basketball's number one player, and the rivalry between Los Angeles and Boston was probably the deepest the professional game has ever seen.

Top 10 Most appearances in playoff games

Player	Apps
1 Kareem Abdul-Jabbar	237
2 Scottie Pippen*	201
3 Danny Ainge	193
4 Magic Johnson	190
5 Robert Parish	184
6 Byron Scott	183
7 Dennis Johnson	180
8 Michael Jordan	179
9 John Stockton*	173
10 John Havlicek	170

* Active during 2000-01 season

After six years with the Milwaukee Bucks (1969–75), Kareem Abdul-Jabbar moved to the Los Angeles Lakers and went on to became the first man to enjoy a 20-year playing career in the NBA.

Top 10 Most field goals in playoff games

Player	Attempts	Goals
1 Kareem Abdul-Jabbar	4,422	2,356
2 Michael Jordan	4,497	2,188
3 Jerry West	3,460	1,622
4 Karl Malone*	3,393	1,581
5 Hakeem Olajuwon*	2,825	1,492
6 Larry Bird	3,090	1,458
7 John Havlicek	3,329	1,451
8 Wilt Chamberlain	2,728	1,425
9 Elgin Baylor	3,161	1,388
10 Scottie Pippen*	2,948	1,308

* Active during 2000-01 season

When Kareem Abdul-Jabbar retired in 1989, he was the all-time NBA leader in 20 categories. He won six NBA titles with the Bucks and the Lakers.

Top 10 Most free throws in playoff games

Player	Attempts	Free throws
1 Michael Jordan	1,766	1,463
2 Jerry West	1,507	1,213
3 Karl Malone*	1,583	1,173
4 Kareem Abdul-Jabbar	1,419	1,050
5 Magic Johnson	1,241	1,040
6 Larry Bird	1,012	901
7 John Havlicek	1,046	874
8 Elgin Baylor	1,101	847
9 Kevin McHale	972	766
10 Scottie Pippen*	1,057	763

* Active during 2000-01 season

Playing against Cleveland on May 1, 1988, Michael Jordan made 24 field goals, which equals the NBA playoff single-game record for field goals.

Top 10 Point scorers in playoff games

Player	Games	Points
1 Michael Jordan	179	5,987
2 Kareem Abdul-Jabbar	237	5,762
3 Jerry West	153	4,457
4 Karl Malone*	163	4,341
5 Larry Bird	164	3,897
6 John Havlicek	172	3,776
7 Hakeem Olajuwon*	140	3,727
8 Magic Johnson	190	3,701
9 Elgin Baylor	134	3,623
10 Wilt Chamberlain	160	3,607

* Active during 2000-01 season

Michael Jordan scored 20 points or more in 29 consecutive NBA finals. His career record in playoff games is 33.6 points. Both are NBA records.

◀ Magic Johnson retired in 1991 but returned to play in the 1992 NBA All-Star game and also the US "Dream Team" at the Barcelona Olympics.

Top 10 Most NBA final appearances

	Team	Titles	Apps
1	Minneapolis/Los Angeles Lakers	13	26
2	Boston Celtics	16	19
3	Syracuse Nationals/Philadelphia 76ers	3	9
4	New York Knicks	2	8
5 =	Chicago Bulls	6	6
=	Philadelphia/San Francisco/Golden State Warriors	3	6
7	Ft. Wayne/Detroit Pistons	2	5
8 =	Baltimore/Washington Bullets	1	4
=	Houston Rockets	2	4
=	St. Louis Hawks	1	4

The Lakers appeared in and won their first final in 1949. Between then and 1954, they won the title five times, with John Kundla coaching them to all five victories. Surprisingly, their next title was not until 1972, and that came on the back of seven defeats in nine years.

Top 10 Scoring averages in playoff games

	Player	Games	Points	Average
1	Michael Jordan	179	5,987	33.4
2	Allen Iverson*	40	1,213	30.3
3	Jerry West	153	4,457	29.1
4	Shaquille O'Neal*	105	2,956	28.2
5 =	Elgin Baylor	134	3,623	27.0
=	George Gervin	59	1,592	27.0
7 =	Karl Malone*	163	4,341	26.6
=	Hakeem Olajuwon*	140	3,727	26.6
9	Dominique Wilkins	55	1,421	25.8
10	Bob Pettit	88	2,240	25.5

* Active during 2000–01 season

▶ Basketball's biggest earner, Michael Jordan. In 2000, he earned more than $35 million from the sport, even though he was no longer an active player at the time.

The highest-placed active player, Allen Iverson, had an eventful start to his pro career in the 1996–97 season when he set a 76ers all-time rookie record with 1,787 points and went on to become the first 76er to win the Rookie of the Year title.

BASKETBALL

TEAMS & ARENAS

- ● NBA team payrolls
- ● Most NBA games played
- ● Most points in the NBA
- ● Most NBA games won
- ● Biggest NBA arenas
- ● Shirt numbers most often retired
- ● Newest current NBA teams

> "Flip a coin between Atlanta and Houston and hope it doesn't come down.
>
> **Scottie Pippen,** of Chicago in 1996–97, when asked which team had the ugliest uniform"

Top 10 NBA team payrolls

	Team	Payroll ($)*
1	New York Knicks	85,457,889
2	Portland Trail Blazers	83,758,700
3	New Jersey Nets	75,172,371
4	Philadelphia 76ers	58,073,366
5	Dallas Mavericks	57,363,430
6	Milwaukee Bucks	56,224,266
7	Phoenix Suns	56,187,219
8	Sacramento Kings	54,921,012
9	Washington Wizards	54,776,087
10	Minnesota Timberwolves	54,559,632

* 2001–02 season

Two players earned more than $20 million each: Kevin Garnett, Minnesota Timberwolves ($22,400,000) and Shaquille O'Neal, Los Angeles Lakers ($21,428,572). Allan Houston was the Nicks' biggest earner in the 2001–02 season, with a salary of $12,750,000, making him the 7th-biggest earner in the NBA.

Top 10 Most points in the NBA*

	Team	Points
1	Los Angeles Lakers	508,468
2	Boston Celtics	504,482
3	Philadelphia 76ers	474,166
4	New York Knicks	470,939
5	Golden State Warriors	470,687
6	Detroit Pistons	454,833
7	Atlanta Hawks	452,293
8	Sacramento Kings	451,029
9	Chicago Bulls	321,536
10	Seattle Super Sonics	316,674

* Since the launch of the NBA championship in 1946–47

Between 1957 and 1969 Boston Celtics dominated the NBA, winning 11 Championships. During that 13-year period they were known, unsurprisingly, as "The Dynasty."

Top 10 Most NBA games played*

	Team	Matches
1	Los Angeles Lakers	4,748
2	Boston Celtics	4,738
3	New York Knicks	4,627
4	Golden State Warriors	4,489
5	Philadelphia 76ers	4,473
6	Detroit Pistons	4,401
7	Atlanta Hawks	4,379
8	Sacramento Kings	4,307
9	Chicago Bulls	3,103
10	Seattle Super Sonics	2,973

* Since the launch of the NBA championship in 1946–47

The Los Angeles Lakers, then known as the Minneapolis Lakers, played their first NBA game in 1948. They ended the season with a 44–16 record and went on to beat the Washington Capitols 4–2 to win the NBA final. The coach of that winning team was John Kundla.

Top 10 Most NBA games won*

	Team	Wins
1	Los Angeles Lakers	2,923
2	Boston Celtics	2,841
3	Philadelphia 76ers	2,424
4	New York Knicks	2,390
5	Atlanta Hawks	2,197
6	Detroit Pistons	2,102
7	Golden State Warriors	2,090
8	Sacramento Kings	1,982
9	Chicago Bulls	1,640
10	Seattle Super Sonics	1,592

* Since the launch of the NBA championship in 1946–47

The Los Angeles Lakers, with 61.6 percent, have the best win average. The most games the Lakers have won in a regular season is 69, in 1971–72. Their worst season was 1957–58, when they won just 19 matches.

Top 10 Biggest NBA arenas

	Arena	Team	Capacity
1	The Palace of Auburn Hills	Detroit Pistons	22,076
2	United Center	Chicago Bulls	21,711
3	MCI Center	Washington Wizards	20,674
4	Gund Arena	Cleveland Cavaliers	20,562
5	The Alamodome	San Antonio Spurs	20,557
6	First Union Center	Philadelphia 76ers	20,444
7	The Pyramid	Memphis Grizzlies	20,142
8	Continental Airlines Arena, East Rutherford	New Jersey Nets	20,049
9	The Rose Garden	Portland Trail Blazers	19,980
10	Charlotte Coliseum	Charlotte Hornets	19,925

Just after finishing the season with an all-time low 16–66 record, the Detroit Pistons won a franchise best 63 games in 1988–89 and then went on to win their first Championship in 1989. This coincided with the move at the start of the season to their new home, The Palace of Auburn Hills.

Top 10 Shirt numbers most often retired

	Shirt number	No. of teams retired by
1 =	15	7
=	22	7
=	32	7
4	13	6
5 =	1	5
=	2	5
=	6	5
=	10	5
=	23	5
=	24	5
=	25	5
=	33	5
=	44	5

Three of the six retired Number 13 shirts belonged to Wilt Chamberlain.

The 10 Newest current NBA teams

	Team	First season
1 =	Memphis Grizzlies	1995–96
=	Toronto Raptors	1995–96
3 =	Minnesota Timberwolves	1989–90
=	Orlando Magic	1989–90
5 =	Charlotte Hornets	1988–89
=	Miami Heat	1988–89
7	Dallas Mavericks	1980–81
8	Utah Jazz	1974–75
9 =	Cleveland Cavaliers	1970–71
=	Los Angeles Clippers	1970–71
=	Portland Trail Blazers	1970–71

When they joined the NBA the Clippers were based in Buffalo. They moved to San Diego in 1978, before moving to Los Angeles in 1984. The Memphis Grizzlies were based in Vancouver when they joined the NBA and the Utah Jazz were the New Orleans Jazz in their first season.

◀ The most successful NBA team of all time, the LA Lakers. They have won 13 of the 26 NBA finals in which they have appeared.

BASKETBALL

SINGLE-SEASON RECORD-BREAKERS

- Assist averages in a single NBA season
- Most points in a single NBA game
- Players heading the annual field goal percentages most frequently
- Players heading the annual scoring list most frequently
- Scoring averages in a single season

WILT CHAMBERLAIN

In his first NBA game for the Philadelphia Warriors in the 1959–60 season, Wilt Chamberlain scored 43 points on 17-of-20 shooting, grabbed 28 rebounds, and blocked 17 shots against the Nicks. He was that season's MVP and Rookie of the Year with an average of 37.6, a record-scoring average for both awards.

Top 10 Assist averages in a single NBA season*

	Player/team	Season	Average
1	John Stockton, Utah Jazz	1989-90	14.5
2	John Stockton, Utah Jazz	1990-91	14.2
3	Isiah Thomas, Detroit Pistons	1984-85	13.9
4	John Stockton, Utah Jazz	1987-88	13.8
5	John Stockton, Utah Jazz	1991-92	13.7
6	John Stockton, Utah Jazz	1988-89	13.6
7	Kevin Porter, Detroit Pistons	1978-79	13.4
8	Magic Johnson, Los Angeles Lakers	1983-84	13.1
9	Magic Johnson, Los Angeles Lakers	1988-89	12.8
10 =	Magic Johnson, Los Angeles Lakers	1984-85	12.6
=	John Stockton, Utah Jazz	1993-94	12.6

* Based on average assists per game

John Stockton has spent his entire NBA career with the Utah Jazz, making his debut in 1984–85. In the 10 seasons from 1987–88, he averaged 10 or more assists per game every season and was the annual leader in assists nine years in succession, overtaking the eight-time leading record set by Bob Cousy, which had been set more than 30 years earlier.

Top 10 Most points in a single NBA game

	Player	Match	Date	Points
1	Wilt Chamberlain	Philadelphia Warriors vs. New York Knicks	Mar. 2, 1962	100
2	Wilt Chamberlain*	Philadelphia Warriors vs. Los Angeles Lakers	Dec. 8, 1961	78
3 =	Wilt Chamberlain	Philadelphia Warriors vs. Chicago Packers	Jan. 13, 1962	73
=	Wilt Chamberlain	San Francisco Warriors vs. New York Knicks	Nov. 16, 1962	73
=	David Thompson	Denver Nuggets vs. Detroit Pistons	Apr. 9, 1978	73
6	Wilt Chamberlain	San Francisco Warriors vs. Los Angeles Lakers	Nov. 3, 1962	72
7 =	Elgin Baylor	Los Angeles Lakers vs. New York Knicks	Nov. 15, 1960	71
=	David Robinson	San Antonio Spurs vs. Los Angeles Clippers	Apr. 24, 1994	71
9	Wilt Chamberlain	San Francisco Warriors vs. Syracuse Nationals	Mar. 10, 1963	70
10	Michael Jordan#	Chicago Bulls vs. Cleveland Cavaliers	Mar. 28, 1990	69

* Triple overtime game

Overtime game

Wilt Chamberlain broke more than one record on the night of March 2, 1962. In addition to becoming the first and so far only man to score 100 points in a game, he set a record for field goals (36), free throws (28 of 32), most points for a quarter (31), and most points for a half (59). The Warriors' 169–147 win over the Knickerbockers was also a record for the most points aggregate in a game, beating by four the Celtics' 173–139 win over the Lakers in 1959.

> Ask not what your teammates can do for you. Ask what you can do for your teammates.
>
> Magic Johnson

Top 10 Players heading the annual field goal percentages most frequently

	Player	First/last season	No.
1	Wilt Chamberlain	1961–73	9
2	Shaquille O'Neal	1994–2001	5
3	Artis Gilmore	1981–84	4
4	Neil Johnston	1953–57	3
5 =	Bob Feerick	1947–48	2
=	Johnny Green	1970–71	2
=	Alex Groza	1950–51	2
=	Cedric Maxwell	1979–80	2
=	Kevin McHale	1987–88	2
=	Gheorge Muresan	1996–97	2
=	Kenny Sears	1959–60	2
=	Buck Williams	1991–92	2

Top 10 Players heading the annual scoring list most frequently

	Player	First/last season	No.
1	Michael Jordan	1987–98	10
2	Wilt Chamberlain	1960–66	7
3	George Gervin	1978–82	4
4 =	Neil Johnston	1953–55	3
=	Bob McAdoo	1974–76	3
=	George Mikan	1949–51	3
7 =	Kareem Abdul-Jabbar*	1971–72	2
=	Paul Arizin	1952–57	2
=	Adrian Dantley	1981–84	2
=	Allen Iverson	1999–2001	2
=	Shaquille O'Neal	1995–2000	2
=	Bob Pettit	1956–59	2

* Kareem Abdul-Jabbar won one title under his birth name of Lew Alcindor in 1971

Top 10 Scoring averages in a single season

	Player/team	Season	Average
1	Wilt Chamberlain, Philadelphia Warriors	1961–62	50.4
2	Wilt Chamberlain, San Francisco Warriors	1962–63	44.8
3	Wilt Chamberlain, Philadelphia Warriors	1960–61	38.4
4	Elgin Baylor, Los Angeles Lakers	1961–62	38.3
5	Wilt Chamberlain, Philadelphia Warriors	1959–60	37.6
6	Michael Jordan, Chicago Bulls	1986–87	37.1
7	Wilt Chamberlain, San Francisco Warriors	1963–64	36.9
8	Rick Barry, San Francisco Warriors	1966–67	35.6
9	Michael Jordan, Chicago Bulls	1987–88	35.0
10 =	Kareem Abdul–Jabbar, Milwaukee Bucks	1971–72	34.8
=	Elgin Baylor, Los Angeles Lakers	1960–61	34.8

◀ The NBA's free throw expert, John Stockton of the Utah Jazz.

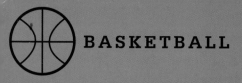

BASKETBALL

ALL-TIME GREATS

- ● Most points in an NBA career
- ● Most field goals in an NBA career
- ● Most free throws in an NBA career
- ● Most assists in an NBA career
- ● Most rebounds in an NBA career
- ● Scoring averages in an NBA career

> Michael Jordan is one of the greatest athletes in any sport in any era, and all of us are fortunate that we saw him play, because the greats are like that—spectacularly individual.
>
> **Spike Lee,** filmmaker and basketball enthusiast

Top 10 Most points in an NBA career

	Player	Years	Games	Points
1	Kareem Abdul-Jabbar	20	1,560	38,387
2	Karl Malone*	16	1,273	32,919
3	Wilt Chamberlain	14	1,045	31,419
4	Michael Jordan	13	930	29,277
5	Moses Malone	19	1,329	27,409
6	Elvin Hayes	16	1,303	27,313
7	Oscar Robertson	14	1,040	26,710
8	Dominique Wilkins	15	1,074	26,668
9	Hakeem Olajuwon*	17	1,177	26,511
10	John Havlicek	16	1,270	26,395

* Active during 2000-01 season

Michael Jordan came out of retirement in 2001 and on January 4, 2002, became only the fourth man in NBA history to top 30,000 points. His new mark came on a free throw, with 5 minutes 25 seconds remaining in the second quarter. It was his 960th career game.

Top 10 Most field goals in an NBA career

	Player	Years	Attempts	Field goals
1	Kareem Abdul-Jabbar	20	28,307	15,837
2	Wilt Chamberlain	14	23,497	12,681
3	Karl Malone*	16	23,122	12,102
4	Elvin Hayes	16	24,272	10,976
5	Michael Jordan	13	21,686	10,958
6	Alex English	15	21,036	10,659
7	Hakeem Olajuwon*	17	20,573	10,555
8	John Havlicek	16	23,930	10,513
9	Dominique Wilkins	15	21,589	9,963
10	Robert Parish	21	17,914	9,614

* Active during 2000-01 season

For all his scoring exploits, Kareem Abdul-Jabbar only twice headed the annual NBA scoring list, in 1971, and the following year. He was also top of the field goal percentage list, but only once, in 1977.

Top 10 Most free throws in an NBA career

	Player	Years	Attempts	Free throws
1	Karl Malone*	16	11,703	8,636
2	Moses Malone	19	11,090	8,531
3	Oscar Robertson	14	9,185	7,694
4	Jerry West	14	8,801	7,160
5	Dolph Schayes	16	8,273	6,979
6	Adrian Dantley	15	8,351	6,832
7	Michael Jordan	13	8,115	6,798
8	Kareem Abdul-Jabbar	20	9,304	6,712
9	Charles Barkley	16	8,643	6,349
10	Bob Pettit	11	8,119	6,182

* Active during 2000-01 season

Going into the 2001–02 season, Karl Malone was the all-time leader in free throws, second in career points, and third in field goals made. He appeared on the All-NBA first team 11 times 1989–99, and appeared on two US Olympic teams, in 1992 and 1996.

Top 10 Most assists in an NBA career

	Player	Years	Games	Assists
1	John Stockton*	17	1,340	14,503
2	Magic Johnson	13	906	10,141
3	Oscar Robertson	14	1,040	9,887
4	Mark Jackson*	14	1,090	9,235
5	Isiah Thomas	13	979	9,061
6	Maurice Cheeks	15	1,101	7,392
7	Lenny Wilkens	15	1,077	7,211
8	Rod Strickland*	13	894	7,027
9	Bob Cousy	14	924	6,955
10	Guy Rodgers	12	892	6,917

* Active during 2000-01 season

John Stockton went into 2001–02 as the NBA leader not only in assists, but also in steals, with 2,976. He had a personal best 28 assists in a single game against San Antonio on January 15, 1991.

Top 10 Most rebounds in an NBA career

	Player	Years	Games	Rebounds
1	Wilt Chamberlain	14	1,045	23,924
2	Bill Russell	13	963	21,620
3	Kareem Abdul-Jabbar	20	1,560	17,440
4	Elvin Hayes	16	1,303	16,279
5	Moses Malone	19	1,329	16,212
6	Robert Parish	21	1,611	14,715
7	Nate Thurmond	14	964	14,464
8	Walt Bellamy	14	1,043	14,241
9	Wes Unseld	13	984	13,769
10	Hakeem Olajuwon*	17	1,177	13,381

* Active during 2000-01 season

Hakeem Olajuwon, the only active player on this list, became the first player in NBA history to accumulate both 2,000 blocks and 2,000 steals, thanks to a steal against Seattle on November 20, 1999. All were achieved with the Houston Rockets, for whom he made his debut in 1984–85.

Top 10 Scoring averages in an NBA career

	Player	Years	Games	Points	Average
1	Michael Jordan	13	930	29,277	31.5
2	Wilt Chamberlain	14	1,045	31,419	30.1
3	Shaquille O'Neal*	9	608	16,812	27.7
4	Elgin Baylor	14	846	23,149	27.4
5	Jerry West	14	932	25,192	27.0
6	Bob Pettit	11	792	20,880	26.4
7	George Gervin	10	791	20,708	26.2
8	Karl Malone*	16	1,273	32,919	25.9
9	Oscar Robertson	14	1,040	26,710	25.7
10	Dominique Wilkins	15	1,074	26,668	24.8

* Active during 2000-01 season

Between them, Michael Jordan and Wilt Chamberlain topped the annual scoring average 17 times. Jordan topped it 10 times with Chicago between 1987 and 1998, while Chamberlain topped it seven times, with Philadelphia and San Francisco, all consecutive, between 1960 and 1966.

◀ Another score for Karl Malone of the Utah Jazz as he closes in on Kareem Abdul-Jabbar's all-time scoring record.

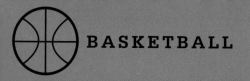

COACHES, AWARDS & DRAFTS

- Greatest NBA coaches

- First men to win Rookie and MVP awards in the NBA

- Coaches of the year with the biggest seasonal improvement

- Coaches with the most NBA titles

- Coaches with the most wins in the NBA

- MVP winners with the best scoring average

BEST OF THE BEST

Lenny Wilkens and John Wooden are the only two men to be honored by Basketball's Hall of Fame as both player and coach. As part of its 50th anniversary celebration in the 1996–97 season, the NBA named its 50 Greatest Players and also its 50 Greatest Coaches. Wilkens was the only person to appear on both lists.

Top 10 Greatest NBA coaches*

	Coach
1	Red Auerbach
2	Chuck Daly
3	Bill Fitch
4	Red Holzman
5	Phil Jackson
6	John Kundla
7	Don Nelson
8	Jack Ramsay
9	Pat Riley
10	Lenny Wilkens

* As named by the NBA as part of its 50th anniversary celebrations in 1996; listed alphabetically

With a career record of 1,037–548, and as the mastermind behind the Boston Celtics domination of the sport in the 1960s with eight straight NBA Championships 1959–66, it is not surprising that the NBA voted Arnold "Red" Auerbach the "Greatest Coach of All Time."

Top 10 First men to win Rookie and MVP awards in the NBA

	Player	Rookie year	First MVP
1	Bob Pettit	1955	1956
2	Wilt Chamberlain	1960	1960
3	Oscar Robertson	1961	1964
4	Wes Unseld	1969	1969
5	Willis Reed	1965	1970
6	Lew Alcindor*	1970	1971
7	Dave Cowens	1971	1973
8	Bob McAdoo	1973	1975
9	Larry Bird	1980	1984
10	Michael Jordan	1985	1988

* Alcindor changed his name to Kareem Abdul-Jabbar at the end of the 1970–71 season

Chamberlain and Unseld are the only men to have won both awards in the same season. Bob Pettit won two MVP awards, in 1956 and 1959. He appeared on the All-NBA first team 10 times between 1955 and 1964, and was the first player to score 20,000 points in the NBA.

Top 10 Coaches of the year with the biggest seasonal improvement*

	Coach/team	Year	Improvement from W–L	Improvement to W–L
1	Bill Fitch, Boston Celtics	1980	29–53	61–21
2	Cotton Fitzsimmons, Phoenix Suns	1989	28–54	55–27
3	Phil Jackson, Chicago Bulls	1996	47–35	72–10
4 =	Bill Sharman, Los Angeles Lakers	1972	48–34	69–13
=	Gene Shue, Baltimore Bullets	1969	36–46	57–25
6 =	Larry Bird, Indiana Pacers	1998	39–43	58–24
=	Pat Riley, Miami Heat	1997	42–40	61–21
8 =	Richie Guerin, St. Louis Hawks	1968	39–42	56–26
=	Alex Hannum, San Francisco Warriors	1964	31–49	48–32
=	Doug Moe, Denver Nuggets	1988	37–45	54–28

* Based on best win-loss improvement on season before award-winning season

The outstanding coach of the year, as voted by a panel of writers and broadcasters, was first presented in 1963 and won by Harry Gallatin of St. Louis. The trophy was renamed the Red Auerbach Trophy in 1967, in honor of the great Boston Celtics coach. Don Nelson (1983, 1995, 1992) and Pat Riley (1990, 1993, 1997) are the only men to win the award three times. No one has won the trophy back-to-back. Bill Fitch's record-breaking season was his first of four seasons in charge of the Boston Celtics, who he led to the Divisional title.

◄ Coach Red Auerbach seen with just one of the many trophies that he won during his time with Boston Celtics.

Top 10 Coaches with the most NBA titles

	Player/team	First/last titles	Total no of titles
1	Red Auerbach, Boston Celtics	1957–66	9
2	Phil Jackson,* Chicago Bulls/Los Angeles Lakers	1991–2001	8
3	John Kundla, Minnesota Lakers	1949–54	5
4	Pat Riley,* Los Angeles Lakers	1982–88	4
5 =	Chuck Daly, Detroit Pistons	1989–90	2
=	Alex Hannum, St. Louis Hawks/Philadelphia 76ers	1958–67	2
=	Tommy Heinsohn, Boston Celtics	1974–76	2
=	Red Holzman, New York Knicks	1970–73	2
=	K. C. Jones, Boston Celtics	1984–86	2
=	Bill Russell, Boston Celtics	1968–69	2
=	Rudy Tomjanovich,* Houston Rockets	1994–95	2

* Active during 2000-01 season

In nine years as Chicago Bulls head coach, Phil Jackson guided the team to six NBA titles. After a year out of the game, he returned in 2000 and led the Los Angeles Lakers to the title in his first season as their coach, following that up with a second title a year later.

Top 10 Coaches with the most wins in the NBA

	Coach	Years	Regular season wins	Play-off wins	Total wins
1	Lenny Wilkens*	28	1,226	78	1,304
2	Pat Riley*	19	1,049	155	1,204
3	Red Auerbach	20	938	99	1,037
4	Don Nelson*	23	979	55	1,034
5	Bill Fitch	25	944	55	999
6	Dick Motta	25	935	56	991
7	Jack Ramsay	21	864	44	908
8	Cotton Fitzsimmons	21	832	35	867
9	Jerry Sloan*	16	784	76	860
10	Larry Brown*	18	788	61	849

* Active during 2000-01 season

Top 10 MVP winners with the best scoring average

	Player/team	Year	Average
1	Wilt Chamberlain, Syracuse Nationals	1960	37.6
2	Michael Jordan, Chicago Bulls	1988	35.0
3	Kareem Abdul-Jabbar, Milwaukee Bucks	1972	34.8
4	Bob McAdoo, Buffalo Braves	1975	34.5
5	Wilt Chamberlain, Philadelphia 76ers	1966	33.5
6	Michael Jordan, Chicago Bulls	1991	31.5
7	Oscar Robertson, Cincinnati Royals	1964	31.4
8 =	Allen Iverson, Philadelphia 76ers	2001	31.1
=	Moses Malone, Houston Rockets	1982	31.1
10	Michael Jordan, Chicago Bulls	1996	30.4

First awarded in 1956, the Most Valuable Player trophy has been judged by a panel of journalists and broadcasters since 1981. The winner receives the Maurice Podoloff Trophy, which is named after the first commissioner of the NBA. Kareem Abdul-Jabbar (formerly Lew Alcindor) has won the title a record six times.

▶ During his 28 years of coaching, Lenny Wilkens has been with Seattle (twice), Portland, Cleveland, Atlanta, and Toronto, which he joined in 2000.

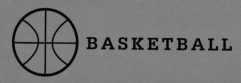

BASKETBALL

- Points in an ABA career
- Point scorers in the WNBA
- Medal-winning countries at the Olympic Games
- Medal-winning countries at the World Championships

> "Without a most valuable team I could not be the Most Valuable Player.
>
> **Cynthia Cooper,** of the Houston Comets, after winning her second successive WNBA MVP Award in 1998"

Top 10 Points in an ABA career

	Player	Points
1	Louie Dampier	13,726
2	Dan Issel	12,823
3	Ron Boone	12,153
4	Mel Daniels	11,739
5	Julius "Dr. J" Erving	11,662
6	Freddie Lewis	11,660
7	Don Freeman	11,544
8	Mack Calvin	10,620
9	Stew Johnson	10,538
10	Roger Brown	10,498

The ABA (American Basketball Association) was a rival organization to the NBA, with just 10 teams. It folded at the end of the 1975–76 season after only nine years.

Top 10 Point scorers in the WNBA*

	Player	Games	Points
1	Cynthia Cooper	89	1,987
2	Jennifer Gillom	90	1,549
3	Lisa Leslie	88	1,494
4	Andrea Stinson	90	1,323
5 =	Vicky Bullett	90	1,127
=	Wendy Palmer	87	1,127
7	Tina Thompson	87	1,103
8	Sheryl Swoopes	70	1,102
9	Sophia Witherspoon	90	1,091
10	Eva Nemcova	89	1,087

* The Women's National Basketball Association (WNBA) is owned and run by the NBA and was inaugurated in 1997

Source: WNBA

◀ As a result of a decision to allow NBA players to compete in the Olympics, the US "Dream Team" at the Barcelona Games contained such notables as Michael Jordan, Magic Johnson, and Larry Bird.

Top 10 Medal-winning countries at the Olympic Games*

	Country	G (men)	S (men)	B (men)	G (women)	S (women)	B (women)	G (combined)	S (combined)	B (combined)	Total
1	United States	12	1	1	4	1	1	16	2	2	20
2	USSR/Unified Team	2	4	3	3	0	1	5	4	4	13
3	Yugoslavia	1	4	1	0	1	1	1	5	2	8
4	Brazil	0	0	3	0	1	1	0	1	4	5
5	Lithuania	0	0	3	0	0	0	0	0	3	3
6 =	Australia	0	0	0	0	0	1	0	1	1	2
=	Bulgaria	0	0	0	0	1	1	0	1	1	2
=	China	0	0	0	0	1	1	0	1	1	2
=	France	0	2	0	0	0	0	0	2	0	2
=	Uruguay	0	0	2	0	0	0	0	0	2	2

G – gold medals, S – silver medals, B – bronze medals

* Based on total of gold, silver, and bronze medals won in the men's and women's competitions

Teresa Edwards (US) is the only person to have won five Olympic medals for basketball. She won gold in 1984, 1992, 1996, and 2000, and bronze in 1988. The United States dominated the Olympic basketball competition from 1936, when it was first held, to 1968. They won seven straight gold medals and went 62 straight games without defeat. The nearest any country came to beating them was in 1948, when Argentina lost by just two points, 57–59. However, the US team's amazing run came to an end in controversial circumstances in Munich in 1972, when they were beaten 51–50 by the Soviet team.

Top 10 Medal-winning countries at the World Championships*

	Country	G (men)	S (men)	B (men)	G (women)	S (women)	B (women)	G (combined)	S (combined)	B (combined)	Total
1	USSR/Russia	3	5	2	6	3	0	9	8	2	19
2	United States	3	3	3	6	1	1	9	4	4	17
3	Yugoslavia	4	3	2	0	1	0	4	4	2	10
4	Brazil	2	2	2	1	0	1	3	2	3	8
5	Czechoslovakia	0	0	0	0	2	4	0	2	4	6
6	Chile	0	0	2	0	1	0	0	1	2	3
7 =	Bulgaria	0	0	0	0	1	1	0	1	1	2
=	Canada	0	0	0	0	0	2	0	0	2	2
=	China	0	0	0	0	1	1	0	1	1	2
=	South Korea	0	0	0	0	2	0	0	2	0	2

G – gold medals, S – silver medals, B – bronze medals

* Based on total of gold, silver, and bronze medals won in the men's and women's competitions

The men's basketball World Championship was first held in Buenos Aires, Argentina, in 1950. The first women's World Championship took place in Santiago, Chile, in 1953. The first men's champions were the hosts, Argentina, and the first women's champions the United States. The States won their first men's title in 1954, but had to wait until 1986 for their second title.

◀ Cynthia Cooper of the Houston Comets goes up for two during the championship game against the New York Liberty at The Summit in Houston, Texas.

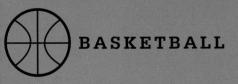
COLLEGE BASKETBALL

- NCAA Championships

- Best scoring averages in an NCAA Division I career

- All-time NCAA Division I wins

- Point scorers in an NCAA Division I career

- Most points in an NCAA Division I season

- Highest scoring NCAA Championship finals

- Most points in a single NCAA Division I game

Top 10 NCAA Championships*

	Team	Wins
1	UCLA	11
2	Kentucky	7
3	Indiana	5
4 =	Duke	3
=	North Carolina	3
6 =	Cincinnati	2
=	Kansas	2
=	Louisville	2
=	Michigan State	2
=	North Carolina State	2
=	Oklahoma A&M#	2
=	San Francisco	2

* Since 1939

\# Now Oklahoma State

The first National Championships were held in 1939 under the aegis of the National Association of Basketball Coaches. Since 1940, it has been an officially sanctioned NCAA tournament.

Top 10 Best scoring averages in an NCAA Division I career

	Player/team	Average
1	Pete Maravich, LSU	44.2
2	Austin Carr, Notre Dame	34.6
3	Oscar Robertson, Cincinnati	33.8
4	Calvin Murphy, Niagara	33.1
5	Dwight Lamar, SW Louisiana	32.7
6	Frank Selvy, Furman	32.5
7	Rick Mount, Purdue	32.3
8	Darryl Floyd, Furman	32.1
9	Nick Werkman, Seton Hall	32.0
10	Willie Humes, Idaho State	31.5

Pete Maravich and Oscar Robertson are the only men to top the NCAA Division I scoring list three times, and both did so in consecutive years. Robertson achieved his titles between 1958–60, while Maravich did so a decade later, between 1968 and 1970.

TOP SOPHOMORES

Only four sophomores have won the NCAA scoring title: Oscar Robertson, Cincinnati (1958), Pete Maravich, LSU (1968), Johnny Neumann, Ole Miss (1971), and Larry Fogle, Canisius (1974). Robertson (1959) and Maravich (1969) are the only men to have won the title as both sophomores and juniors.

> **I** couldn't imagine not playing basketball. To me, basketball is what life is all about.
>
> **Bill Walton,** college and pro basketball player

Top 10 All-time NCAA Division I wins

	Team	Wins
1	Kentucky	1,795
2	North Carolina	1,781
3	Kansas	1,738
4	Duke	1,649
5	St. John's	1,621
6	Temple	1,571
7	Syracuse	1,549
8	Penn State	1,508
9	Indiana	1,494
10	Oregon State	1,491

While Kentucky has been NCAA champion seven times, they have won the Final Four title on only four occasions: in 1958, when they beat Seattle, in 1978 against Duke, in 1996 against Syracuse, and in 1998 with a win over Utah.

Top 10 Point scorers in an NCAA Division I career

	Player/team	Points
1	Pete Maravich, LSU	3,667
2	Freeman Williams, Port State	3,249
3	Lionel Simmons, La Salle	3,217
4	Alphonso Ford, Missouri/Val State	3,165
5	Harry Kelly, Texas Southern	3,066
6	Hersey Hawkins, Bradley	3,008
7	Oscar Robertson, Cincinnati	2,973
8	Danny Manning, Kansas	2,951
9	Alfrederick Hughes, Loyola-Chicago	2,914
10	Elvin Hayes, Houston	2,884

After a successful college basketball career, Pete Maravich went into the NBA in 1970, playing for the Atlanta Hawks. He moved to the New Orleans Jazz in 1974, and in 1977 was the scoring leader with an average of 31.1. He finished his career with the Boston Celtics in 1979–80.

Top 10 Most points in an NCAA Division I season

	Player/team	Year	Games	Points
1	Pete Maravich, LSU	1970	31	1,381
2	Elvin Hayes, Houston	1968	33	1,214
3	Frank Selvy, Furman	1954	29	1,209
4	Pete Maravich, LSU	1969	26	1,148
5	Pete Maravich, LSU	1968	26	1,138
6	Bo Kimble, Loyola (CA)	1990	32	1,131
7	Hersey Hawkins, Bradley	1988	31	1,125
8	Austin Carr, Notre Dame	1970	29	1,106
9	Austin Carr, Notre Dame	1971	29	1,101
10	Otis Birdsong, Houston	1977	36	1,090

None of the players in this list played on a Championship-winning team during their record-breaking season. The only one to play in a final four series was Elvin Hayes, with Houston in 1968, when they finished fourth. Hayes went on to spend 16 seasons in the NBA.

Top 10 Highest-scoring NCAA Championship finals

	Winner	Runner-up	Year	Score	Total points
1	Kentucky	Duke	1978	94–88	182
2	UCLA	Duke	1964	98–83	181
3	UCLA	Kentucky	1975	92–85	177
4	UNLV	Duke	1990	103–73	176
5	UCLA	Michigan	1965	91–80	171
6	La Salle	Bradley	1954	92–76	168
7	UCLA	Arkansas	1995	89–78	167
8	Michigan State	Florida	2000	89–76	165
9	UCLA	Purdue	1969	92–72	164
10	Arizona	Kentucky*	1997	84–79	163

* Overtime game

Despite being the highest-scoring championship game, the 1978 Kentucky versus Duke match failed to break any Final Four records for either individuals or teams. The nearest to a record was the 18 field goals of Jack Givens (Kentucky), which is third in the all-time list.

Top 10 Most points in a single NCAA Division I game

	Player	Game	Year	Points
1	Kevin Bradshaw	US International vs. Loyola (CA)	1991	72
2	Pete Maravich	LSU vs. Alabama	1970	69
3	Calvin Murphy	Niagara vs. Syracuse	1969	68
4 =	Jay Handlan	Wash & Lee vs. Furman	1951	66
=	Pete Maravich	LSU vs. Tulane	1969	66
=	Anthony Roberts	Oral Roberts vs. NC A&T	1977	66
7 =	Scott Haffner	Evansville vs. Dayton	1989	65
=	Anthony Roberts	Oral Roberts vs. Oregon	1977	65
9	Pete Maravich	LSU vs. Kentucky	1970	64
10 =	Hersey Hawkins	Bradley vs. Detroit	1988	63
=	Johnny Neumann	Ole Miss vs. LSU	1971	63

Although scoring a record 72 points against Loyola in 1991, Kevin Bradshaw was still on the losing side. Loyola beat US International on their home court 186 points to 140, and their 186 remains a record for a single NCAA Division One game.

◀ Cedric Bozeman (#21) of UCLA dribbles against Jamal Sampson (#31) of Cal during the Pacific 10 Tournament at the Staples Center in Los Angeles, California in March 2002.

HOCKEY

At the Start

Games resembling hockey are depicted in early Greek friezes and medieval manuscripts, while hockey on ice developed in the Netherlands in the 17th century as *kalv* and somewhat later in England as *bandy*, played on frozen football fields and iced-over canals. "Hurley-on-ice" (from hurling, an ancient Irish game) was played in Windsor, Nova Scotia, in about 1800. It remained no more than a popular pastime until the first formal match was played at the newly opened Victoria Skating Rink in Montreal in 1875. The "McGill [University] Rules" were introduced and the sport spread rapidly across North America and the rest of the world, becoming an Olympic event in 1920.

HOCKEY

- Most Stanley Cup wins
- Most Stanley Cup appearances
- Goal scorers in Stanley Cup playoffs
- Goaltenders in Stanley Cup playoffs
- Point scorers in Stanley Cup playoffs
- Best goals against averages by a goaltender in Stanley Cup playoffs

> Some people skate to the puck. I skate to where the puck is going to be.
> — Wayne Gretzky

STANLEY CUP RECORDS

Top 10 Most Stanley Cup wins*

	Team	Years	Wins
1	Montreal Canadiens	1916–93	24
2	Toronto Maple Leafs	1918–67	13
3	Detroit Red Wings	1936–98	9
4 =	Boston Bruins	1929–72	5
=	Edmonton Oilers	1984–90	5
6 =	Montreal Victorias	1895–98	4
=	Montreal Wanderers	1906–10	4
=	New York Islanders	1980–83	4
=	New York Rangers	1933–94	4
=	Ottawa Senators	1920–27	4

* Since 1918, after the abolition of the challenge match format

The Stanley Cup was originally a challenge trophy—any amateur team in Canada could challenge for the trophy over a single match. This was later changed to a best-of-three series. Following the formation of the professional National Hockey Association in 1910–11, the trophy was presented to their first champions, but challenges were allowed from any other team. Following the formation of a new league, the Pacific Coast Hockey Association (PCHA) in 1912–13, there began the first end-of-season series of games between the champions of the respective leagues.

Top 10 Most Stanley Cup appearances*

	Team	Years	Apps
1	Montreal Canadiens	1919–1993	32
2 =	Detroit Red Wings	1936–98	21
=	Toronto Maple Leafs	1918–67	21
4	Boston Bruins	1927–90	17
5 =	Chicago Blackhawks	1931–92	10
=	New York Rangers	1928–94	10
7	Philadelphia Flyers	1974–97	7
8	Edmonton Oilers	1983–90	6
9 =	New York Islanders	1980–84	5
=	Vancouver Millionaires	1918–24	5

* Since 1918, after the abolition of the challenge match format

The Montreal Canadiens' first Stanley Cup appearance post-1918 was in 1919 against Seattle. However, the series was canceled with the scores leveled at 2–2 after many of the Montreal players caught the Spanish influenza that was sweeping the country at the time. One of their players, English-born Joe Hall, died a few days later, and the series was never completed.

Top 10 Goal scorers in Stanley Cup playoffs

	Player	Games	Goals
1	Wayne Gretzky	208	122
2	Mark Messier*	236	109
3	Jari Kurri	200	106
4	Glenn Anderson	225	93
5	Brett Hull*	163	90
6	Mike Bossy	129	85
7	Maurice Richard	133	82
8	Claude Lemieux*	221	80
9	Jean Beliveau	162	79
10	Mario Lemieux*	107	76

* Active during 2001 season

Despite playing with a sore shoulder, Mark Messier helped the Edmonton Oilers to their first Stanley Cup final in 1983, where they lost to the Islanders. However, a year later Messier and the Oilers were Stanley Cup winners.

Top 10 Goaltenders in Stanley Cup playoffs

	Player	Games	Wins
1	Patrick Roy*	219	137
2	Grant Fuhr	150	92
3	Billy Smith	132	88
4	Ken Dryden	112	80
5	Ed Belfour*	141	79
6	Mike Vernon*	138	77
7	Jacques Plante	112	71
8	Andy Moog	132	68
9	Martin Brodeur*	109	65
10	Tom Barrasso	119	61

* Active during 2001 season

Patrick Roy has been on four winning Stanley Cup teams, with Montreal in 1986 and 1993, and with Colorado in 1996 and 2001.

◀ Ray Bourque of the Colorado Avalanche and teammate Patrick Roy raise the Stanley Cup in 2001 after they beat New Jersey 3–1.

Top 10 Point scorers in Stanley Cup playoffs

Player	Games	Goals	Assists	Points
1 Wayne Gretzky	208	122	260	382
2 Mark Messier*	236	109	186	295
3 Jari Kurri	200	106	127	233
4 Glenn Anderson	225	93	121	214
5 Paul Coffey*	194	59	137	196
6 Bryan Trottier	221	71	113	184
7 Ray Bourque*	214	41	139	180
8 Doug Gilmore*	170	56	122	178
9 Jean Beliveau	162	79	97	176
10 Denis Savard	169	66	109	175

* Active during 2001 season

Wayne Gretzky was wearing ice skates from the age of two. He turned to professional hockey at age 17 with the Indianapolis Racers in the WHA, but after just eight games he was traded to the Edmonton Oilers. He went on to make history, breaking 60 NHL records.

Top 10 Best goals against averages by a goaltender in Stanley Cup playoffs*

Player	Games	Goals against	Average
1 Martin Brodeur#	109	217	1.91
2 George Hainsworth	52	112	1.93
3 Turk Broda	101	211	1.98
4 Dominik Hasek#	74	157	2.09
5 Ed Belfour#	141	308	2.14
6 Jacques Plante	112	240	2.16
7 Chris Osgood#	68	144	2.17
8 Patrick Roy	219	516	2.29
9 Ken Dryden	112	274	2.40
10 Bernie Parent	71	174	2.43

* Minimum qualification: 50 games played

Active during 2001 season

Chris Benedict had an all-time average of 1.80, but played in only 48 games.

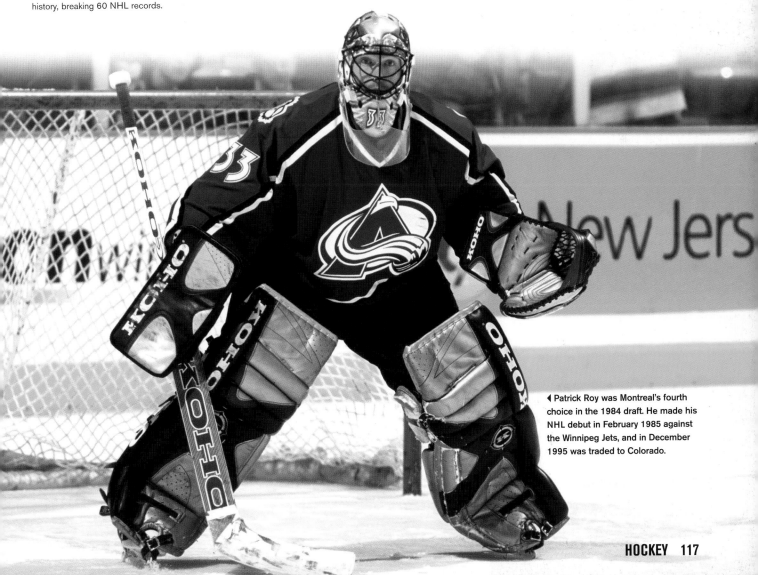

◀ Patrick Roy was Montreal's fourth choice in the 1984 draft. He made his NHL debut in February 1985 against the Winnipeg Jets, and in December 1995 was traded to Colorado.

SEASON RECORD-BREAKERS

- Most points in a single game
- Wins by a goaltender in a season
- Most assists in a season
- Goal scorers in a season
- NHL games to produce the most goals

STAR SIBLINGS

On February 22, 1981, playing for Quebec against Washington, the Czech-born brothers Peter and Anton Stastny each scored eight points. Not only is eight points in a game one of the highest marks in NHL history, but to be achieved by brothers is even more remarkable. Moreover, they were both in their first season in the NHL.

Top 10 Most points in a single game

	Player	Match	Date	Goals	Assists	Points
1	Darryl Sittler	Toronto vs. Boston	Feb. 7, 1976	6	4	10
2 =	Tom Bladon	Philadelphia vs. Cleveland	Dec. 11, 1977	4	4	8
=	Paul Coffey	Edmonton vs. Detroit	Mar. 14, 1986	2	6	8
=	Wayne Gretzky	Edmonton vs. New Jersey	Nov. 19, 1983	3	5	8
=	Wayne Gretzky	Edmonton vs. Minnesota	Jan. 4, 1984	4	4	8
=	Mario Lemieux	Pittsburgh vs. St. Louis	Oct. 15, 1988	2	6	8
=	Mario Lemieux	Pittsburgh vs. New Jersey	Dec. 31, 1988	5	3	8
=	Bernie Nicholls	Los Angeles vs. Toronto	Dec. 1, 1988	2	6	8
=	Bert Olmstead	Montreal vs. Chicago	Jan. 9, 1954	4	4	8
=	Maurice Richard	Montreal vs. Detroit	Dec. 28, 1944	5	3	8
=	Anton Stastny	Quebec vs. Washington	Feb. 22, 1981	3	5	8
=	Peter Stastny	Quebec vs. Washington	Feb. 22, 1981	4	4	8
=	Bryan Trottier	NY Islanders vs. NY Rangers	Dec. 23, 1978	5	3	8

The most goals in one game is seven, by Joe Malone for Quebec against Toronto on January 31, 1920.

Top 10 Wins by a goaltender in a season

	Player/team	Season	Wins
1	Bernie Parent, Philadelphia Flyers	1973–74	47
2 =	Bernie Parent, Philadelphia Flyers	1974–75	44
=	Terry Sawchuk, Detroit Red Wings	1950–51	44
=	Terry Sawchuk, Detroit Red Wings	1951–52	44
5 =	Tom Barrasso, Pittsburgh Penguins	1992–93	43
=	Ed Belfour, Chicago Blackhawks	1990–91	43
=	Martin Brodeur, New Jersey Devils	1997–98	43
=	Martin Brodeur, New Jersey Devils	1999–2000	43
9 =	Martin Brodeur, New Jersey Devils	2000–01	42
=	Ken Dryden, Montreal Canadiens	1975–76	42
=	Jacques Plante, Montreal Canadiens	1955–56	42
=	Jacques Plante, Montreal Canadiens	1961–62	42
=	Mike Richter, New York Rangers	1993–94	42
=	Roman Turek, St. Louis Blues	1999–2000	42

Bernie Parent made headlines after the 1971–72 season by becoming the first big-name goalie to sign for the WHA when he joined the Miami Screaming Eagles. The Eagles moved to Philadelphia before playing a game and were renamed the Blazers. Parent played just one season with them.

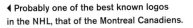

◀ Probably one of the best known logos in the NHL, that of the Montreal Canadiens.

Top 10 Most assists in a season

	Player/team	Season	Games	Assists
1	Wayne Gretzy, Edmonton Oilers	1985-86	80	163
2	Wayne Gretzy, Edmonton Oilers	1984-85	80	135
3	Wayne Gretzy, Edmonton Oilers	1982-83	80	125
4	Wayne Gretzy, Los Angeles Kings	1990-91	78	122
5	Wayne Gretzy, Edmonton Oilers	1986-87	79	121
6	Wayne Gretzy, Edmonton Oilers	1981-82	80	120
7	Wayne Gretzy, Edmonton Oilers	1983-84	74	118
8 =	Wayne Gretzy, Los Angeles Kings	1988-89	78	114
=	Mario Lemieux, Pittsburgh Penguins	1988-89	76	114
10 =	Wayne Gretzy, Edmonton Oilers	1980-81	80	109
=	Wayne Gretzy, Edmonton Oilers	1987-88	64	109

Top 10 Goal scorers in a season

	Player/team	Season	Games	Goals
1	Wayne Gretzy, Edmonton Oilers	1981-82	80	92
2	Wayne Gretzy, Edmonton Oilers	1983-84	74	87
3	Brett Hull, St. Louis Blues	1990-91	78	86
4	Mario Lemieux, Pittsburgh Penguins	1988-89	76	85
5 =	Phil Esposito, Boston Bruins	1970-71	78	76
=	Alexander Mogilny, Buffalo Sabres	1992-93	77	76
=	Teemu Selanne, Winnipeg Jets	1992-93	84	76
8	Wayne Gretzy, Edmonton Oilers	1984-85	80	73
9	Brett Hull, St. Louis Blues	1989-90	80	72
10 =	Wayne Gretzy, Edmonton Oilers	1982-83	80	71
=	Jari Kurri, Edmonton Oilers	1984-85	73	71

In nine seasons with the Edmonton Oilers, Wayne Gretzky only once scored less than 50 goals in a regular season and that was in 1987–88, when he scored 40.

Top 10 NHL games to produce the most goals

	Teams	Score	Date	Total goals
1 =	Edmonton Oilers vs. Chicago Blackhawks	12-9	Dec. 11, 1985	21
=	Montreal Canadiens vs. Toronto St. Patricks	14-7	Jan. 10, 1920	21
3 =	Edmonton Oilers vs. Minnesota North Stars	12-8	Jan. 4, 1984	20
=	Toronto Maple Leafs vs. Edmonton Oilers	11-9	Jan. 8, 1986	20
5 =	Boston Bruins vs. New York Rangers	10-9	Mar. 4, 1944	19
=	Boston Bruins vs. Detroit Red Wings	10-9	Mar. 16, 1944	19
=	Montreal Wanderers vs. Toronto Arenas	10-9	Dec. 19, 1917	19
=	Montreal Canadiens vs. Quebec Bulldogs	16-3	Mar. 3, 1920	19
=	Montreal Canadiens vs. Hamilton Tigers	13-3	Feb. 26, 1921	19
=	Vancouver Canucks vs. Minnesota North Stars	10-9	Oct. 7, 1983	19

The 16 goals scored by the Montreal Canadiens against the Quebec Bulldogs in 1920 is the most goals scored by one side in a single game.

◀ When people talk about hockey records, the name of one man crops up time and time again: Wayne Gretzky, the game's greatest player.

ALL-TIME HOCKEY GREATS

- Most games in an NHL career
- Most goals in an NHL career
- Goaltenders in an NHL career
- Most shutouts in an NHL career
- NHL annual leaders in a career
- Points scored in an NHL career

> By the age of 18, the average American has witnessed 200,000 acts of violence on television, most of them occurring during Game 1 of the NHL playoff series.
>
> **Steve Rushin,** sports writer

Top 10 Most games in an NHL career

	Player	Years	Games
1	Gordie Howe	1946–80	1,767
2	Larry Murphy*	1980–2001	1,615
3	Ray Bourque*	1979–2001	1,612
4	Mark Messier*	1979–2001	1,561
5	Alex Delvecchio	1950–74	1,549
6	John Buyck	1955–78	1,540
7	Ron Francis*	1981–2001	1,489
8	Wayne Gretzky	1979–99	1,487
9	Tim Horton	1949–74	1,446
10	Scott Stevens*	1982–2001	1,434

* Active during 2000–01 season

Gordie Howe, who holds the record for the most seasons (26) and games played (1,767) in the NHL, retired in 1971 but then returned to play alongside his sons Mark and Marty for Houston in the newly formed World Hockey Association.

Top 10 Most goals in an NHL career

	Player	Years	Games	Goals
1	Wayne Gretzky	20	1,487	894
2	Gordie Howe	26	1,767	801
3	Marcel Dionne	18	1,348	731
4	Phil Esposito	18	1,282	717
5	Mark Gartner	19	1,432	708
6	Mark Messier*	22	1,561	651
7	Brett Hull*	16	1,019	649
8	Mario Lemieux*	13	788	648
9	Steve Yzerman*	18	1,310	645
10	Bobby Hull	16	1,063	610

* Active during 2000–01 season

Wayne Gretzky's very first goal in the NHL was against Vancouver on October 14, 1979. The goalie who had the distinction of letting in that first goal was Glen Hanlon.

Top 10 Goaltenders in an NHL career

	Player	Years	Games	Wins
1	Patrick Roy*	17	903	484
2	Terry Sawchuk	21	971	447
3	Jacques Plante	18	837	434
4	Tony Esposito	16	886	423
5	Glenn Hall	18	906	407
6	Grant Fuhr	19	868	403
7	Mike Vernon*	18	763	383
8 =	Andy Moog	18	713	372
=	John Vanbiesbrouck*	19	877	372
10	Rogie Vachon	16	795	355

* Active during 2000–01 season

The first of Patrick Roy's 484 career wins was in the 1985 season when he came on for one period for the Montreal Canadiens against Winnipeg Jets. He faced just two shots but got a credit for the win.

Top 10 Most shutouts in an NHL career

	Player	Years	Games	Shutouts
1	Terry Sawchuk	21	971	103
2	George Hainsworth	11	465	94
3	Glenn Hall	18	906	84
4	Jacques Plante	18	837	82
5 =	Alex Connell	12	417	81
=	Tiny Thompson	12	553	81
7	Tony Esposito	16	886	76
8	Lorne Chabot	11	411	73
9	Harry Lumley	16	804	71
10	Roy Worters	12	484	66

* Active during 2000–01 season

As a 12-year-old, Terry Sawchuk broke his arm playing rugby. It healed badly and one arm was two inches shorter than the other, but it did not stop him going on to play more NHL games than any other goalie.

▶ The leading active NHL point scorer of 2001, Mark Messier (right), in action for the New York Rangers against the New Jersey Devils.

DID YOU KNOW? No one has topped the points, goals, and assists lists in a season as often as Wayne Gretzky, who headed all three lists five times between 1982 and 1987.

Top 10 NHL annual leaders in a career*

	Player	Points leader	Goals leader	Assists leader	Total
1	Wayne Gretzky	10	5	16	31
2 =	Phil Esposito	5	6	3	14
=	Gordie Howe	6	5	3	14
4	Mario Lemieux	6	3	3	12
5	Bobby Hull	3	7	0	10
6	Jaromir Jagr	5	0	3	8
7 =	Charlie Conacher	2	5	0	7
=	Stan Mikita	4	0	3	7
=	Bobby Orr	2	0	5	7
10 =	Bill Cook	2	3	0	5
=	Guy Lafleur	3	1	1	5
=	Maurice Richard	0	5	0	5

* Accumulative total of Art Ross Trophy wins for being top point scorer, top goal scorer, and most assists

Top 10 Point scorers in an NHL career

	Player	Years	Games	Goals	Assists	Points
1	Wayne Gretzky	20	1,487	894	1,963	2,857
2	Gordie Howe	26	1,767	801	1,049	1,850
3	Mark Messier*	22	1,561	651	1,130	1,781
4	Marcel Dionne	18	1,348	731	1,040	1,771
5	Ron Francis*	20	1,489	487	1,137	1,624
6	Steve Yzerman*	18	1,310	645	969	1,614
7	Phil Esposito	18	1,282	717	873	1,590
8	Ray Bourque*	22	1,612	410	1,169	1,579
9	Mario Lemieux*	13	788	648	922	1,570
10	Paul Coffey*	21	1,409	396	1,135	1,531

* Active during 2001 season

COACHES, AWARDS & STADIUMS

- First winners of the President's Trophy
- Biggest NHL arenas
- Most NHL awards
- Winners of the Hart Trophy
- Oldest NHL arenas
- Coaches in the Stanley Cup
- NHL coaches

> Every player who is sitting here who lifted up the Cup for the first time will tell you the same thing. There is no feeling like lifting up the Stanley Cup.
> **Wayne Gretzky**

The 10 First winners of the President's Trophy*

	Player	Year(s)
1	Edmonton Oilers	1986, 1987#
2	Calgary Flames	1988, 1989#
3	Boston Bruins	1990
4	Chicago Blackhawks	1991
5	New York Rangers	1992
6	Pittsburgh Penguins	1993
7	Colorado Avalanche	1994, 1997, 2001#
8	Detroit Red Wings	1995, 1996
9	Dallas Stars	1998, 1999#
10	St. Louis Blues	2000

* Up to the 2000–01 season

\# Won Stanley Cup in the same season

The President's Trophy is presented to the team with the best regular season record in the NHL. It was presented to the NHL by the NHL Board of Governors and was first awarded in the 1985–86 season.

Top 10 Most NHL awards*

	Player	Total
1	Wayne Gretzky	19
2	Bobby Orr	12
3	Dominik Hasek	10
4	Mario Lemieux	8
5 =	Frank Boucher	7
=	Doug Harvey	7
=	Jacques Plante	7
8 =	Ray Bourque	6
=	Ken Dryden	6
=	Bill Duman	6
=	Gordie Howe	6

* Based on total major awards won: Hart Memorial Trophy, Calder Memorial Trophy, Vezina Trophy, Lady Byng Memorial Trophy, James Norris Memorial Trophy, Frank Selke Trophy, and Lester B. Pearson Award

The most prestigious annual award in the NHL is the Hart Memorial Trophy. It was presented to the NHL by Dr. David Hart, the father of Cecil Hart, the former coach of the Montreal Canadiens. The original trophy was retired to the NHL Hall of Fame in 1960 and replaced by the Hart Memorial Trophy. It is presented to the player judged by a panel of journalists to be the most valuable player of the year to his team.

Top 10 Biggest NHL arenas*

	Stadium/location	Home team	Capacity
1	Molson Center	Montreal Canadiens	21,273
2	United Center	Chicago Blackhawks	20,500
3	Joe Louis Arena	Detroit Red Wings	19,983
4	MCI Center	Washington Capitals	19,700
5	National Car Rental Center, Sunrise	Florida Panthers	19,542
6	First Union Center	Philadelphia Flyers	19,519
7	Ice Palace	Tampa Bay Lightning	19,500
8	Savvis Center	St. Louis Blues	19,260
9	Continental Airlines Arena, East Rutherford	New Jersey Devils	19,040
10	Phillips Arena	Atlanta Thrashers	19,008

* Based on capacity during 2000–01 season

Top 10 Winners of the Hart Trophy

	Player	Years	Wins
1	Wayne Gretzky	1980–89	9
2	Gordie Howe	1952–63	6
3	Eddie Shore	1933–38	4
4 =	Bobby Clarke	1973–76	3
=	Mario Lemieux	1988–96	3
=	Howie Morenz	1928–32	3
=	Bobby Orr	1970–72	3
8 =	Jean Beliveau	1956–64	2
=	Bill Cowley	1941–43	2
=	Phil Esposito	1969–74	2
=	Dominic Hasek	1997–98	2
=	Bobby Hull	1965–66	2
=	Guy Lafleur	1977–78	2
=	Mark Messier	1990–92	2
=	Stan Mikita	1967–68	2
=	Nels Stewart	1926–30	2

Source: National Hockey League

Top 10 Oldest NHL arenas

	Stadium	Home team	Year
1	Mellon Arena	Pittsburgh Penguins	1961
2	Madison Square Garden	New York Rangers	1964
3	Nassau Veterans Memorial Coliseum, Uniondale	New York Islanders	1972
4	Skyreach Center	Edmonton Oilers	1974
5	Joe Louis Arena	Detroit Red Wings	1979
6	Continental Airlines Arena, Rutherford	New Jersey Devils	1981
7	Pengrowth Saddledome	Calgary Flames	1983
8	America West Arena	Phoenix Coyotes	1992
9	Arrowhead Pond	Mighty Ducks of Anaheim	June 1993
10	Compaq Center at San Jose	San Jose Sharks	Sep 1993

Known as the "Igloo" by Penguins fans, the Mellon Arena opened on September 17, 1961. However, it was not until the summer of 1967 that the Penguins moved in, and they played their first game there on October 11, 1967, when they lost 2–1 to the Canadiens.

Top 10 Coaches in the Stanley Cup*

	Coach	Team(s)	Years	Wins
1 =	Toe Blake	Montreal Canadiens	1956–68	8
=	Scotty Bowman	Montreal Canadiens, Pittsburgh Penguins, Detroit Red Wings	1973–98	8
3	Hap Day	Toronto Maple Leafs	1942–49	5
4 =	Al Arbour	New York Islanders	1980–83	4
=	Punch Imlach	Toronto Maple Leafs	1962–67	4
=	Dick Irvin	Toronto Maple Leafs, Montreal Canadiens	1932–53	4
=	Glen Sather	Edmonton Oilers	1984–88	4
8 =	Jack Adams	Detroit Red Wings	1936–43	3
=	Pete Green	Ottawa Senators	1920–23	3
=	Tommy Ivan	Detroit Red Wings	1950–54	3
=	Lester Patrick	Victoria Cougars, New York Rangers	1925–33	3

* Based on winning teams coached 1918–2001

Top 10 NHL coaches*

	Coach	Years	Regular season	Playoffs	Total
1	Scotty Bowman#	29	1193	207	1400
2	Al Arbour	22	781	121	904
3	Dick Irvin	26	690	100	790
4	Mike Keenan#	15	539	91	630
5	Billy Reay	16	542	57	599
6	Toe Blake	13	500	82	582
7	Pat Quinn#	15	484	75	559
8	Glen Sather	11	464	89	553
9	Bryan Murray	13	484	34	518
10	Roger Neilson	15	459	51	510

* Based on number of wins

\# Active during 2000-01 season

Bowman coached eight Stanley Cup winning teams: Montreal in 1973 and 1976–79, Pittsburgh in 1992, and Detroit in 1997 and 1998.

◄ Coach Scotty Bowman of the Detroit Red Wings wins the Jack Adams Trophy during the NHL awards ceremony in 1996.

- Biggest hockey arenas in Europe

- Most European Championship gold medals

- Medal-winning countries at the Olympic Games

- Countries outside the US and Canada with the most ice rinks

- Medal-winning countries at the men's World Championships

Top 10 Biggest hockey arenas in Europe*

	Arena/country	Capacity
1	Cologne Arena, Germany	18,000
2	Allmend Eisstadion, Bern, Switzerland	16,771
3	Manchester Evening News Arena, England	16,500
4	Sportovni Hala, Prague, Czech Republic	14,660
5	Globe Arena, Stockholm, Sweden	13,850
6	Hartwall Arena, Helsinki, Finland	13,665
7	Scandinavium, Gothenburg, Sweden	12,306
8	Elysee Arena, Turku, Finland	11,820
9 =	Hallenstadion, Zurich, Switzerland	11,500
=	Luzhniki Sports Palace, Moscow, Russia	11,500

* Based on capacity during 2000–01 season

Top 10 Most European Championship gold medals

	Country	Golds
1	USSR	27
2 =	Czechoslovakia	11
=	Sweden	11
4 =	UK	4
=	Switzerland	4
6	Bohemia	3
7 =	Austria	2
=	Germany	2
9 =	Belgium	1
=	France	1

The European Championships were held 1910–91.

SURPRISE OLYMPIC WIN

One of the biggest Winter Olympic shocks was in 1936 when the UK won the hockey tournament. In the semifinal, they defeated the Canadians, thereby ending Canada's run of 20 Olympic matches without defeat.

> In a land so inescapably and inhospitably cold, hockey is the chance of life, and an affirmation that despite the deathly chill of winter we are alive.
>
> **Stephen Leacock,** Canadian humorist, on why hockey is so popular in Canada

Top 10 Medal-winning countries at the Olympic Games

	Country	G (men)	S (men)	B (men)	G (women)	S (women)	B (women)	G (combined)	S (combined)	B (combined)	Total
1	Canada	6	4	2	1	1	0	7	5	2	14
2 =	US	2	6	1	1	1	0	3	7	1	11
=	USSR	7	2	2	0	0	0	7	2	2	11
4 =	Czechoslovakia/Czech Republic	1	4	3	0	0	0	1	4	3	8
=	Sweden	1	2	4	0	0	1	1	2	5	8
6	Finland	0	1	2	0	0	1	0	1	3	4
7 =	Germany	0	0	2	0	0	0	0	0	2	2
=	Switzerland	0	0	2	0	0	0	0	0	2	2
=	UK	1	0	1	0	0	0	1	0	1	2
10	Unified Team	1	0	0	0	0	0	1	0	0	1

G – gold medals, S – silver medals, B – bronze medals

Hockey was first contested at the Summer Olympics in 1920. It has been contested at the Winter Olympics since 1924 for men and since 1998 for women.

Top 10 Countries outside the US and Canada with the most ice rinks

	Country	Indoor	Outdoor	Total
1	Sweden	274	350	624
2	Germany	199	48	247
3	Switzerland	73	45	118
4	Czech Republic	97	20	117
5	Russia	92	14	106
6	Japan	85	20	105
7	Finland	94	5	99
8	Austria	19	79	98
9	France	86	5	91
10	Italy	45	19	64

Source: International Ice Hockey Federation (IIHF)

Despite being second on the list with 247 rinks, Germany has never won an Olympic gold medal. All they have to show for all those rinks are two bronze medals; one in Lake Placid in 1932 and the other in Innsbruck in 1976.

Top 10 Medal-winning countries at the men's World Championships

	Country	Gold	Silver	Bronze	Total
1	Czechoslovakia/Czech Republic	10	12	19	41
2	Canada	21	10	9	40
3	Sweden	7	16	13	36
4	USSR/Russia	23	7	5	35
5	US	2	9	4	15
6	Switzerland	0	1	8	9
7	Finland	1	5	1	7
8	UK	1	2	2	5
9	Germany	0	2	2	4
10	Austria	0	0	2	2

The World Championship for men has been contested since 1930, although the Olympic champions of 1920, 1924, and 1928 were also deemed to be world champions. Between 1932 and 1968, the Olympic champions were also declared world champions. In the Olympic years of 1972, 1976, and 1992 the International Ice Hockey Federation (IIHF) ran its own World Championships, but there were no championships in the Olympic years of 1980, 1984, and 1988.

The only other country to have won a medal is Slovakia, with one bronze.

The women's World Championship has been held sporadically since 1990, but annually since 1999. During this period, Canada has won all seven gold medals, the United States all seven silver medals, while Finland (six) and Russia (one) have been the only bronze medal winners.

◄ Theo Fiery of Canada celebrates after defeating the US 5–2 during the men's hockey gold medal game of the 2002 Salt Lake Winter Olympics.

NCAA HOCKEY

- Most NCAA titles
- Most NCAA Coach of the Year titles
- Most appearances in the NCAA tournament
- Most wins in the NCAA tournament
- NCAA coaches
- Most points in NCAA Championship games

COACHING TROPHY

The trophy awarded to the NCAA Coach of the Year is the Penrose Memorial Trophy. This trophy was named after Spencer T. Penrose, the man who built the Broadmoor hotel and leisure complex in Colorado Springs, home to the NCAA Championship from 1948 to 1957.

Top 10 Most NCAA titles

	Team	Years	Wins
1	Michigan	1948–98	9
2	North Dakota	1959–2000	7
3 =	Denver	1958–69	5
=	Wisconsin	1973–90	5
5	Boston University	1971–95	4
6 =	Lake Superior State	1988–94	3
=	Michigan Tech.	1962–75	3
=	Minnesota	1974–79	3
9 =	Boston College	1949–2001	2
=	Colorado College	1950–57	2
=	Cornell	1967–70	2
=	Maine	1993–99	2
=	Michigan State	1966–86	2
=	RPI	1954–85	2

Top 10 Most NCAA Coach of the Year titles

	Name	Years	Total
1 =	Len Ceglarski	1966*, 1973, 1985	3
=	Charlie Holt	1969, 1974, 1979	3
3 =	Dean Blais	1997, 2001	2
=	Rick Comley	1980, 1991	2
=	Eddie Jeremiah	1951, 1967	2
=	Snooks Kelly	1959, 1972	2
=	John MacInnes	1970, 1976	2
=	Joe Marsh	1989, 2000	2
=	Jack Parker	1975, 1978	2
=	Jack Riley	1957, 1960	2
=	Cooney Weiland	1955, 1971	2

* Shared title

Eddie Jeremiah won his second title in 1967, 16 years after his first. It was a fitting second title, since it capped his final year of 30 as Dartmouth coach.

The 10 Most appearances in the NCAA tournament*

	Team	Years appearing
1 =	Boston University	25
=	Minnesota	25
3	Michigan	24
4	Boston College	22
5	Michigan State	21
6 =	Clarkson	18
=	Wisconsin	18
8	North Dakota	17
9	Harvard	16
10	St. Lawrence	15

* Appearances in end-of-season tournament

Of the two top teams, Minnesota has the slightly better record in NCAA tournament matches with 39–28–0 to Boston's 32–27–0.

The 10 Most wins in the NCAA tournament*

	Team	Wins
1	Minnesota	39
2	Michigan	38
3	Boston University	32
4	North Dakota	30
5	Wisconsin	28
6	Michigan State	24
7	Boston College	23
8 =	Lake Superior State	20
=	Maine	20
10	Denver	17

* Wins in all end-of-season tournament matches

The highest-scoring NCAA championship game was in 1957, when Colorado College beat Michigan 13–6 for an aggregate of 19 goals.

▶ Kurt Millerg gets one past Derek Heriofsky, the goalkeeper of Boston University, at the NCAA Division I Hockey Championship.

> It was a great period... I guess I turned into a great goal-scorer all of a sudden. Last year those shots would have hit the post and bounced into our own net.
>
> **Matt Murley** of Rensselaer after he scored his 100th career point against UMass–Amherst, November 2000

Top 10 NCAA coaches*

	Coach/college	Years	Wins
1	Vic Heyliger, Michigan	1948–56	6
2	Murray Armstrong, Denver	1958–69	5
3 =	Herb Brooks, Minnesota	1974–79	3
=	Gino Gasparini, North Dakota	1980–87	3
=	Ned Harkness, RPI/Cornell	1954–70	3
=	Bob Johnson, Wisconsin	1973–81	3
=	John MacInnes, Michigan Tech.	1962–75	3
8 =	Red Berenson, Michigan	1996–98	2
=	Dean Blais, North Dakota	1997–2000	2
=	Jeff Jackson, Lake Superior State	1992–94	2
=	Jack Kelley, Boston University	1971–72	2
=	Jack Parker, Boston University	1978–95	2
=	Jeff Sauer, Wisconsin	1983–90	2
=	Shawn Walsh, Maine	1993–99	2
=	Jerry York, Bowling Green/Boston College	1984–2001	2

* Based on most Championship wins

Top 10 Most points in NCAA Championship games

	Player/college	Year	Goals	Assists	Points
1 =	Tony Amonte, Boston University	1990	7	6	13
=	Aaron Broten, Minnesota	1981	6	7	13
3	Tony Hrkac, North Dakota	1987	3	9	12
4 =	Lane MacDonald, Harvard	1986	4	7	11
=	Mitch Messier, Michigan State	1986	5	6	11
=	Dave Trombley, Clarkson	1991	3	8	11
7 =	Rob Gaudreau, Providence	1989	6	4	10
=	Gerald Tallaire, Lake Superior State	1994	3	7	10
9 =	Dick Dougherty, Minnesota	1954	6	3	9
=	Pat Flatley, Wisconsin	1983	3	6	9
=	Tony Frasca, Colorado College	1950	3	6	9
=	John Mayasich, Minnesota	1954	4	5	9
=	Bob McCusker, Colorado College	1957	7	2	9
=	Bill McFarland, Michigan	1954	4	5	9
=	Jim Montgomery, Maine	1993	5	4	9
=	Chris Ray, Colorado College	1950	5	4	9
=	Bill Watson, Minnesota–Duluth	1985	3	6	9

AUTO SPORTS

At the Start

In 1878, a 33-hour contest between two steam wagons over the 201 miles (323 kilometres) from Green Bay to Madison, Wisconsin, marks the world's first auto race. Sixteen years later, in 1894, 25 cars competed in a race from Paris to Rouen, France, with the Comte de Dion as victor. In the United States the following year, Frank Duryea won the 54-mile (87-km) round-trip race between Chicago and Evanston, Illinois with an average speed of 7.5 mph (12 km/h). Road races were progressively replaced by those on tracks, the first of which took place on a harness racetrack in Cranston, Rhode Island, in 1896. The first Grand Prix was the French Grand Prix, which was held in 1906. The first US Grand Prix was organized by the Automobile Club of America (ACA) in 1908 and raced in Savannah, Georgia.

NASCAR RECORDS

- Most wins in a NASCAR season
- NASCAR race winners in the modern era
- Fastest winning speeds in the Daytona 500
- NASCAR career money winners
- Longest NASCAR race circuits
- Drivers with the most Winston Cup race wins

> It's the largest picnic in the world.
>
> **Peter Golenboch**, sports writer, on the Daytona 500

Top 10 Most wins in a NASCAR season

	Driver	Season	Wins
1	Richard Petty	1967	27
2	Richard Petty	1971	21
3 =	Tim Flock	1955	18
=	Richard Petty	1970	18
5	Bobby Isaac	1969	17
6 =	David Pearson	1968	16
=	Richard Petty	1968	16
8 =	Ned Jarrett	1964	15
=	David Pearson	1966	15
10 =	Buck Baker	1956	14
=	Richard Petty	1963	14

Source: NASCAR

All these wins were in the Grand National Series. The best total since the launch of the Winston Cup Series in 1972 is 13 by Richard Petty in 1975 and Jeff Gordon in 1998.

Top 10 NASCAR race winners in the modern era

	Driver	Total
1	Darrell Waltrip	84
2	Dale Earnhardt	77
3	Cale Yarborough	69
4	Richard Petty	60
5	Jeff Gordon	58
6	Bobby Allison	55
7	Rusty Wallace	54
8	David Pearson	45
9	Bill Elliott	41
10	Mark Martin	32

NASCAR's "Modern Era" started in 1972. This was the year that the NASCAR founder, Bill France, handed over the reigns to his son, Bill Jr. They also completed a sponsorship deal with R. J. Reynolds to rename the series the Winston Cup. A new point system was also introduced.

Top 10 Fastest winning speeds in the Daytona 500

	Driver	Car	Year	Winning speed (mph)	Winning speed (km/h)
1	Buddy Baker	Oldsmobile	1980	177.602	285.823
2	Bill Elliott	Ford	1987	176.263	283.668
3	Dale Earnhardt*	Chevrolet	1998	172.712	277.953
4	Bill Elliott	Ford	1985	172.265	277.234
5	Richard Petty	Buick	1981	169.651	273.027
6	Derrike Cope	Chevrolet	1990	165.761	266.766
7	Michael Waltrip	Chevrolet	2001	161.783	260.364
8	Jeff Gordon	Chevrolet	1999	161.551	259.991
9	A. J. Foyt	Mercury	1972	161.550	259.990
10	Richard Petty	Plymouth	1966	160.627	258.449

* Killed on final turn of last lap of 2001 Daytona 500

Source: NASCAR

First held in 1959, the Daytona 500 is raced every February at the Daytona International Speedway, Daytona Beach, Florida. One of the most prestigious races of the NASCAR season, it covers 200 laps of the 2½-mile (4-km) high-banked oval circuit.

Top 10 NASCAR career money winners*

	Driver	Career earnings ($)
1	Jeff Gordon	45,748,580
2	Dale Earnhardt	41,742,384
3	Dale Jarrett	33,274,832
4	Rusty Wallace	29,657,719
5	Mark Martin	29,165,332
6	Bill Elliott	27,306,174
7	Terry Labonte	26,536,692
8	Bobby Labonte	25,953,024
9	Ricky Rudd	24,530,223
10	Jeff Burton	22,958,499

* To end of 2001 season
Source: NASCAR

All drivers were active in 2001. Dale Earnhardt lost his life in a tragic accident during the 2001 Daytona 500.

Top 10 Longest NASCAR race circuits*

	Circuit	miles	km
1	Talladega Superspeedway	2.66	4.28
2 =	Daytona International Speedway	2.50	4.02
=	Indianapolis Motor Speedway	2.50	4.02
=	Pocono Raceway	2.50	4.02
5	Watkins Glen International	2.45	3.94
6 =	California Speedway	2.00	3.22
=	Michigan International Speedway	2.00	3.22
=	Sears Point Raceway	2.00	3.22
9	Atlanta Motor Speedway	1.54	2.48
10 =	Chicagoland Speedway	1.50	2.41
=	Homestead-Miami Speedway	1.50	2.41
=	Kansas Speedway	1.50	2.41
=	Las Vegas Motor Speedway	1.50	2.41
=	Lowe's Motor Speedway at Charlotte	1.50	2.41
=	Texas Motor Speedway	1.50	2.41

* In the 2002 season
Source: NASCAR

Top 10 Drivers with the most Winston Cup race wins

	Driver	Career	Wins
1	Richard Petty	1958–92	200
2	David Pearson	1960–86	105
3 =	Bobby Allison	1975–88	84
=	Darrell Waltrip	1975–92	84
5	Cale Yarborough	1957–88	83
6	Dale Earnhardt	1979–2000	76
7	Jeff Gordon	1994–2001	58
8 =	Lee Petty	1949–64	54
=	Rusty Wallace	1986–2001	54
10 =	Ned Jarrett	1953–66	50
=	Junior Johnson	1953–66	50

Source: NASCAR

The Winston Cup is a season-long series of races organized by NASCAR. These races, which take place over enclosed circuits such as the Daytona speedway, are among the most popular motor races in the US. Cale (William Caleb) Yarborough, who also won the Daytona 500 on four occasions, is the only driver to win three successive titles.

▼ Richard Petty, seven-time winner of the Winston Cup series, a record he holds with the late Dale Earnhardt.

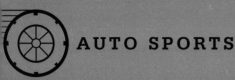

AUTO SPORTS

- CART career money winners of all time
- Drivers with the most wins in CART races 1909–2001
- Drivers with the most wins in CART races 1979–2001
- CART drivers in the 2001 season
- Drivers with the most poles in CART races 1979–2001
- Drivers with the most poles in CART races 1909–2001
- Last back-to-back winners of the CART series
- Longest circuits used for the 2002 Fedex CART Series

A. J. FOYT

A. J. Foyt is the only man in history to win the big four auto races: 12 Hours of Sebring, Indianapolis 500, Daytona 500, and Le Mans 24 Hours.

CART RECORDS

Top 10 CART career money winners of all time*

Driver#	Career earnings ($)
1 Al Unser, Jr.	18,828,406
2 Michael Andretti	17,409,368
3 Bobby Rahal	16,344,008
4 Emerson Fittipaldi, Brazil	14,293,625
5 Mario Andretti	11,552,154
6 Rick Mears	11,050,807
7 Jimmy Vasser	10,124,994
8 Danny Sullivan	8,884,126
9 Paul Tracy, Canada	8,331,520
10 Arie Luyendyk, Netherlands	7,732,188

* As of December 31, 2001
# All US unless otherwise stated
Source: Championship Auto Racing Teams

Michael Andretti is the only current driver on this list. He, like Unser, comes from a famous racing family—his father Mario was not only a successful CART driver but was, in 1978, only the second driver from the US to win the Formula One world title. Michael's 15-year-old son Marco, currently enjoying a Karting career, seems likely to follow in the footsteps of his famous father and grandfather.

Top 10 Drivers with most wins in CART races 1909–2001*

Driver	Career	Wins
1 A. J. Foyt	1960–81	67
2 Mario Andretti	1965–93	52
3 Michael Andretti	1986–2001	41
4 Al Unser	1965–87	39
5 Bobby Unser	1966–81	35
6 Al Unser, Jr.	1984–95	31
7 Rick Mears	1978–91	29
8 Johnny Rutherford	1965–86	27
9 Rodger Ward	1953–66	26
10 Gordon Johncock	1965–83	25

Source: Championship Auto Racing Teams

Two generations of the Unser family dominate the CART scene: Al and Bobby, both of whom figure in this list, are brothers, while Al's son, Al Jr., also makes a showing here and as all-time money winner. In 1998, after pursuing other auto sports, Bobby's son Robby also entered Indy car racing.

Michael Andretti, who started his CART career in 1983, is the only current driver in this list.

> Every car has a lot of speed in it. The trick is getting the speed out of it.
>
> A. J. Foyt, Jr.

Top 10 Drivers with the most wins in CART races 1979-2001

	Driver/country*	Wins
1	Michael Andretti#	41
2	Al Unser, Jr.	31
3	Rick Mears	26
4	Bobby Rahal	24
5	Emerson Fittipaldi, Brazil	22
6	Mario Andretti	19
7	Paul Tracy,# Canada	18
8	Danny Sullivan	17
9	Alex Zanardi, Italy	15
10 =	Juan Montoya, Colombia	10
=	Johnny Rutherford	10
=	Tom Sneva	10
=	Bobby Unser	10

* All US unless otherwise stated
# Active in the 2001 season

Top 10 CART drivers in the 2001 season*

	Driver/country	Points
1	Gil de Ferran, France	199
2	Kenny Brack, Sweden	163
3	Michael Andretti, US	147
4	Helio Castroneves, Brazil	141
5	Cristiano da Matta, Brazil	140
6	Max Papis, Italy	107
7	Dario Franchitti, UK	105
8	Scott Dixon, New Zealand	98
9	Tony Kanaan, Brazil	93
10	Patrick Carpentier, Canada	91

* Based on points gained in the 2001 FedEx Championship

Before moving into CART racing, Gil de Ferran started his competitive career in Karting in Brazil. From there he progressed through Formula Ford to Formula Three and Formula 3000 before joining the CART circuit in 1995.

Top 10 Drivers with the most poles in CART races 1979-2001

	Driver/country*	Poles
1	Rick Mears	39
2	Michael Andretti#	32
3	Mario Andretti	30
4	Danny Sullivan	19
5	Bobby Rahal	18
6	Emerson Fittipaldi, Brazil	17
7	Gil de Ferran,# France	16
8 =	Juan Montoya, Colombia	14
=	Bobby Unser	14
10	Paul Tracy,# Canada	13

* All US unless otherwise stated
# Active in the 2001 season

This list includes pole leaders since the launch of CART (Championship Auto Racing Teams) in 1979. Prior to that, it was the AAA (American Automobile Association) series from 1909–55, and the USAC (United States Auto Club) series 1956–78.

Top 10 Drivers with the most poles in CART races 1909-2001*

	Driver/country#	Poles
1	Mario Andretti	67
2	A. J. Foyt	53
3	Bobby Unser	49
4	Rick Mears	40
5	Michael Andretti†	32
6	Al Unser	27
7	Johnny Rutherford	23
8	Gordon Johncock	20
9 =	Rex Mays	19
=	Danny Sullivan	19

* Since the start of the AAA (American Automobile Association)
# All US
† Active in the 2001 season

Mario Andretti also took pole in his first Formula One race at Watkins Glen in October 1968. It was his first race at "The Glen."

The 10 Last back-to-back winners of the CART series

	Driver/country*	Years
1	Gil de Ferran, France	2000-01
2	Alex Zanardi, Italy	1997-98
3	Bobby Rahal	1986-87
4	Rick Mears	1981-82
5	Joe Leonard	1971-72
6	Mario Andretti	1965-66
7	A. J. Foyt	1960-61
8	Jimmy Bryan	1956-57
9	Ted Horn#	1947-48
10	Rex Mays	1940-41

* US unless otherwise stated
# Ted Horn won three consecutive titles 1946-48, the only man to achieve this feat

Launched in 1909 as the AAA (American Automobile Association) Championship, the event became officially known as the FedEx Championship in 1997. The first winner was George Robertson and the first man to win back-to-back championships was Tommy Milton in 1920-21. A. J. Foyt has won a record seven championships.

Top 10 Longest circuits used for the 2002 FedEx CART Series

	Circuit/location	Length (miles)
1	Road America, Elkhart Lake, Wisconsin	4.048
2	Circuit Gilles Villeneuve, Montreal, Canada	2.747
3	Autodromo Hermanos Rodriguez, Mexico City	2.480
4	Mid-Ohio Sports Car Course, Lexington, Ohio	2.258
5 =	Gold Coast, Southport, Queensland, Australia	2.238
=	Laguna Seca, Monterey, California	2.238
7	Burke Lakefront Airport, Cleveland, Ohio	2.106
8	Fundidora Park, Monterrey, Mexico	2.100
9	California Speedway, Fontana, California	2.029
10	Eurospeedway, Klettwitz, Germany	2.023

In addition to those in the list, there are four other races held outside the United States in the 2002 FedEx Series: the Rockingham Motor Speedway, Corby, England; Concorde Pacific Place, Vancouver, Canada; the Exhibition Place, Toronto, Canada; and the Twin Ring Motegi, Tochigi, Japan.

◄ The sight all racing drivers long to see— the checkered flag at the finish.

INDIANAPOLIS 500 RECORDS

- Fastest winning speeds in the Indianapolis 500

- Drivers with the most starts in the Indianapolis 500

- Drivers with the most Indianapolis 500 poles

- Drivers with the most wins in the Indianapolis 500

- Lowest starting positions by winners of the Indianapolis 500

- Indianapolis 500 winning engines

WITHOUT STOPPING

Only four cars have completed the Indy 500 without a pit stop. The respective drivers were: Dave Evans in the Cummins Diesel (1931, finished 13th), Cliff Bergere in the Noc Out Hose Clamp (1941, 5th), Jimmy Jackson in the Howard Kleck (1949, 6th), and Johnny Mantz in the Agajanian (1949, 7th).

Top 10 Fastest winning speeds in the Indianapolis 500

	Driver/country*	Car	Year	Speed (mph)	Speed (km/h)
1	Arie Luyendyk, Netherlands	Lola-Chevrolet	1990	185.981	299.307
2	Rick Mears	Chevrolet-Lumina	1991	176.457	283.980
3	Bobby Rahal	March-Cosworth	1986	170.722	274.750
4	Juan Montoya, Colombia	G Force-Aurora	2000	167.607	269.730
5	Emerson Fittipaldi, Brazil	Penske-Chevrolet	1989	167.581	269.695
6	Rick Mears	March-Cosworth	1984	163.612	263.308
7	Mark Donohue	McLaren-Offenhauser	1972	162.962	262.619
8	Al Unser	March-Cosworth	1987	162.175	260.995
9	Tom Sneva	March-Cosworth	1983	162.117	260.902
10	Gordon Johncock	Wildcat-Cosworth	1982	162.029	260.760

* All US unless otherwise stated

Source: Indianapolis Motor Speedway

The Indianapolis 500, known affectionately as the "Indy," was first held on Memorial Day, May 30, 1911, and was won by Ray Harroun, driving a bright yellow 447-cubic-inch six-cylinder Marmon Wasp at an average speed of 74.59 mph (120.04 km/h). The race takes place over 200 laps of the 2½-mile (4-km) Indianapolis Speedway, which, from 1927 to 1945, was owned by World War I flying ace Eddie Rickenbacker. Over the years, the speed has steadily increased: Harroun's race took 6 hours 42 minutes 6 seconds to complete, while Arie Luyendyk's record-breaking win was achieved in just 2 hours 18 minutes 18.248 seconds. Luyendyk also holds the track record of 237.498 mph (382.20 km/h), set in 1996.

Top 10 Drivers with the most starts in the Indianapolis 500

	Driver	Starts
1	A. J. Foyt	35
2	Mario Andretti	29
3	Al Unser	27
4 =	Gordon Johncock	24
=	Johnny Rutherford	24
6	George Snider	22
7	Gary Bettenhausen	21
8	Bobby Unser	19
9 =	Roger McCluskey	18
=	Lloyd Ruby	18
=	Tom Sneva	18

Source: Indianapolis Motor Speedway

A. J. Foyt's first Indy 500 was in 1958. He completed 148 laps before spinning out. He had 10 top five finishes and led in 13 races for 555 laps. His total career earnings from the Indy 500 was $2,640,576. A. J. Foyt also completed a record 12,272.5 miles in his 35-race Indianapolis 500 career.

Top 10 Drivers with the most Indianapolis 500 poles

	Driver/country*	Poles
1	Rick Mears	6
2 =	A. J. Foyt	4
=	Rex Mays	4
4 =	Mario Andretti	3
=	Arie Luyendyk, Netherlands	3
=	Johnny Rutherford	3
=	Tom Sneva	3
8 =	Scott Brayton	2
=	Bill Cummings	2
=	Ralph DePalma	2
=	Leon Duray	2
=	Parnelli Jones	2
=	Jimmy Murphy	2
=	Duke Nalon	2
=	Eddie Sachs	2
=	Bobby Unser	2

* All US unless otherwise stated

Source: Indianapolis Motor Speedway

> A gigantic, grimy lawn party, a monstrous holiday compounded of dust and danger and noise, the world's biggest carnival.
>
> **Red Smith,** sports writer, on the Indianapolis 500

Top 10 Drivers with the most wins in the Indianapolis 500

	Driver*	Years	Wins
1 =	A. J. Foyt	1961, 1964, 1967, 1977	4
=	Rick Mears	1979, 1984, 1988, 1991	4
=	Al Unser	1970-71, 1978, 1987	4
4 =	Louie Meyer	1928, 1933, 1936	3
=	Mauri Rose	1941, 1947-48	3
=	Johnny Rutherford	1974, 1976, 1980	3
=	Wilbur Shaw	1937, 1939-40	3
=	Bobby Unser	1968, 1975, 1981	3
9 =	Emerson Fittipaldi, Brazil	1989, 1993	2
=	Gordon Johncock	1973, 1982	2
=	Arie Luyendyk, Netherlands	1990, 1997	2
=	Tommy Milton	1921, 1923	2
=	Al Unser, Jr.	1992, 1994	2
=	Bill Vukovich	1953-54	2
=	Rodger Ward	1959, 1962	2

* All US unless otherwise stated

Source: Indianapolis Motor Speedway

Top 10 Lowest starting positions by winners of the Indianapolis 500*

	Driver	Year	Position
1 =	Ray Harroun	1911	28th
=	Louie Meyer	1936	28th
3	Fred Frame	1932	27th
4	Johnny Rutherford	1974	25th
5 =	Kelly Petillo	1935	22nd
=	George Souders	1927	22nd
7 =	Lora Corum/Joe Boyer#	1924	21st
8 =	Frank Lockhart	1926	20th
=	Tommy Milton	1921	20th
=	Al Unser	1987	20th

* Based on starting position on the grid

\# Joint drivers

Source: Indianapolis Motor Speedway

Top 10 Indianapolis 500 winning engines

	Engine	First/last win	Wins
1	Offenhauser	1935-76	27
2	Miller	1922-38	12
3	Cosworth	1978-87	10
4	Ford	1965-96	8
5	Chevy Indy	1988-93	6
6	Oldsmobile/Aurora	1997-2001	5
7 =	Duesenberg	1924-27	3
=	Peugeot	1913-19	3
9 =	Frontenac	1920-21	2
=	Maserati	1939-40	2
=	Mercedes	1915-94	2

Source: Indianapolis Motor Speedway

▶ Races can be won or lost on the speed of wheel changes. Anything over 10 seconds is slow these days – and that's for four wheels!

FORMULA ONE RECORDS

- Countries to host the most Grand Prix races
- Formula One drivers with the most World titles
- Formula One drivers with the most career wins
- Formula One drivers to compete in most Grand Prix races
- Constructors with the most titles

ENZO FERRARI

Enzo Ferrari, the man behind the greatest name in auto racing, was himself a racecar driver, finishing second in the 1920 Targa Florio, one of the sport's foremost road races. He was driving an Alfa Romeo.

Top 10 Countries to host the most Grand Prix races*

	Country/Grand Prix	First/last races	Total races
1	Italy (Italian GP 52; San Marino 21; Pescara GP 1)	1950–2001	74
2	United States (United States GP 27; Indianapolis 500 11; Detroit GP 7; United States GP (West) 8; Las Vegas GP 2; Indianapolis GP 2; Dallas GP 1)	1950–2001	58
3	Germany (German GP 49; European GP 6; Luxembourg GP 2)	1951–2001	57
4	Great Britain (British GP 52; European GP 3)	1950–2001	55
5	France (French GP 51; Swiss GP 1)	1950–2001	52
6 =	Belgium	1950–2001	48
=	Monaco	1950–2001	48
8 =	Canada	1967–2001	33
=	Spain (Spanish GP 31; European GP 2)	1951–2001	33
10	Netherlands	1952–85	30

* For Formula One World Championship races; as of March 1, 2002

Since the launch of the Formula One World Championship in 1950, one race each year has been designated the Grand Prix d'Europe (European Grand Prix). The first race to carry such a title—but no extra points—was the inaugural race at Silverstone, Northamptonshire, England on May 13, 1950. The first separate European Grand Prix was raced at Brands Hatch, Longfield, England, in 1983, and won by Nelson Piquet (Brazil) in a Brabham–BMW.

Top 10 Formula One drivers with the most World titles

	Driver/country	Years	Races won	World titles
1	Juan Manuel Fangio, Argentina	1951–57	24	5
2 =	Alain Prost, France	1985–93	51	4
=	Michael Schumacher, Germany	1994–2001	53	4
4 =	Jack Brabham, Australia	1959–60	14	3
=	Niki Lauda, Austria	1975–84	25	3
=	Nelson Piquet, Brazil	1981–87	23	3
=	Ayrton Senna, Brazil	1988–91	41	3
=	Jackie Stewart, UK	1969–71	27	3
9 =	Alberto Ascari, Italy	1952–53	13	2
=	Jim Clark, UK	1963–65	25	2
=	Emerson Fittipaldi, Brazil	1972–74	14	2
=	Mika Häkkinen, Finland	1998–99	20	2
=	Graham Hill, UK	1962–68	14	2

Argentinean-born Juan Manuel Fangio was runner-up in the first World Championship in 1950, but won by six points over Alberto Ascari (Italy) the following year. He was runner-up again in 1953, but then won four years in succession, 1954–57. In the last three of those years, the driver second to Fangio was UK's Stirling Moss, one of the best drivers never to win the world title. When fellow Briton Mike Hawthorn won the world title in 1958, Moss was "bridesmaid" yet again, just one point behind Hawthorn.

◀ Brazilian driver Ayrton Senna, one of the most talented drivers ever in Formula One.

Top 10 Formula One drivers with the most career wins

	Driver/country	Career	Wins*
1	Michael Schumacher, Germany	1991–	53
2	Alain Prost, France	1980–93	51
3	Ayrton Senna, Brazil	1984–94	41
4	Nigel Mansell, UK	1980–95	31
5	Jackie Stewart, UK	1965–73	27
6 =	Jim Clark, UK	1960–68	25
=	Niki Lauda, Austria	1971–85	25
8	Juan Manuel Fangio, Argentina	1950–58	24
9	Nelson Piquet, Brazil	1978–91	23
10	Damon Hill, UK	1992–99	22

* As of March 1, 2002

Michael Schumacher started his Formula One career with Jordan in 1991 but after one race moved to Benetton. He won his first Grand Prix, the 1992 Belgian Grand Prix, in his first full season.

Top 10 Formula One drivers to compete in most Grands Prix*

	Driver/country	Starts
1	Riccardo Patrese, Italy	256
2	Gerhard Berger, Austria	210
3	Andrea de Cesaris, Italy	208
4	Nelson Piquet, Brazil	204
5	Jean Alesi, France	201
6	Alain Prost, France	199
7	Michele Alboreto, Italy	194
8	Nigel Mansell, UK	187
9 =	Graham Hill, UK	176
=	Jacques Laffite, France	176

* As of March 1, 2002

Riccardo Patrese started his career with the Shadow team in 1977 and picked up one point for finishing sixth in the season's final race, the Japanese Grand Prix. His final season was in 1993, the year after his best finish in the drivers' championship, when he finished second to UK's Nigel Mansell.

Top 10 Constructors with the most titles

	Constructor	First/last title	Titles
1	Ferrari	1961–2001	11
2	Williams	1980–97	9
3	McLaren	1974–98	8
4	Lotus	1963–78	7
5 =	Brabham	1966–67	2
=	Cooper	1959–60	2
7 =	Benetton	1995	1
=	BRM	1962	1
=	Matra	1969	1
=	Tyrrell	1971	1
=	Vanwall	1958	1

While the World Championship for drivers was launched in 1950, the first championship for constructors was not initiated until 1958.

▼ The man who put Ferrari back on the Formula One map in the 1990s, Germany's Michael Schumacher.

AUTO SPORTS

ENDURANCE RACES & RALLYING

- Most wins in the 24 Hours of Daytona
- Most wins in the Le Mans 24 Hours
- Constructors in the World Rally Championships
- Car models in the World Rally Championships
- Drivers in the World Rally Championships

JACKY ICKX

Six-time Le Mans winner Jacky Ickx was also a talented Formula One driver, winning eight World Championship races in 116 drives between 1966 and 1979. He was twice runner-up in the world drivers' championship; to Jackie Stewart (UK) in 1969 and to the posthumous winner of the title, Jochen Rindt (Austria) in 1970.

Top 10 Most wins in the 24 Hours of Daytona

	Driver*	First/last win	Total
1	Hurley Haywood	1973–91	5
2 =	Peter Gregg	1973–78	4
=	Pedro Rodriguez	1963–71	4
=	Bob Wollek, France	1983–91	4
5 =	Derek Bell, UK	1986–89	3
=	Butch Leitzinger	1994–99	3
=	Rolf Stommelen, Germany	1978–82	3
8 =	Mauro Baldi, Italy	1998–2001	2
=	Elliott Forbes-Robinson	1987–89	2
=	A. J. Foyt	1983–85	2
=	Al Holbert	1986–87	2
=	Ken Miles	1965–66	2
=	Brian Redman, UK	1976–81	2
=	Lloyd Ruby	1965–66	2
=	Didier Theys, Belgium	1998–2001	2
=	Al Unser, Jr.	1986–87	2
=	Andy Wallace, UK	1997–99	2

* All US unless otherwise stated

First held as a three-hour race in 1962 and won by Dan Gurney in a Lotus Ford, this event has changed format over the years. Since 1973, it has been a 24-hour race. There was no race in 1974 as a result of a national energy crisis.

Top 10 Most wins in the Le Mans 24 Hours

	Driver/country	First/last win	Wins
1	Jacky Ickx, Belgium	1969–82	6
2	Derek Bell, UK	1975–87	5
3 =	Yannick Dalmas, France	1992–99	4
=	Olivier Gendebien, Belgium	1958–62	4
=	Henri Pescarolo, France	1972–84	4
6 =	Woolf Barnato, UK	1928–30	3
=	Luigi Chinetti, Italy/US	1932–49	3
=	Hurley Haywood, US	1977–94	3
=	Phil Hill, US	1958–62	3
=	Al Holbert, US	1983–87	3
=	Tom Kristensen, Norway	1997–2001	3
=	Klaus Ludwig, West Germany	1979–85	3

The first Le Mans endurance race was held on May 26–27, 1923 and won by André Lagache and René Leonard in a Chenard & Walcker at an average speed of 57.21 mph (92.07 km/h). The record-winning speed is 138.13 mph (222.30 km/h), set in 1971 by Gijs van Lennep (Netherlands) and Helmut Marko, (Austria) in a Porsche 917. The original Le Mans circuit measured 10.73 miles (17.26 kilometers).

Top 10 Constructors in the World Rally Championships*

	Constructor	Wins
1	Lancia	74
2	Toyota	43
3	Ford	40
4 =	Mitsubishi	34
=	Peugeot	34
=	Subaru	34
7	Audi	24
8	Fiat	21
9	Nissan/Datsun	9
10	Opel	6
=	Renault	6
=	Renault-Alpine	6

* As of March 1, 2002

The first Lancia driver to win the World Rally Championships was Juha Kankkunen in 1987. The first Lancia to win the manufacturers' title was in 1972.

Top 10 Car models in the World Rally Championships*

	Model	Wins
1	Subaru Impreza WRC	22
2	Audi Quattro	21
3	Fiat 131 Abarth	18
4 =	Ford Escort RS	17
=	Lancia Stratos	17
6	Toyota Celica Turbo 4wd	16
7	Peugeot 206 WRC	15
8	Lancia Delta Integrale	14
9 =	Lancia Delta Integrale 16V	13
=	Toyota Celica GT-Four	13

* As of March 1, 2002

Subaru's 34 championship wins have come with just three cars: the Impreza WRC, Impreza 555 (11 wins), and the Legacy RS (one win). They won the constructors' title in 1997 with the WRC, and in 1995 and 1996 with the 555.

Top 10 Drivers in the World Rally Championships*

	Driver/country	Wins
1	Tommi Mäkinen, Finland	24
2 =	Juha Kankkunen, Finland	23
=	Colin McRae, UK	23
=	Carlos Sainz, Spain	23
5	Didier Auriol, France	20
6	Markku Alen, Finland	19
7	Hannu Mikkola, Finland	18
8	Massimo Biasion, Italy	17
9	Bjorn Waldegaard, Sweden	16
10	Walter Röhrl, Germany	14

* As of January 1, 2002

Launched in 1977 under the aegis of the Féderation International de l'Automobile (FIA), the World Rally Championship begins each year in January with the Monte Carlo Rally, after which a further 13 rallies are held across the world. Kankkunen (1986–87, 1991, 1993) and Mäkinen (1996–99) have each won the World Rally Driver's Championship a record four times.

◄ Spain's leading rally driver, Carlos Sainz, in his Lancia during the 1993 Monte Carlo Rally.

ON TWO WHEELS

- Fastest-ever Daytona 200 races
- Most World Motorcycling titles
- Most Isle of Man TT wins
- Most consecutive World Motorcycling titles
- Most World Trials Championship titles

Top 10 Fastest-ever Daytona 200 races

	Rider*	Bike	Year	Average speed (km/h)	Average speed (mph)
1	Matt Mladin, Australia	Suzuki	2000	182.87	113.63
2	Miguel Duhamel, Canada	Honda	1999	182.61	113.47
3	Kenny Roberts	Yamaha	1984	182.08	113.14
4	Scott Russell	Yamaha	1998	179.89	111.78
5	Kenny Roberts	Yamaha	1983	178.52	110.93
6	Scott Russell	Kawasaki	1992	178.11	110.67
7	Graeme Crosby, New Zealand	Yamaha	1982	175.58	109.10
8	Steve Baker	Yamaha	1977	175.18	108.85
9	Miguel Duhamel, Canada	Honda	1996	175.13	108.82
10	Johnny Cecotto, Venezuela	Yamaha	1976	175.05	108.77

* All US unless otherwise stated

The Daytona 200, which was first held in 1937, forms a round in the AMA (American Motorcyclist Association) Grand National Dirt Track series. It is raced over 57 laps of the 3.56-mile (5.73-km) Daytona International Speedway. In addition to those riders named here, the only other non-United States winners have been: Billy Matthews (Canada) 1941, 1950; Jaarno Saarinen (Finland) 1973; Giacomo Agostini (Italy) 1974; and Patrick Pons (France) 1980.

In 500, you have more advantage with a new tire than with a new bike.

Valentino Rossi, Italy's former 125cc and 250cc champion, who became 500cc champion in 2001, winning 11 of 16 races

▼ Italy's Giacomo Agostini in action during the British Grand Prix (500cc), which he won five years in succession, 1968–72.

DID YOU KNOW? The United Kingdom's 500cc world champion Barry Sheen also won World Championship races at 125cc and 50cc.

Top 10 Most World Motorcycling titles*

	Rider/country	Title	500cc	350cc	250cc	125cc	50/80cc	Total
1	Giacomo Agostini, Italy	1966–75	8	7	0	0	0	15
2	Angel Nieto, Spain	1969–84	0	0	0	7	6	13
3 =	Mike Hailwood, UK	1961–67	4	2	3	0	0	9
=	Carlo Ubbiali, Italy	1951–60	0	0	3	6	0	9
5 =	Phil Read, UK	1964–74	2	0	4	1	0	7
=	John Surtees, UK	1956–60	4	3	0	0	0	7
7 =	Geoff Duke, UK	1951–55	4	2	0	0	0	6
=	Jim Redman, Southern Rhodesia	1962–65	0	4	2	0	0	6
9 =	Michael Doohan, Australia	1994–98	5	0	0	0	0	5
=	Anton Mang, West Germany	1980–87	0	2	3	0	0	5

* Solo classes only

The first World Road Race Championship season was in 1949, and the British Grand Prix on the Isle of Man was the very first race. Harold Daniell (UK) won the 500cc race, Freddie Frith (UK) the 350cc, and Manliff Barrington (Ireland) the 250cc. After six rounds, the inaugural world champions were: 500cc: Leslie Graham (UK) on an AJS; 350cc: Freddie Frith (UK) on a Velocette; 250cc: Bruno Ruffo (Italy) on a Guzzi; 125cc: Nello Pagani (Italy) on a Mondial; Sidecar: Eric Oliver (UK) on a Norton. AJS won the inaugural manufacturers' title.

Top 10 Most Isle of Man TT wins

	Rider/country*	First/last wins	Wins
1	Joey Dunlop	1977–2000	26
2	Mike Hailwood	1961–79	14
3 =	Steve Hislop	1987–94	11
=	Phillip McCallen	1992–97	11
5 =	Giacomo Agostini, Italy	1966–75	10
=	Stanley Woods	1923–39	10
7 =	Mick Boddice#	1983–89	9
=	Dave Saville#	1985–90	9
=	Siegfried Schauzu,# West Germany	1967–75	9
10 =	Rob Fisher#	1994–2000	8
=	Charles Mortimer	1970–78	8
=	Phil Read	1961–77	8

* All UK unless otherwise stated

\# Wins in sidecar class

Top 10 Most consecutive World Motorcycling titles*

	Rider/country	Class	Years	Consecutive wins
1	Giacomo Agostini, Italy	500cc	1966–72	7
=	Giacomo Agostini, Italy	350cc	1968–74	7
3	Michael Doohan, Australia	500cc	1994–98	5
4 =	Max Biaggi, Italy	250cc	1994–97	4
=	Stefan Dorflinger, Switzerland	50/80cc	1982–85	4
=	Mike Hailwood, UK	500cc	1962–65	4
=	Angel Nieto, Spain	125cc	1981–84	4
=	Jim Redman, Southern Rhodesia	350cc	1962–65	4
9 =	Hans Georg Anscheidt, West Germany	50cc	1966–68	3
=	Jorge Martínez Aspar, Spain	80cc	1986–88	3
=	Angel Nieto, Spain	50cc	1975–77	3
=	Walter Villa, Italy	50cc	1974–76	3
=	Carlo Ubbiali, Italy	125cc	1958–60	3

* Solo classes only

Giacomo Agostini's reign as World 500cc champion was ended by Phil Read (UK) in 1973. Agostini finished third that year and was fourth in 1974, when Read won again. However, Agostini claimed his eighth 500cc title in 1975 when he beat Read into second place by just eight points.

Top 10 Most World Trials Championship titles

	Rider/country	First/last title	Wins
1	Jordi Tarrés, Spain	1987–95	7
2	Doug Lampkin, UK	1997–2001	5
3 =	Eddy Lejeune, Belgium	1982–84	3
=	Thierry Michaud, France	1985–88	3
=	Yrjo Vesterinen, Finland	1976–78	3
6 =	Tommi Ahvala, Finland	1992	1
=	Gilles Burgat, France	1981	1
=	Marc Colomer, Spain	1996	1
=	Ulf Karlson, Sweden	1980	1
=	Martin Lampkin, UK	1975	1
=	Bernie Schreiber, US	1979	1

The World Trials Championship evolved from the famous Scottish Six-Day Trial, which was launched in 1909. An International Six-Day Trial was first held in 1913, but it was not until 1973 that the World Championship was launched.

OLYMPICS

At the Start

The Olympic Games, which were part of a religious festival held every four years, may have been staged even earlier, but the first on record took place in 776 BC. Originally, running was the only event, but in successive Games, jumping, discus and javelin throwing, wrestling, boxing, and chariot-racing were added, for a total of 23 events. In AD 393, the Games were banned as a pagan ritual by order of the Christian emperor Theodosius I. Various revivals were mooted, and an Olympic festival was first held in Much Wenlock, England, in 1849. This event encouraged French sports enthusiast Baron Pierre de Coubertin to launch the modern Olympic movement, which led, in 1896, to the revival of the Games.

THE OLYMPIC CHAMPIONS

- Men with most the Olympic medals
- Women with the most Olympic medals
- All-time medal-winning countries
- Individual gold medal winners at the Summer Olympics
- First athletes to win medals at five or more Summer Olympics

> I've had an incredible career, and it's time to stop. To be able to end your career with an Olympic gold medal... is a dream. I feel like I've been blessed.
>
> **Carl Lewis,** after winning his 9th Olympic gold medal, 1992

Top 10 Men with the most Olympic medals*

	Athlete/country	Sport	Years	G	S	B	Total
1	Nikolai Andrianov, USSR	Gymnastics	1972–80	7	5	3	15
2 =	Edoardo Mangiarotti, Italy	Fencing	1936–60	6	5	2	13
=	Takashi Ono, Japan	Gymnastics	1952–64	5	4	4	13
=	Boris Shakhlin, USSR	Gymnastics	1956–64	7	4	2	13
5 =	Sawao Kato, Japan	Gymnastics	1968–76	8	3	1	12
=	Alexei Nemov, Russia	Gymnastics	1996–2000	4	2	6	12
=	Paavo Nurmi, Finland	Athletics	1920–28	9	3	0	12
8 =	Matt Biondi, US	Swimming	1984–92	8	2	1	11
=	Viktor Chukarin, USSR	Gymnastics	1952–56	7	3	1	11
=	Carl Osburn, US	Shooting	1912–24	5	4	2	11
=	Mark Spitz, US	Swimming	1968–72	9	1	1	11

* At the Summer Olympics 1896–2000

G – gold medals, S – silver medals, B – bronze medals

Top 10 Women with the most Olympic medals*

	Athlete/country	Sport	Years	G	S	B	Total
1	Larissa Latynina, USSR	Gymnastics	1956–64	9	5	4	18
2	Vera Cáslavská, Czechoslovakia	Gymnastics	1960–68	7	4	0	11
3 =	Polina Astakhova, USSR	Gymnastics	1956–64	5	2	3	10
=	Birgit Fischer-Schmidt, East Germany	Canoeing	1980–2000	7	3	0	10
=	Agnes Keleti, Hungary	Gymnastics	1952–56	5	3	2	10
=	Jenny Thompson, US	Swimming	1992–2000	8	1	1	10
7 =	Nadia Comaneci, Romania	Gymnastics	1976–80	5	3	1	9
=	Dara Torres, US	Swimming	1984–2000	4	1	4	9
=	Lyudmila Turishcheva, USSR	Gymnastics	1968–76	4	3	2	9
10 =	Shirley Babashoff, US	Swimming	1972–76	2	6	0	8
=	Kornelia Ender, East Germany	Swimming	1972–76	4	4	0	8
=	Dawn Fraser, Australia	Swimming	1956–64	4	4	0	8
=	Sofia Muratova, USSR	Gymnastics	1956–60	2	2	4	8

* At the Summer Olympics 1896–2000

G – gold medals, S – silver medals, B – bronze medals

▶ Larissa Latynina of Russia in action during the women's compulsory exercises in the gymnastics event at the 1964 Olympic Games in Tokyo.

◄ The official logo of the 2000 Sydney Olympics. Logos have been used since the 1932 Los Angeles Games.

Top 10 All-time medal-winning countries

	Country	Gold	Silver	Bronze	Total
1	US	872	658	586	2,116
2	Russia*	498	409	371	1,278
3	Germany#	214	242	280	736
4	UK	180	233	225	638
5	France	188	193	217	598
6	Italy	179	143	157	479
7	Sweden	136	156	177	469
8	East Germany	159	150	136	445
9	Hungary	150	135	158	443
10	Australia	102	110	138	350

* Including USSR (1952–88) and Unified Team (1992)

\# Including West Germany (1968–88)

Top 10 Individual gold medal winners at the Summer Olympics

	Athlete/country	Sport	Years	Gold medals
1	Ray Ewry, US	Athletics	1900–08	10
2 =	Larissa Latynina, USSR	Gymnastics	1956–64	9
=	Carl Lewis, US	Athletics	1984–96	9
=	Paavo Nurmi, Finland	Athletics	1920–28	9
=	Mark Spitz, US	Swimming	1968–72	9
6 =	Matt Biondi, US	Swimming	1984–92	8
=	Sawao Kato, Japan	Gymnastics	1968–76	8
=	Jenny Thompson, US	Swimming	1992–2000	8
9 =	Nikolai Andrianov, USSR	Gymnastics	1972–80	7
=	Vera Cáslavská, Czechoslovakia	Gymnastics	1964–68	7
=	Viktor Chukarin, USSR	Gymnastics	1952–56	7
=	Birgit Fischer-Schmidt, East Germany	Canoeing	1980–2000	7
=	Aladár Gerevich, Hungary	Fencing	1932–60	7
=	Boris Shakhlin, USSR	Gymnastics	1956–64	7

All Ewry's golds were in the standing jumps—long jump, high jump, and triple jump—that once formed part of the track and field competition. Born in 1873, Ewry contracted polio as a boy and seemed destined to be confined to a wheelchair for life, but through a determined effort to overcome his handicap, he exercised and developed his legs to such a remarkable degree that he went on to become an outstanding athlete. Spitz's seven gold medals in 1972 is a record number for medals won at one celebration.

Top 10 First athletes to win medals at five or more Summer Olympics

	Athlete/country	Sport	Years
1	Heikki Ilmari Savolainen, Finland	Gymnastics	1928–52
2	Aladár Gerevich,* Hungary	Fencing	1932–56
3	Edoardo Mangiarotti, Italy	Fencing	1936–60
4	Gustav Fischer, Switzerland	Dressage	1952–68
5	Hans Günther Winkler,# West Germany	Show jumping	1956–72
6	Ildikó Ságiné-Rejtö (née Uljaki-Rejtö), Hungary	Fencing	1960–76
7	John Michael Plumb, US	Three-day event	1964–84
8	Reiner Klimke, West Germany	Dressage	1964–88
9 =	Teresa Edwards, US	Basketball	1984–2000
=	Birgit Fischer-Schmidt, East Germany	Canoeing	1980–2000
=	Stephen Redgrave, UK	Rowing	1984–2000

* Also won medal at the 1960 Games

\# Also won medal at the 1976 Games

MEDAL-WINNING COUNTRIES 1896–1928

- Countries at the 1896 Olympic Games
- Countries at the 1900 Olympic Games
- Countries at the 1904 Olympic Games
- Countries at the 1906 Olympic Games
- Countries at the 1908 Olympic Games
- Countries at the 1912 Olympic Games
- Countries at the 1920 Olympic Games
- Countries at the 1924 Olympic Games
- Countries at the 1928 Olympic Games

IN TWO COUNTRIES

The 12-foot dinghy sailing event at the 1920 Olympics is the only event in Olympic history to have been staged in two countries. The first race was in Belgium but, because the only two competitors were Dutch, the last two races took place in the Netherlands.

Top 10 Countries at the 1896 Olympic Games

	Country	G	S	B	Total
1	Greece*	10	19	18	47
2	US	11	6	2	19
3	Germany	7	5	3	15
4	France	5	4	2	11
5 =	Denmark	1	2	4	7
=	UK	3	3	1	7
7	Hungary	2	1	3	6
8	Austria	2	0	3	5
9	Switzerland	1	2	0	3
10	Australia	2	0	0	2

* Host country

G – gold medals, S – silver medals, B – bronze medals

The first modern Olympic champion was James Connolly (US) in the hop, step, and jump (now the triple jump) on April 6,1896. Connolly was the first Olympic champion since the ancient Games of AD 369.

Top 10 Countries at the 1900 Olympic Games

	Country	G	S	B	Total
1	France*	26	37	32	95
2	US	18	14	15	47
3	UK	16	6	8	30
4	Belgium	6	5	5	16
5	Switzerland	6	1	1	8
6	Germany	3	2	2	7
7 =	Australia	2	0	4	6
=	Austria	0	3	3	6
=	Denmark	1	3	2	6
=	Hungary	1	3	2	6
=	Netherlands	1	2	3	6

* Host country

G – gold medals, S – silver medals, B – bronze medals

Women competed for the first time in 1900, and the first women's Olympic champion was Charlotte Cooper (UK) in the singles lawn tennis event.

Top 10 Countries at the 1904 Olympic Games

	Country	G	S	B	Total
1	US*	79	84	82	245
2	Germany	4	4	4	12
3	Canada	4	1	1	6
4 =	Cuba	4	0	0	4
=	Hungary	2	1	1	4
6	Austria	1	1	1	3
7 =	Greece	1	0	1	2
=	Switzerland	1	0	1	2
=	UK	0	1	1	2
10	Ireland	1	0	0	1

* Host country

G – gold medals, S – silver medals, B – bronze medals

One of the most remarkable competitors at the 1904 St. Louis Olympics was the American gymnast George Eyser. He won six medals despite having a wooden leg.

Top 10 Countries at the 1906 Olympic Games

	Country	G	S	B	Total
1	France	15	9	16	40
2	Greece*	8	13	12	33
3 =	UK	8	11	5	24
=	US	12	6	6	24
5	Italy	7	6	3	16
6 =	Germany	4	6	5	15
=	Switzerland	5	6	4	15
8	Sweden	2	5	7	14
9	Hungary	2	5	3	10
10	Austria	3	3	2	8

* Host country

G – gold medals, S – silver medals, B – bronze medals

The 1906 Olympics were Intercalated Games in Greece to celebrate the 10th anniversary of the founding of the modern Olympics.

> The important thing in the Olympic Games is not to win but to take part, just as the most important thing in life is not the triumph but the struggle.
>
> **Pierre de Coubertin**, the founder of the modern Olympics at the 1908 Games

Top 10 Countries at the 1908 Olympic Games

	Country	G	S	B	Total
1	UK*	54	46	38	138
2	US	23	12	12	47
3	Sweden	8	6	11	25
4	France	5	5	9	19
5	Canada	3	3	10	16
6	Germany	3	5	5	13
7	Hungary	3	4	2	9
8 =	Belgium	1	5	2	8
=	Norway	2	3	3	8
10 =	Australia	1	2	2	5
=	Denmark	0	2	3	5
=	Finland	1	1	3	5

* Host country

G – gold medals, S – silver medals, B – bronze medals

Top 10 Countries at the 1912 Olympic Games

	Country	G	S	B	Total
1	Sweden*	23	24	17	64
2	US	25	18	20	63
3	UK	10	15	16	41
4	Finland	9	8	9	26
5	Germany	5	13	7	25
6	France	7	4	3	14
7	Denmark	1	6	5	12
8	Norway	3	2	5	10
9 =	Canada	3	2	3	8
=	Hungary	3	2	3	8

* Host country

G – gold medals, S – silver medals, B – bronze medals

The cycling road race in the 1912 Stockholm Olympics was 199 miles (320 km) in length and is the longest race of any kind in Olympic history.

Top 10 Countries at the 1920 Olympic Games

	Country	G	S	B	Total
1	US	41	27	27	95
2	Sweden	19	20	25	64
3	UK	14	15	13	42
4	France	9	19	13	41
5	Belgium*	13	11	11	35
6	Finland	15	10	9	34
7	Norway	13	9	9	31
8	Italy	13	5	5	23
9	Denmark	3	9	1	13
10 =	Netherlands	4	2	5	11
=	Switzerland	2	2	7	11

* Host country

G – gold medals, S – silver medals, B – bronze medals

Victor Boin became the first man to swear the athletes' Olympic Oath when it was introduced in 1920.

Top 10 Countries at the 1924 Olympic Games

	Country	G	S	B	Total
1	US	45	27	27	99
2	France*	13	15	10	38
3	Finland	14	13	10	37
4	UK	9	13	12	34
5	Sweden	4	13	12	29
6	Switzerland	7	8	10	25
7	Italy	8	3	5	16
8	Belgium	3	7	3	13
9 =	Czechoslovakia	1	4	5	10
=	Netherlands	4	1	5	10
=	Norway	5	2	3	10

* Host country

G – gold medals, S – silver medals, B – bronze medals

The Olympic motto of "Citius, Altius, Fortius" (Swifter, Higher, Stronger) was introduced in 1924, as was the closing ceremony ritual of raising the flag of the IOC host country alongside that of the next host country.

Top 10 Countries at the 1928 Olympic Games

	Country	G	S	B	Total
1	US	22	18	16	56
2	Germany	10	7	14	31
3 =	Finland	8	8	9	25
=	Sweden	7	6	12	25
5	France	6	10	5	21
6	UK	3	10	7	20
7 =	Italy	7	5	7	19
=	Netherlands*	6	9	4	19
9 =	Canada	4	4	7	15
=	Switzerland	7	4	4	15

* Host country

G – gold medals, S – silver medals, B – bronze medals

The now-standard practice of Greece leading the parade of athletes at the opening ceremony with the host country bringing up the rear was first adopted at the 1928 Games.

▲ The official poster from the 1904 Olympic Games, held in St. Louis, Missouri.

OLYMPICS

MEDAL-WINNING COUNTRIES 1932–1968

● Countries at the 1932 Olympic Games

● Countries at the 1936 Olympic Games

● Countries at the 1948 Olympic Games

● Countries at the 1952 Olympic Games

● Countries at the 1956 Olympic Games

● Countries at the 1960 Olympic Games

● Countries at the 1964 Olympic Games

● Countries at the 1968 Olympic Games

THE OLYMPIC TORCH

The Olympic torch relay was introduced for the 1936 Olympic Games. It was the idea of Dr. Carl Diem. The first relay saw the torch make its 1,864-mile (3,000-km) journey from Olympia through seven countries, Greece, Bulgaria, Yugoslavia, Hungary, Czechoslovakia, Austria, and Germany.

Top 10 Countries at the 1932 Olympic Games

	Country	G	S	B	Total
1	US*	41	32	30	103
2	Italy	12	12	12	36
3	Finland	5	8	12	25
4	Sweden	9	5	9	23
5	Germany	3	12	5	20
6	France	10	5	4	19
7	Japan	7	7	4	18
8	UK	4	7	5	16
9 =	Canada	2	5	8	15
=	Hungary	6	4	5	15

* Host country

G – gold medals, S – silver medals, B – bronze medals

The 1932 Olympics lasted just 16 days. Previously no Summer Games had lasted less than 79 days. Since 1932 all subsequent Games have lasted between 15 and 18 days.

Top 10 Countries at the 1936 Olympic Games

	Country	G	S	B	Total
1	Germany*	33	26	30	89
2	US	24	20	12	56
3	Italy	8	9	5	22
4	Sweden	6	5	9	20
5 =	Finland	7	6	6	19
=	France	7	6	6	19
7	Japan	6	4	8	18
8	Netherlands	6	4	7	17
9	Hungary	10	1	5	16
10	Switzerland	1	9	5	15

* Host country

G – gold medals, S – silver medals, B – bronze medals

As a result of the UK's dropping out of the Top 10 (in 11th place with 14 medals), the United States is the only country to have appeared in the Top 10 every year since the launch of the Games in 1896.

Top 10 Countries at the 1948 Olympic Games

	Country	G	S	B	Total
1	US	38	27	19	84
2	Sweden	16	11	17	44
3 =	France	10	6	13	29
=	Italy	8	12	9	29
5	Hungary	10	5	12	27
6	UK*	3	14	6	23
7 =	Denmark	5	7	8	20
=	Finland	8	7	5	20
=	Switzerland	5	10	5	20
10	Netherlands	5	2	9	16

* Host country

G – gold medals, S – silver medals, B – bronze medals

US athlete Bob Mathias won the decathlon in 1948 at the age of 17, just four months after taking up the event. He is the youngest male athlete to win a track and field event in Olympic history.

Top 10 Countries at the 1952 Olympic Games

	Country	G	S	B	Total
1	US	40	19	17	76
2	Soviet Union	22	30	18	70
3	Hungary	16	10	16	42
4	Sweden	12	13	10	35
5	Germany	0	7	17	24
6	Finland*	6	3	13	22
7	Italy	8	9	4	21
8	France	6	6	6	18
9	Switzerland	2	6	6	14
10	Czechoslovakia	7	3	3	13

* Host country

G – gold medals, S – silver medals, B – bronze medals

Germany's 5th position is the highest-ever position by a country not winning a gold medal, and is the biggest medal haul without a gold among the total.

◀ Germany's Konrad Frey, winner of the parallel bars and pommel horse events at the 1936 Berlin Olympic Games.

Top 10 Countries at the 1956 Olympic Games

	Country	G	S	B	Total
1	USSR	37	29	32	98
2	US	32	25	17	74
3	Australia*	13	8	14	35
4	Hungary	9	10	7	26
5	Italy	8	8	9	25
6	UK	6	7	11	24
7	West Germany	5	9	6	20
8 =	Japan	4	10	5	19
=	Sweden	8	5	6	19
10	Finland	3	1	11	15

* Host country

G – gold medals, S – silver medals, B – bronze medals

Due to quarantine restrictions in Australia, the equestrian events in 1956 were held in Sweden five months before the opening of the Games in Melbourne—the first Games to be held in the Southern Hemisphere.

Top 10 Countries at the 1960 Olympic Games

	Country	G	S	B	Total
1	USSR	43	29	31	103
2	US	34	21	16	71
3	Italy*	13	10	13	36
4	West Germany	10	10	6	26
5	Australia	8	8	6	22
6 =	Hungary	6	8	7	21
=	Poland	4	6	11	21
8	UK	2	6	12	20
9	East Germany	3	9	7	19
10	Japan	4	7	7	18

* Host country

G – gold medals, S – silver medals, B – bronze medals

Top 10 Countries at the 1964 Olympic Games

	Country	G	S	B	Total
1	US	36	26	28	90
2	USSR	30	31	25	86
3	West Germany	7	14	14	35
4	Japan*	16	5	8	29
5	Italy	10	10	7	27
6	Poland	7	6	10	23
7	Hungary	10	7	5	22
8	East Germany	3	11	5	19
9 =	Australia	6	2	10	18
=	UK	4	12	2	18

* Host country

G – gold medals, S – silver medals, B – bronze medals

Top 10 Countries at the 1968 Olympic Games

	Country	G	S	B	Total
1	US	45	28	34	107
2	USSR	29	32	30	91
3	Hungary	10	10	12	32
4 =	East Germany	9	9	7	25
=	Japan	11	7	7	25
=	West Germany	5	10	10	25
7	Poland	5	2	11	18
8	Australia	5	7	5	17
9	Italy	3	4	9	16
10 =	France	7	3	5	15
=	Romania	4	6	5	15

G – gold medals, S – silver medals, B – bronze medals

Mexico, the host country, finished in joint 13th place with nine medals (three gold, three silver, three bronze). They were the first hosts not to finish in the Top 10.

▶ Jesse Owens starting off in the 200 meters at the 1936 Berlin Games. It was to be one of four events Owens won at those Olympics.

MEDAL-WINNING COUNTRIES 1972–2000

- Countries at the 1972 Olympic Games
- Countries at the 1976 Olympic Games
- Countries at the 1980 Olympic Games
- Countries at the 1984 Olympic Games
- Countries at the 1988 Olympic Games
- Countries at the 1992 Olympic Games
- Countries at the 1996 Olympic Games
- Countries at the 2000 Olympic Games

> I'm looking forward to gloating over the performances of the US athletes.
>
> **Larry Ellis**, US men's coach, before the 1984 Los Angeles Olympics

Top 10 Countries at the 1972 Olympic Games

	Country	G	S	B	Total
1	USSR	50	27	22	99
2	US	33	31	30	94
3	East Germany	20	23	23	66
4	West Germany*	13	11	16	40
5	Hungary	6	13	16	35
6	Japan	13	8	8	29
7 =	Bulgaria	6	10	5	21
=	Poland	7	5	9	21
9 =	Italy	5	3	10	18
=	UK	4	5	9	18

* Host country

G – gold medals, S – silver medals, B – bronze medals

The 1972 Olympics were marred by events on September 5, when eight Palestinian terrorists broke into the Olympic village and killed two members of the Israeli team. The also took nine members of the team hostage, and, in a bloody battle, they too were all killed, along with five of the terrorists and one policeman. It was the blackest day in Olympic history.

Top 10 Countries at the 1976 Olympic Games

	Country	G	S	B	Total
1	USSR	49	41	35	125
2	US	34	35	25	94
3	East Germany	40	25	25	90
4	West Germany	10	12	17	39
5	Romania	4	9	14	27
6	Poland	7	6	13	26
7	Japan	9	6	10	25
8 =	Bulgaria	6	9	7	22
=	Hungary	4	5	13	22
10 =	Cuba	6	4	3	13
=	Italy	2	7	4	13
=	UK	3	5	5	13

* Host country

G – gold medals, S – silver medals, B – bronze medals

Canada finished in 13th place with 11 medals (five silver, six bronze). They are the only host country not to win a gold medal. Following a tour by the New Zealand All Blacks rugby team to South Africa in 1976, 32 countries boycotted the Olympics because the IOC would not bar New Zealand from the Games.

Top 10 Countries at the 1980 Olympic Games

	Country	G	S	B	Total
1	USSR*	80	69	46	195
2	East Germany	47	37	42	126
3	Bulgaria	8	16	17	41
4 =	Hungary	7	10	15	32
=	Poland	3	14	15	32
6	Romania	6	6	13	25
7	UK	5	7	9	21
8	Cuba	8	7	5	20
9	Italy	8	3	4	15
10 =	Czechoslovakia	2	3	9	14
=	France	6	5	3	14

* Host country

G – gold medals, S – silver medals, B – bronze medals

The United States and 63 other countries boycotted the 1980 Olympic Games because of the USSR's invasion of Afghanistan on December 27, 1979.

Top 10 Countries at the 1984 Olympic Games

	Country	G	S	B	Total
1	US*	83	61	30	174
2	West Germany	17	19	23	59
3	Romania	20	16	17	53
4	Canada	10	18	16	44
5	UK	5	11	21	37
6 =	China	15	8	9	32
=	Italy	14	6	12	32
=	Japan	10	8	14	32
9	France	5	7	16	28
10	Australia	4	8	12	24

* Host country

G – gold medals, S – silver medals, B – bronze medals

The Soviet Union and 13 other Eastern Bloc countries did not attend the Games, choosing to boycott them in retaliation for the United States' boycott of the 1980 Games.

◀ American shot-putter Randy Barnes in action during the 1988 Seoul Olympics, where he won silver. He won the gold medal at Atlanta in 1996.

Top 10 Countries at the 1988 Olympic Games

	Country	G	S	B	Total
1	USSR	55	31	46	132
2	East Germany	37	35	30	102
3	US	36	31	27	94
4	West Germany	11	14	15	40
5	Bulgaria	10	12	13	35
6	South Korea*	12	10	11	33
7	China	5	11	12	28
8 =	UK	5	10	9	24
=	Romania	7	11	6	24
10	Hungary	11	6	6	23

* Host country

G – gold medals, S – silver medals, B – bronze medals

Top 10 Countries at the 1992 Olympic Games

	Country	G	S	B	Total
1	Unified Team	45	38	29	112
2	US	37	34	37	108
3	Germany	33	21	28	82
4	China	16	22	16	54
5	Cuba	14	6	11	31
6	Hungary	11	12	7	30
7 =	France	8	5	16	29
=	South Korea	12	5	12	29
9	Australia	7	9	11	27
10 =	Japan	3	8	11	22
=	Spain*	13	7	2	22

* Host country

G – gold medals, S – silver medals, B – bronze medals

Top 10 Countries at the 1996 Olympic Games

	Country	G	S	B	Total
1	Unified Team	45	38	29	112
2	US*	44	32	25	101
3	Germany	20	18	27	65
4	Russia	26	21	16	63
5	China	16	22	12	50
6	Australia	9	9	23	41
7	France	15	7	15	37
8	Italy	13	10	12	35
9	South Korea	7	15	5	27
10	Cuba	9	8	8	25

* Host country

G – gold medals, S – silver medals, B – bronze medals

Top 10 Countries at the 2000 Olympic Games

	Country	G	S	B	Total
1	US	39	25	33	97
2	Russia	32	28	28	88
3	China	28	16	15	59
4	Australia*	16	25	17	58
5	Germany	14	17	26	57
6	France	13	14	11	38
7	Italy	13	8	13	34
8	Cuba	11	11	7	29
9 =	UK	11	10	7	28
=	Korea	8	9	11	28

* Host country

G – gold medals, S – silver medals, B – bronze medals

The Sydney Olympics were the biggest to date, with 10,651 athletes (6,582 men and 4,069 women) competing in 300 events. The Games were opened by Sir William Deane, Governor General of Australia, and the Olympic flame was lit by Australian track star Cathy Freeman.

▶ China's Linghui Kong in action in the Table Tennis Men's Singles Final on his way to a gold medal at the 2000 Sydney Olympics.

THE WINTER GAMES

- Most medals won by men at the Winter Olympics
- Most medals won by women at the Winter Olympics
- Medal-winning countries at the Winter Olympics
- Sports at which the US has won the most Winter Olympic medals

EARLY EVENTS

The Winter Olympics did not start until 1924, but figure skating was included in the Summer program in 1908 and 1920, while hockey was part of the 1920 Antwerp Olympics.

Top 10 Most medals won by men at the Winter Olympics

	Athlete/country	Event	G	S	B	Total
1	Bjorn Dählie, Norway	Cross-country	8	4	0	12
2	Sixten Jernberg, Sweden	Cross-country	4	3	2	9
3 =	Kjetil André Aamodt, Norway	Alpine skiing	3	2	2	7
=	Peter Angerer, Germany/West Germany	Biathlon	3	2	2	7
=	Ivar Ballangrud, Norway	Speed skating	4	2	1	7
=	Rico Gross, Germany	Biathlon	3	3	1	7
=	Veikko Hakulinen, Finland	Cross-country	3	3	1	7
=	Eero Mäntyranta, Finland	Cross-country	3	2	2	7
=	Bogdan Musiol, Germany/East Germany	Bobsled	1	5	1	7
=	Clas Thunberg, Finland	Speed skating	5	1	1	7

G – gold medals, S – silver medals, B – bronze medals

Norway's Bjorn Dählie won his 12 Olympic medals in the three Games between 1992 and 1998. He was just 30 when he won his last medal, but injury forced him to retire at the age of 33 in March 2001. He was nicknamed the "Nannestad Express" after his home town.

Top 10 Most medals won by women at the Winter Olympics

	Athlete/country	Event	G	S	B	Total
1	Raisa Smetanina, USSR/Unified Team	Cross-country	4	5	1	10
2 =	Stefania Belmondo, Italy	Cross-country	2	3	4	9
=	Lyubov Egorova, Unified Team/Russia	Cross-country	6	3	0	9
=	Larissa Lazutina, Unified Team/Russia	Cross-country	5	3	1	9
5 =	Karin Kania (née Enke), East Germany	Speed skating	3	4	1	8
=	Galina Kulakova, USSR	Cross-country	4	2	2	8
=	Gunda Neimann-Stirnemann, Germany	Speed skating	3	4	1	8
7 =	Andrea Ehrig (née Mitscherlich, formerly Schöne), East Germany	Speed skating	1	5	1	7
=	Marja-Liisa Kirvesniemi (née Hämäläinen), Finland	Cross-country	3	0	4	7
=	Claudia Pechstein, Germany	Speed skating	4	1	2	7
=	Elena Valbe, Unified Team/Russia	Cross-country	3	0	4	7

G – gold medals, S – silver medals, B – bronze medals

Born on February 29, 1952, Russia's Raisa Smetanina appeared in five Olympics for the Soviet Union and the Unified Team in 1992. Her first medal was silver in the 5-km cross-country in Innsbruck in 1976. She came away from those Games with two golds and a silver, and won silver and gold in 1980, two silvers in 1984, a bronze and silver in 1988, and her 10th and last medal, a gold in the 4 x 5-km relay, in 1992.

◀ The most successful athlete in Winter Olympic history, Bjorn Dählie of Norway.

Top 10 Medal-winning countries at the Winter Olympics*

	Country	G	S	B	Total
1	Russia/USSR/Unified Team	113	82	78	273
2	Norway	94	93	73	260
3	US	70	70	51	191
4	Germany/West Germany	68	67	52	187
5	Austria	41	57	66	164
6	Finland	41	51	49	141
7	East Germany	39	37	35	111
8	Sweden	36	28	38	102
9	Switzerland	32	33	36	101
10	Canada	30	28	37	95

G – gold medals, S – silver medals, B – bronze medals

* Includes medals won in figure skating and hockey in the Summer Games prior to the launch of the Winter Olympics in 1924

Top 10 Sports at which the US has won the most Winter Olympic medals*

	Sport	G	S	B	Total
1	Speed skating	26	16	14	56
2	Figure skating	13	13	15	41
3	Alpine skiing	10	15	4	29
4	Bobsleigh	6	5	6	17
5	Hockey	3	7	1	11
6 =	Freestyle skiing	4	4	1	9
=	Short track speed skating	3	3	3	9
8	Snowboarding	2	1	4	7
9	Skeleton	3	3	0	6
10	Luge	0	2	2	4

G – gold medals, S – silver medals, B – bronze medals

* Includes medals won in figure skating and hockey in the Summer Games prior to the launch of the Winter Olympics in 1924

▲ Apolo Anton "Chunky" Ohno, gold medalist in the 1,500-meter speed skating event at Salt Lake City 2002. He was 14 when he won his first US title.

PARALYMPICS

- Paralympics with the most competitors
- Medal-winning countries at the Summer Paralympics
- Medal-winning countries at the Winter Paralympics
- Medal-winning countries at the 2000 Sydney Summer Paralympics
- Medal-winning countries at the 2002 Salt Lake City Winter Paralympics

Top 10 Paralympics with the most competitors

	Venue/country	Year	Countries	Competitors
1	Stoke Mandeville, England/Long Island, New York	1984	42	4,080
2	Sydney, Australia	2000	127	3,843
3	Atlanta, Georgia	1996	103	3,193
4	Seoul, Korea	1988	61	3,053
5	Barcelona, Spain	1992	82	3,020
6	Arnhem, Netherlands	1980	42	2,500
7	Toronto, Canada	1976	42	1,600
8	Heidelberg, Germany	1972	44	1,000
9	Tel Aviv, Israel	1968	29	750
10	Rome, Italy	1960	23	400

The 1984 Games were split, with one group of athletes competing in New York in June and the wheelchair athletes competing in Stoke Mandeville in July and August. President Reagan led the opening ceremony in New York and Prince Charles led the Stoke Mandeville opening ceremony.

SIR LUDWIG GUTTMAN

Four years prior to the first international Games in Stoke Mandeville in 1952, Sir Ludwig Guttmann, a neurosurgeon, organized a sports competition there involving World War II veterans with spinal cord injuries. This was the forerunner to the now very popular Paralympics. Guttmann, who was Jewish, had fled Germany during the war.

◀ The UK's Tanni Grey-Thompson has amassed nine golds, four silvers, and a bronze medal in her Paralympic career. She has also won five London Marathons.

Top 10 Medal-winning countries at the Summer Paralympics*

Country	Gold medals	Silver medals	Bronze medals	Total
1 US	576	523	522	1,621
2 UK	389	401	387	1,177
3 Germany/West Germany	404	385	361	1,150
4 Canada	311	250	262	823
5 France	279	264	241	784
6 Australia	240	248	228	716
7 Netherlands	219	179	153	551
8 Poland	194	184	148	526
9 Sweden	197	190	135	522
10 Spain	156	137	152	445

* Excluding medals won at the 1960 Rome and 1968 Tel Aviv Games–the International Paralympic Committee has not maintained records of medals won at these Games

The first international games for the disabled were held in Stoke Mandeville, England, in 1952, when 130 athletes from just two countries competed. The first Paralympics to take place at the same venue as the Olympic Games was in Rome in 1960. Since then, the Paralympics have been held every four years, and, since Seoul in 1988, at the same venue as the Summer Olympics. Four hundred athletes from 23 countries took part in 1960. In Sydney in 2000, a total of 3,843 athletes from 127 nations competed. The most medals won at one Games is 388 by the United States in the "dual" Paralympics of 1984. Their total of 131 gold medals is also a record for one Games.

Top 10 Medal-winning countries at the Winter Paralympics

Country	Gold medals	Silver medals	Bronze medals	Total
1 Austria	103	102	96	301
2 Germany/West Germany	101	97	93	291
3 Norway	118	84	68	270
4 US	89	92	62	243
5 Finland	75	45	55	175
6 Switzerland	48	56	51	155
7 France	39	40	41	120
8 Russia	39	39	27	105
9 Canada	22	33	36	91
10 Sweden	24	32	34	90

The first Winter Paralympics were held in Örnsköldsvik, Sweden, in 1976, when Austria was the leading country with 35 medals. West Germany and Switzerland were the leading gold-medal countries, with nine each. The most medals won at one Games is 82, by Austria in Innsbruck in 1984, and their tally of 41 golds is also a Games record.

Top 10 Medal-winning countries at the 2000 Sydney Summer Paralympics

Country	Gold medals	Silver medals	Bronze medals	Total
1 Australia	63	39	47	149
2 UK	41	43	47	131
3 US	36	39	34	109
4 Spain	39	30	38	107
5 Canada	38	33	25	96
6 Germany	15	42	38	95
7 France	30	28	28	86
8 China	34	22	16	72
9 Poland	19	22	12	53
10 Czech Republic	15	15	13	43

A staggering 300 World and Paralympic records were broken in the 18 events at the Sydney Games. There were outstanding performances from the United Kingdom's Tanni Grey-Thompson, who won gold medals in the 100-, 200-, 400-, and 800-meter races, and from US swimmer Jason Wening, who won his third consecutive gold medal in the 400-meter freestyle, breaking his own world record at the same time. He returned from the Games with his undefeated record in the 400 meters, stretching back to 1991, still intact.

Top 10 Medal-winning countries at the 2002 Salt Lake City Winter Paralympics

Country	Gold medals	Silver medals	Bronze medals	Total
1 US	10	22	11	43
2 Germany	17	1	15	33
3 Austria	9	10	10	29
4 Russia	7	9	5	21
5 = France	2	11	6	19
= Norway	10	3	6	19
7 Canada	6	4	5	15
8 = Switzerland	6	4	2	12
= Ukraine	0	6	6	12
10 = Italy	3	3	3	9
= Slovakia	0	3	6	9
= Sweden	0	6	3	9

More than 500 athletes from 35 countries competed in the VIIIth Paralympic Winter Games in Salt Lake City, Utah, March 7–16, 2002.

WATER SPORTS

At the Start

Competitive swimming and diving have been practiced since early times—the Romans built swimming baths and included the sport as part of every boy's education. Swimming was also highly regarded in Imperial Japan. The first organized swimming events took place in 1837 in London, where the Amateur Swimming Association was founded in 1869. In the United States, swimming as a sport dates from 1888. Sailing competitions were recorded as early as 1661, while rowing has a similarly long history, and has been considered a competitive sport since the early 18th century, with the addition in relatively modern times of such pursuits as water-skiing.

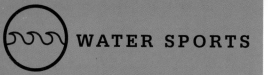

OLYMPIC SWIMMING GREATS

- Most Olympic medals in men's swimming events
- Most Olympic medals in women's swimming events
- Longest-standing Olympic swimming records
- Fastest-ever men's 100-meter freestyle in the Olympics

THE FIRST OLYMPICS

Swimming was featured at the first modern Olympics in 1896 and has been included ever since. In the inaugural Games, the races took place in open waters in the Bay of Zea at Phaleron and were watched by around 40,000 spectators on the shore. There were only four swimming events in 1896, including the 100-meter freestyle for sailors, which was restricted to members of the Greek Navy.

Top 10 Most Olympic medals in men's swimming events

Swimmer/country	Gold medals	Silver medals	Bronze medals	Total
1 = Matt Biondi, US	8	2	1	11
= Mark Spitz, US	9	1	1	11
3 = Zoltán Halmay, Hungary	3	5	1	9
= Alexander Popov, Unified Team/Russia	4	5	0	9
5 = Charles Daniels, US	5	1	2	8
= Gary Hall, Jr., US	4	3	1	8
= Roland Matthes, East Germany	4	2	2	8
= Henry Taylor, UK	4	1	3	8
9 Tom Jager, US	5	1	1	7
10 = Frank Beaurepaire, Australia	0	3	3	6
= Michael Gross, West Germany	3	2	1	6
= John Jarvis, UK	3	1	2	6
= Murray Rose, Australia	4	1	1	6
= Don Schollander, US	5	1	0	6
= Johnny Weissmuller,* US	5	0	1	6

* Total includes one medal in water polo

Top 10 Most Olympic medals in women's swimming events

Swimmer/country	Gold medals	Silver medals	Bronze medals	Total
1 Jenny Thompson, US	8	1	1	10
2 = Shirley Babashoff, US	2	6	0	8
= Kornelia Ender, East Germany	4	4	0	8
= Dawn Fraser, Australia	4	4	0	8
= Dagmar Hase, Germany	2	5	1	8
= Susie O'Neill, Australia	2	4	2	8
= Dara Torres, US	4	0	4	8
= Franziska van Almsick, Germany	0	4	4	8
9 Krisztina Egerszegi, Hungary	5	1	1	7
10 = Daniela Hunger, East Germany/Germany	3	1	2	6
= Angel Martino, US	3	0	3	6
= Kristin Otto, East Germany	6	0	0	6
= Andrea Pollack, East Germany	3	3	0	6
= Amy van Dyken, US	6	0	0	6

◄ Mark Spitz in 1967, at age 17. The following year he won the first of his record 11 Olympic medals.

The 10 Longest-standing Olympic swimming records

	Event	Time (min:sec)	Swimmer/country	Date
1	200-meter freestyle (women)	1:57.65	Heike Friedrich, East Germany	21 Sep 1988
2	400-meter freestyle (women)	4:03.85	Janet Evans, US	22 Sep 1988
3	200-meter breaststroke (men)	2:10.16	Mike Barrowman, US	29 July 1992
4	50-meter freestyle (men)	0:21.91	Alexander Popov, Unified Team	30 July 1992
5	200-meter backstroke (women)	2:07.06	Krisztina Egerszegi, Hungary	31 July 1992
6	1,500-meter freestyle (men)	14:43.48	Kieren Perkins, Australia	31 July 1992
7	100-meter breaststroke (women)	1:07.02	Penny Heyns, South Africa	21 July 1996
8	400-meter freestyle (men)	3:40.59	Ian Thorpe, Australia	16 Sep 2000
9	4 x 100-meter freestyle relay (men)	3:13.67	Australia	16 Sep 2000
10	400-meter individual medley (women)	4:33.59	Yana Klochkova, Ukraine	16 Sep 2000

The women's 400-meter freestyle final at the Seoul Olympics was a showdown between Heike Friedrich and Janet Evans. Friedrich had won 13 consecutive major finals, including five golds at the 1985 European Championships as a 15-year-old, and four golds at the 1986 World Championships. She had won the 200-meter freestyle in Seoul in a new Olympic record time, which still stands, but in the 400 meters she was about to meet her match in diminutive US swimmer Janet Evans. Evans was pushed all the way by Friedrich and her German compatriot Anke Möhring, but with two laps to go, Evans pulled away and won in a world record time, and two seconds clear of her rival. Amazingly, she swam the second half of the race faster than the first.

Top 10 Fastest-ever men's 100-meter freestyle in the Olympics

	Swimmer/country	Year	Time (sec)
1	Pieter van den Hoogenband, Netherlands	2000	47.84
2	Pieter van den Hoogenband, Netherlands	2000	48.30
3	Matt Biondi, US	1988	48.63
4	Pieter van den Hoogenband, Netherlands	2000	48.64
5	Alexander Popov, Russia	2000	48.69
6	Gary Hall, Jr., US	2000	48.73
7 =	Michael Klim, Australia	2000	48.74
=	Alexander Popov, Russia	1996	48.74
9 =	Michael Klim, Australia	2000	48.80
10	Gary Hall, Jr., US	1996	48.81

Gary Hall, Jr., who makes two appearances in this list, comes from a family of swimmers. His grandfather, Charles Keating, was an All-America swimmer at the University of Cincinnati, and his uncle, Charles Keating, Jr., was a member of the 1976 US Olympic team, while his father, Gary Hall, Sr., won silver medals at the 1968 and 1972 Olympics and a bronze in the 1976 Olympics.

▼ Matt Biondi (below) and fellow American Mark Spitz are the most decorated Olympic swimmers.

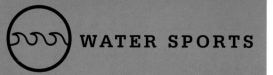
WORLD CHAMPIONS & RECORD HOLDERS

- Longest-standing men's world swimming records
- Longest-standing women's world swimming records
- Women's medal-winning countries at the World Swimming Championships
- Men's medal-winning countries at the World Swimming Championships
- Most men's gold medals at the World Championships

The 10 Longest-standing men's world swimming records*

	Swimmer/country	Event	Time (min:sec)	Date
1	Mike Barrowman, US	200-meter breaststroke	2:10.16	July 29, 1992
2	Jani Sievinen, Finland	200-meter individual medley	1:58.16	Sept. 11, 1994
3	Lenny Krayzelburg, US	100-meter backstroke	0:53.60	Aug. 24, 1999
4	Lenny Krayzelburg, US	200-meter backstroke	1:55.87	Aug. 27, 1999
5	Lenny Krayzelburg, US	50-meter backstroke	0:24.99	Aug. 28, 1999
6	Michael Klim, Australia	100-meter butterfly	0:51.81	Dec. 12, 1999
7	Alexander Popov, Russia	50-meter freestyle	0:21.64	June 16, 2000
8	Australia	400-meter freestyle relay	3:13.67	Sept. 16, 2000
9	Tom Dolan, US	400-meter individual medley	4:11.76	Sept. 17, 2000
10	Pieter van den Hoogenband, Netherlands	100-meter freestyle	0:47.84	Sept. 19, 2000

* Long course world records set in a 50-meter pool

Mike Barrowman's long-standing record in the 200-meter breaststroke is also the longest-standing men's Olympic record. Barrowman went into the final with the five fastest times in the event under his belt. He came out with the sixth, and a gold medal, with a 1.7-second margin of victory over Hungary's Norbert Rózsa.

CHAMPIONSHIP VENUES

The swimming World Championships were first held in Belgrade, Yugoslavia, in 1973 and have generally been held sporadically since then. Championship venues have been: Cali, Colombia (1975); Berlin, West Germany (1978); Guayaquil, Ecuador (1982); Madrid, Spain (1986); Perth, Australia (1991); Rome, Italy (1994); Perth, Australia (1998); Fukuoka, Japan (2001). The 2003 venue is Barcelona, Spain.

The 10 Longest-standing women's world swimming records*

	Swimmer/country	Event	Time (min:sec)	Date
1	East Germany	800-meter freestyle relay	7:55.47	Aug. 18, 1987
2	Janet Evans, US	1,500-meter freestyle	15:52.10	Mar. 26, 1988
3	Janet Evans, US	400-meter freestyle	4:03.85	Sept. 22, 1988
4	Janet Evans, US	800-meter freestyle	8:16.22	Aug. 20, 1989
5	Krisztina Egerszegi, Hungary	200-meter backstroke	2:06.62	Aug. 25, 1991
6	Franziska van Almsick, Germany	200-meter freestyle	1:56.78	Sept. 6, 1994
7	Cihnong He, China	100-meter backstroke	1:00.16	Sept. 10, 1994
8	Yanyan Wu, China	200-meter individual medley	2:09.72	Oct. 17, 1997
9	Penelope Heyns, South Africa	100-meter breaststroke	1:06.52	Aug. 23, 1999
10	Penelope Heyns, South Africa	50-meter breaststroke	0:30.83	Aug. 28, 1999

* Long course world records set in a 50-meter pool

Janet Evans' career has seen her win four Olympic golds and a silver in three Games (1988–96), plus three world championship golds and a silver. She has set world records in three events and set six US national records. Her 45 national titles is a record second only to that of Tracy Caulkins, who has three more. Evans won the coveted Sullivan Award as the top US athlete in 1989.

◀ East Germany's Kornelia Ender, who won four Olympic and a record eight World Championship gold medals.

Top 10 Women's medal-winning countries at the World Swimming Championships*

	Country	Gold medals	Silver medals	Bronze medals	Total
1	US	37	44	34	115
2	East Germany	44	32	15	91
3	China	21	10	7	38
4	Germany/West Germany	6	12	14	32
5	Australia	12	10	8	30
6	Netherlands	4	5	12	21
7	USSR/Russia	4	6	7	17
8	Canada	0	2	10	12
9	Japan	0	3	7	10
10	Hungary	4	2	2	8

* Excluding the long distance events–5 km and 25 km

Top 10 Men's medal-winning countries at the World Swimming Championships*

	Country	Gold medals	Silver medals	Bronze medals	Total
1	US	60	40	28	128
2	USSR/Russia	13	22	21	56
3	Germany/West Germany	11	15	18	44
4	Australia	18	10	8	36
5	Hungary	12	4	9	25
6	East Germany	6	8	10	24
7	UK	3	3	14	20
8	Italy	3	7	7	17
9	Sweden	3	5	8	16
10	Canada	4	6	4	14

Top 10 Most men's gold medals at the World Championships*

	Swimmer/country	Years	Golds
1	Ian Thorpe, Australia	1998–2001	8
2	Jim Montgomery, US	1973–75	7
3 =	Matt Biondi, US	1986–91	6
=	Michael Klim, Australia	1998–2001	6
5 =	Rowdy Gaines, US	1978–82	5
=	Michael Gross, West Germany	1982–90	5
7 =	Joe Bottom, US	1978	4
=	Tamas Darnyi, Hungary	1986–91	4
=	Grant Hackett, Australia	1998–2001	4
=	Tom Jager, US	1986–91	4
=	David McCagg, US	1978–82	4
=	Vladimir Salnikov, Russia	1978–82	4
=	Tim Shaw, US	1975	4

* Long course championships; diving not included

The most golds won by a woman is also eight, by Kornelia Ender (East Germany), 1973–75.

▼ Australia's Ian Thorpe in action on the opening day of the swimming events at Homebush Bay during the 2000 Sydney Olympics. He won three golds to add to the eight he had collected in the World Championships.

YACHTING & WATER-SKIING

- Most Olympic yachting medals
- Medal-winning countries in yachting at the Olympic Games
- Men's world water-skiing titles
- Women's world water-skiing titles

Top 10 Most Olympic yachting medals

	Competitor/country	Years	G	S	B	Total
1 =	Paul Elvström, Denmark	1948–60	4	0	0	4
=	Torben Grael, Brazil	1984–2000	1	1	2	4
=	Valentyn Mankin, Russia	1968–80	3	1	0	4
=	Jochen Schümann, East Germany/Germany	1976–2000	3	1	0	4
5 =	Jesper Bank, Denmark	1988–2000	2	0	1	3
=	Léon Huybrechts, Belgium	1908–24	1	2	0	3
=	Poul Jensen, Denmark	1968–80	2	1	0	3
=	Barbara Kendall, New Zealand	1992–2000	1	1	1	3
=	Rodney Pattisson, UK	1968–76	2	1	0	3
=	Mark Reynolds, US	1988–2000	2	1	0	3

G – gold medals, S – silver medals, B – bronze medals

Valentyn Mankin is the only person to win golds in three different classes: Finn, Tempest, and Star.

Paul Elvström didn't have the best of starts to his Olympic career in the Finn class at the 1948 Olympics, when he failed to finish the first race on day one. However, he clawed his way back to capture the first of his four Olympic gold medals, going on to become the first man to win gold medals at four consecutive Games.

ALL-AROUND WINNERS

The US bronze medalists in the Tempest Class at the 1976 Montreal Olympics both had other claims to fame. Conn Findlay had previously won two golds and a bronze medal in coxed pair rowing events in 1956–64, while his skipper Dennis Conner won the America's Cup in 1980, 1987, and 1988.

Top 10 Medal-winning countries in yachting at the Olympic Games

	Country	Gold medals	Silver medals	Bronze medals	Total
1	USA	17	21	16	54
2	UK	18	12	8	38
3	Sweden	9	12	10	31
4	Norway	16	11	3	30
5	France	11	7	9	27
6	Denmark	11	8	4	23
7	Germany/West Germany	5	6	7	18
8 =	Australia	5	3	8	16
=	Netherlands	4	5	7	16
10 =	New Zealand	6	4	5	15
=	USSR/Unified Team/Russia	4	6	5	15

The United States' first Olympic yachting gold medal was in the Star class at the 1932 Los Angeles Games, when *Jupiter*, skippered by Gilbert Gray of New Orleans, won five of the seven races to win by 11 points from the United Kingdom team. It is appropriate that their first gold should come in the Star class because the Star was a 22-ft-8-in (6.9-metre) boat designed by Francis Sweisguth of New York in 1910.

▶ Action from Rushcutter's Bay, venue for the yachting events at the 2000 Sydney Olympic Games.

Top 10 Men's world water-skiing titles

	Skier/country	Overall	Slalom	Tricks	Jumps	Total
1	Patrice Martin, France	6	0	4	0	10
2 =	Sammy Duval, US	4	0	0	2	6
=	Andy Mapple, UK	0	6	0	0	6
4 =	Bob La Point, US	0	4	1	0	5
=	Jaret Llewellyn, Canada	1	0	1	3	5
=	Alfredo Mendoza, Mexico	2	1	0	2	5
=	Mike Suyderhoud, US	2	1	0	2	5
8 =	George Athans, Canada	2	1	0	0	3
=	Guy de Clercq, Belgium	1	0	0	2	3
=	Wayne Grimditch, US	0	0	2	1	3
=	Mike Hazelwood, UK	1	0	0	2	3
=	Ricky McCormick, US	0	0	1	2	3
=	Billy Spencer, US	1	1	1	0	3

Born in Nantes, France in 1964, Patrice Martin won the first of his 10 world titles (Tricks) in 1979. He won his tenth and last title 20 years later. His long career also saw him win 32 European titles and 13 Masters Tricks titles of the US, France, and England. A bank accountant by occupation, he started water skiing at age two and first competed when he was eight.

Top 10 Women's world water-skiing titles

	Skier/country	Overall	Slalom	Tricks	Jumps	Total
1	Liz Shetter (née Allen), US	3	3	1	4	11
2	Willa McGuire (née Worthington), US	3	2	1	2	8
3	Cindy Todd, US	2	3	0	2	7
4	Deena Mapple (née Brush), US	2	0	0	4	6
5	Yelena Milakova, Russia	3	0	0	2	5
6 =	Marina Doria, Switzerland	1	1	2	0	4
=	Tawn Hahn (née Larsen), US	0	0	4	0	4
=	Helena Kjellander, Sweden	0	4	0	0	4
=	Natalya Ponomaryeva (née Rumyantseva), USSR	1	0	3	0	4
10 =	Maria Victoria Carrasco, Venezuela	0	0	3	0	3
=	Britt Larsen, US	0	0	3	0	3

Liz Shetter won two events at the US National Championships in 1962, at age 11. She went on to win 42 National titles in 13 seasons. In 1969, she set a record by winning all three events—slalom, tricks, and jumps—at the Nationals, the World Championships, and the Masters. She began skiing at age five, after her family moved to Florida in 1955 from West Germany, where her father has been stationed prior to his retirement from the army. Shetter retired in 1975, much to the relief of her rivals.

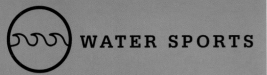

WATER SPORTS

CANOEING & ROWING

- Most medals in Olympic canoeing
- Medal-winning countries in men's rowing in the Olympics
- Medal-winning countries in women's rowing in the Olympics
- Medal-winning countries in men's canoeing in the Olympics
- Medal-winning countries in women's canoeing in the Olympics

Top 10 Most medals in Olympic canoeing

	Competitor/country	Years	G	S	B	Total
1	Birgit Schmidt* (née Fischer), East Germany/Germany	1980–2000	7	3	0	10
2	Gert Fredriksson, Sweden	1948–60	6	1	1	8
3 =	Agneta Andersson,* Sweden	1984–96	3	2	2	7
=	Ivan Patzaichin, Romania	1968–84	4	3	0	7
5 =	Rüdiger Helm, East Germany	1978–80	3	0	3	6
=	Knut Holman, Norway	1992–2000	3	2	1	6
=	Rita Kóbán,* Hungary	1988–2000	2	3	1	6
8 =	Kay Bluhm,* Germany	1992–96	3	1	1	5
=	Ian Ferguson, New Zealand	1984–88	4	1	0	5
=	Olaf Heukrodt, East Germany/Germany	1988–92	1	2	2	5
=	Paul MacDonald, New Zealand	1984–88	3	1	1	5
=	Ramona Portwich,* Germany	1992–96	3	2	0	5

G – gold medals, S – silver medals, B – bronze medals

* Female competitor

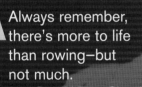

"Always remember, there's more to life than rowing—but not much.
Donald Beer, Olympic rowing medalist "

DID YOU KNOW? Benjamin Spock, who later became famous as the "baby expert," was a member of the 1924 US eights rowing team that won the gold medal.

Top 10 Medal-winning countries in men's rowing in the Olympics

	Country	Gold medals	Silver medals	Bronze medals	Total
1	US	28	22	17	67
2	Germany/West Germany	20	15	15	50
3	UK	21	15	7	43
4	Italy	14	13	10	37
5 =	France	6	14	12	32
=	USSR/Unified Team/Russia	11	14	7	32
7	East Germany	20	4	7	31
8	Switzerland	6	8	9	23
9 =	Australia	6	7	8	21
=	Canada	4	8	9	21

Rowing dates to the 1900 Paris Olympics for men, but as recently as 1976 for women. Some of the discontinued men's rowing events have included: Four-oared Inriggers with Coxswain, Six-man Naval Rowing Boat, and the Seventeen-man Naval Rowing Boat event. The latter two were part of the 1906 Intercalated Games in Athens, when Greece won four of the six medals.

Top 10 Medal-winning countries in women's rowing in the Olympics

	Country	Gold medals	Silver medals	Bronze medals	Total
1	Romania	13	6	5	24
2	East Germany	13	3	1	17
3	USSR/Unified Team/Russia	1	6	6	13
4 =	Canada	4	4	4	12
=	Germany/West Germany	5	2	5	12
=	US	1	7	4	12
7	Bulgaria	2	4	4	10
8	Netherlands	0	3	2	5
9 =	Australia	1	1	2	4
=	China	0	2	2	4

One of the most touching of Olympic stories was at Barcelona in 1992, when Canada's Silken Laumann took bronze in the single sculls. Less than three months before the Olympics her leg was severely damaged in a freak rowing accident. She was told that she needed at least six months' recovery time, but insisted on making the Olympics, despite being able to walk only with the aid of a cane.

Top 10 Medal-winning countries in men's canoeing in the Olympics

	Country	Gold medals	Silver medals	Bronze medals	Total
1	Hungary	12	19	17	48
2	Germany/West Germany	17	11	17	45
3	USSR/Unified Team/Russia	22	13	7	42
4	Romania	9	9	10	28
5	France	4	6	16	26
6	Sweden	11	9	2	22
7	East Germany	8	5	8	21
8	Czechoslovakia/Czech Republic	10	8	2	20
9	Bulgaria	3	3	7	13
10	Canada	3	5	4	12

A Kayak singles race was contested at the 1906 Intercalated Games in Athens, but it was not until 1936 that canoeing became a regular Olympic sport. Sweden has Gerd Fredriksson to thank for its high rank on the all-time canoeing list, because he won six gold medals, one silver, and one bronze between 1948 and 1960. He won the K-1 1,000-meter event at three successive Games. Between 1942 and his retirement in 1964, he won 71 national championships.

◀ Birgit Fischer (front) with Katrina Wagner after winning the K2 final at the 2000 Sydney Olympics. It was Fischer's seventh Olympic gold over a 20-year career.

Top 10 Medal-winning countries in women's canoeing in the Olympics

	Country	Gold medals	Silver medals	Bronze medals	Total
1	Germany/West Germany	8	8	2	18
2	Hungary	2	6	6	14
3	USSR/Unified Team/Russia	8	2	3	13
4	East Germany	6	2	1	9
5	Romania	1	2	4	7
6	Sweden	3	2	1	6
7 =	Bulgaria	1	2	1	4
=	Canada	0	3	1	4
=	Netherlands	0	2	2	4
=	Poland	0	0	4	4

Women's canoeing was first included in the 1948 London Olympics.

Birgit Fischer of Germany (formerly East Germany) is not only the only woman to win 10 Olympic canoeing medals, but also the only woman to win Olympic medals 20 years apart. When she won her first Olympic gold, in the Kayak singles in 1980, she became the youngest Olympic canoe champion at age 18. Had East Germany not boycotted the 1984 Los Angeles Games, she would surely have increased her medal tally.

HORSE RACING

At the Start

Horse racing developed in ancient times from the use of horses in combat and hunting. Horse and chariot racing were introduced into the Olympic Games and remained popular throughout the Roman Empire. There are records of organized horse races from the Middle Ages, and in England annual race meetings were held in York from 1530 and at Chester, Britain's oldest racecourse, from 1540. The Jockey Club was founded in 1750, and the Derby first run in 1780, followed by other races, many of which remain part of the racing calendar. In the United States, such notable races as the Belmont Stakes, Preakness Stakes, and Kentucky Derby date from the 1860s and 1870s. Harness racing with sulkies was first seen in 1829.

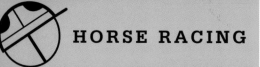
- Fastest winning times in the Kentucky Derby

- Most rides in the Kentucky Derby

- Trainers with the most Kentucky Derby runners

- Latest Triple Crown-winning horses

- Jockeys in Triple Crown races

- Trainers in Triple Crown races

SECRETARIAT

The great Secretariat was foaled at The Meadow, Doswell, Virginia on March 30, 1970. He moved to Florida in January 1972 to be trained by Lucien Laurin, and made his racing debut at Aqueduct on July 4, 1972. Ridden by Paul Feliciano, he finished fourth after being blocked throughout the race – the worst placing of his entire career. Feliciano rode him to his first victory at Aqueduct 11 days later.

Top 10 Fastest winning times in the Kentucky Derby

	Horse	Year	Time (min:sec)
1	Secretariat	1973	1:59.2
2	Monarchos	2001	1:59.4
3	Northern Dancer	1964	2:00.0
4	Spend a Buck	1985	2:00.2
5	Decidedly	1962	2:00.4
6	Proud Clarion	1967	2:00.6
7	Grindstone	1996	2:01.0
8 =	Affirmed	1978	2:01.2
=	Fusaichi Pegasus	2000	2:01.2
=	Lucky Debonair	1965	2:01.2
=	Thunder Gulch	1995	2:01.2

Source: The Jockey Club

The Kentucky Derby is held on the first Saturday in May at Churchill Downs, Louisville, Kentucky. The first leg of the Triple Crown, it was first raced in 1875 over a distance of one mile four furlongs, but after 1896 was reduced to one mile two furlongs. It is said that a hat manufactured by James H. Knapp of South Norwalk, Connecticut, became popular attire at the first Kentucky Derbys, thereby acquiring the name "derby."

Top 10 Most rides in the Kentucky Derby

	Jockey	Years	Starts
1	Bill Shoemaker	1952–88	26
2	Eddie Arcaro	1935–61	21
3	Laffit Pincay, Jr.	1971–94	19
4	Angel Cordero, Jr.	1968–91	17
5 =	Pat Day	1982–98	16
=	Chris McCarron	1976–98	16
7 =	Mack Garner	1916–35	14
=	Jorge Velasquez	1969–96	14
9 =	Johnny Adams	1939–57	13
=	Don Brumfield	1966–87	13
=	Gary Stevens	1985–98	13

Adams is the only one in the list not to have ridden a winner of the race. He came second on two occasions. Bill Shoemaker's first Kentucky Derby victory was on Swaps in 1955. Two years later, he should have won his second Derby but, mistaking a furlong post for the finish line, he stood up to celebrate, only to see Iron Liege storm past his mount Gallant Man to take first place.

Top 10 Trainers with the most Kentucky Derby runners

	Trainers	Years	Runners
1	D. Wayne Lukas	1981–2000	38
2	Dick Thompson	1920–37	24
3	James Rowe, Sr.	1881*–1925	18
4 =	Max Hirsch	1915–51	14
=	Woody Stephens	1949–88	14
6	LeRoy Jolley	1962–92	13
7	Nick Zito	1990–2001	12
8 =	Bob Baffert	1996–2001	11
=	Sunny Jim Fitzsimmons	1930–57	11
=	Ben Jones	1938–52	11

* Year of Rowe's first winner, Hindoo; the year of the first race is unrecorded

In 1995, former high school basketball coach D. Wayne Lukas became the first man to train the winner of all three Triple Crown races with different horses; Thunder Gulch (Derby and Belmont Stakes) and Timber Country (Preakness).

The 10 Latest Triple Crown-winning horses*

	Horse	Year
1	Affirmed	1978
2	Seattle Slew	1977
3	Secretariat	1973
4	Citation	1948
5	Assault	1946
6	Count Fleet	1943
7	Whirlaway	1941
8	War Admiral	1937
9	Omaha	1935
10	Gallant Fox	1930

* Horses that have won the Kentucky Derby, the Preakness, and the Belmont Stakes in the same season

Since Affirmed's victory in 1978, three horses have come close to winning all three races, but missed out by finishing second in one of them. They were: Sunday Silence (1989), Silver Charm (1997), and Real Quiet (1998).

> It's not how many races you win that counts, but that you win the good ones.
>
> **Charlie Whittingham,** thoroughbred horse trainer.

Top 10 Jockeys in Triple Crown races

	Jockey	Kentucky	Preakness	Belmont	Wins
1	Eddie Arcaro	5	6	6	17
2	Bill Shoemaker	4	2	5	11
3 =	Pat Day	1	5	3	9
=	Bill Hartack	5	3	1	9
=	Earle Sande	3	1	5	9
6	Jimmy McLaughlin	1	1	6	8
=	Gary Stevens	3	2	3	8
8 =	Angel Cordero, Jr.	3	2	1	6
=	Chas Kurtsinger	2	2	2	6
=	Ron Turcotte	2	2	2	6

The US Triple Crown consists of the Kentucky Derby (held at Churchill Downs, Louisville, Kentucky, since 1875), Preakness Stakes (held at Pimlico Race Course, Baltimore, Maryland, since 1873), and Belmont Stakes (held at Belmont Park, Elmont, New York, since 1867). The only jockey to complete the Triple Crown twice is Eddie Arcaro, on Whirlaway (1941) and on Citation (1948).

Top 10 Trainers in Triple Crown races

	Trainer	Kentucky	Preakness	Belmont	Wins
1 =	Sunny Jim Fitzsimmons	3	4	6	13
=	D. Wayne Lukas	4	5	4	13
3	Robert Walden	1	7	4	12
4	James Rowe, Sr.	2	1	8	11
5 =	Max Hirsch	3	2	4	9
=	Ben Jones	6	2	1	9
7	Woody Stephens	2	1	5	8
8 =	Sam Hildreth	0	0	7	7
=	Jimmy Jones	2	4	1	7
10 =	Bob Baffert	2	3	1	6
=	Lucien Laurin	2	1	3	6

Sunny Jim Fitzsimmons and Ben Jones are the only two men to have trained two Triple Crown winners. Fitzsimmons' triumphs came with Gallant Fox (1930) and Omaha (1935), while Jones' were with Whirlaway (1941) and Citation (1948).

▼ The Belmont Stakes, part of the Triple Crown, is held at Belmont Park, Elmont, New York.

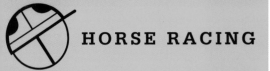

BREEDERS' CUP

- Biggest winning margins in Breeders' Cup races
- Jockeys in the Breeders' Cup
- Money-winning jockeys in the Breeders' Cup
- Trainers with the most starters in the Breeders' Cup
- Fastest winning times in the Breeders' Cup Classic

> A horse gallops with his lungs, perseveres with his heart, and wins with his character.
>
> Federico Tesio, racehorse breeder

Top 10 Biggest winning margins in Breeders' Cup races

	Winning horse	Runner-up	Year/race	Winning distance (lengths)
1	Inside Information	Heavenly Prize	1995 Distaff	13½
2	Countess Diana	Career Collection	1997 Juvenile Fillies	8½
3	Princess Rooney	Life's Magic	1984 Distaff	7
4	Bayakoa (Argentina)	Colonial Waters	1990 Distaff	6¾
5	Life's Magic	Lady's Secret	1985 Distaff	6¼
6	Skip Away	Deputy Commander	1997 Classic	6
7 =	Banks Hill (GB)	Sook Express	2001 Filly and Mare Turf	5½
=	Brave Raj	Tappiano	1986 Juvenile Fillies	5½
=	Favorite Trick	Dawson's Legacy	1997 Juvenile	5½
10 =	Arazi	Bertrando	1991 Juvenile	5
=	Brocco	Blumin Affair	1993 Juvenile	5
=	Meadow Star	Private Treasure	1990 Juvenile Fillies	5

Inside Information's jockey at Belmont Park in 1995 was Mike Smith, who had previously ridden four Breeders' Cup winners, including Lure in the Mile in 1992 and 1993. He has now won a total of eight Cup races, the last being in 1997. He has also enjoyed victory in Europe, winning the Irish 2,000 Guineas on Fourstars Allstar in 1991.

Top 10 Jockeys in the Breeders' Cup

	Jockey	Years	Wins
1 =	Pat Day	1984–2001	12
=	Jerry Bailey	1991–2001	12
3	Chris McCarron	1985–2001	9
4 =	Mike Smith	1992–97	8
=	Gary Stevens	1990–2000	8
6 =	Eddie Delahoussaye	1984–93	7
=	Laffit Pincay, Jr.	1985–93	7
8 =	Jose Santos	1986–97	6
=	Pat Valenzuela	1986–92	6
10	Corey Nakatani	1996–99	5

Source: The Breeders' Cup

Held at a different venue each year, the Breeders' Cup is an end-of-season gathering with eight races run during the day, with the season's best thoroughbreds competing in each category. Staged in October or November, there was nearly $13,000,000 prize money in 2001, with over $2,000,000 going to the winner of the day's senior race, the Classic. Churchill Downs is the most-used venue, with five Breeders' Cups, the first being in 1984.

Top 10 Money-winning jockeys in the Breeders' Cup

	Jockey	Prize winnings ($)
1	Pat Day	21,717,800
2	Chris McCarron	17,669,520
3	Jerry Bailey	13,691,000
4	Gary Stevens	13,324,720
5	Mike Smith	8,194,200
6	Eddie Delahoussaye	7,775,000
7	Laffit Pincay, Jr.	6,811,000
8	Corey Nakatani	6,440,360
9	Angel Cordero, Jr.	6,020,000
10	Jose Santos	5,828,800

In 2001, Pat Day became only the third jockey after Bill Shoemaker and Laffit Pincay, Jr. to win 8,000 career races. Day was born in 1953, and rode his first winner at age 20. His record winnings in the Breeders' Cup have been aided by a record 12 wins, including four in the Classic, in 1984 on Wild Again, in 1990 on Unbridled, on Awesome Again in 1998, and Cat Thief in 1999. His first Breeders' Cup winner was Wild Again, as above.

Top 10 Trainers with the most starters in the Breeders' Cup

	Trainer	Starters
1	D. Wayne Lukas	135
2	Robert Frankel	42
3	William Mott	39
4	Claude R. McGaughey III	35
5	Andre Fabre	34
6	Bob Baffert	29
7	Ronald McAnally	27
8 =	Neil Drysdale	26
=	Flint S. Schulhofer	26
10	Charles Whittingham	24

Despite his record 135 starters, D. Wayne Lukas had to wait until 1999 for his first winner of the Classic. Even then, notwithstanding his record of 14 Breeders' Cup winners, his horse Cat Thief was not favored to win the race, but the jockey ensured that the pundits were wrong by pushing him to the finish.

Top 10 Fastest winning times in the Breeders' Cup Classic

	Horse	Jockey	Year	Track	Time (min:sec)
1	Skip Away	Mike Smith	1997	Hollywood Park	1:59.2
2 =	Cat Thief	Pat Day	1999	Gulfstream Park	1:59.4
=	Cigar	Jerry Bailey	1995	Belmont Park	1:59.4
4 =	A. P. Indy	Eddie Delahoussaye	1992	Gulfstream Park	2:00.2
=	Sunday Silence	Chris McCarron	1989	Gulfstream Park	2:00.2
6	Skywalker	Laffit Pincay, Jr.	1986	Santa Anita Park	2:00.4
7 =	Tiznow	Chris McCarron	2000	Churchill Downs	2:00.6
=	Tiznow	Chris McCarron	2001	Belmont Park	2:00.6
9 =	Arcangues	Jerry Bailey	1993	Santa Anita Park	2:00.8
=	Proud Truth	Jorge Velasquez	1985	Aqueduct	2:00.8

The most prestigious of the Breeders' Cup races, the Classic, is run over 1¼ miles and attracts a prize fund of over $3,500,000. Jockey Chris McCarron has won the race a record five times, including back-to-back wins on Tiznow in 2000 and 2001.

◀ With 12 wins to his name, jockey Pat Day is the most successful rider in the Breeders' Cup.

CHAMPION JOCKEYS

- Jockeys of all time in the UK
- Jockeys in a UK flat-racing season
- Most flat race Jockeys' Championships in the UK
- Most wins in a season by the annual money leader in the US
- Money-winning North American jockeys
- US jockeys with most wins in a career

> Mother always told me my day was coming, but I never realized I'd end up being the shortest knight of the year.
>
> **Gordon Richards**, jockey, on being knighted, 1953

Top 10 Jockeys of all time in the UK

	Jockey	Years	Wins
1	Gordon Richards	1921–54	4,870
2	Lester Piggott	1948–95	4,513
3	Pat Eddery	1969–2001	4,476
4	Willie Carson	1962–96	3,828
5	Doug Smith	1931–67	3,111
6	Joe Mercer	1950–85	2,810
7	Fred Archer	1870–86	2,748
8	Edward Hide	1951–85	2,591
9	George Fordham	1850–84	2,587
10	Eph Smith	1930–65	2,313

When Pat Eddery rode Silver Partriarch to victory in the St. Leger in Doncaster, England on September 13, 1997, he became only the third member of the elite "4,000 Club"–jockeys who have won more than 4,000 races.

Top 10 Jockeys in a UK flat-racing season

	Jockey	Year	Wins
1	Gordon Richards	1947	269
2	Gordon Richards	1949	261
3	Gordon Richards	1933	259
4	Fred Archer	1885	246
5	Fred Archer	1884	241
6	Frankie Dettori	1994	233
7	Fred Archer	1883	232
8	Gordon Richards	1952	231
9	Fred Archer	1878	229
10	Gordon Richards	1951	227

Richards rode over 200 winners in a season 12 times, while Archer did so on eight occasions. The only other men to reach double centuries are Tommy Loates (1893), Pat Eddery (1990), Michael Roberts (1992), Frankie Dettori (1995), and Kieren Fallon (1997, 1998, and 1999).

Top 10 Most flat race Jockeys' Championships in the UK

	Jockey	First title	Last title	Total
1	Gordon Richards	1925	1953	26
2	George Fordham	1855	1871	14
3 =	Fred Archer	1874	1886	13
=	Elnathan "Nat" Flatman	1840	1852	13
5 =	Pat Eddery	1974	1996	11
=	Lester Piggott	1960	1982	11
7	Steve Donoghue	1914	1923	10
8	Morny Cannon	1891	1897	6
9 =	Willie Carson	1972	1983	5
=	Doug Smith	1954	1959	5

Apart from Pat Eddery (No. 5=), the best total of other current jockeys is four wins by Kieren Fallon, between 1997 and 2001. Gordon Richards' last jockeys' title was in 1953, the year he eventually won the Derby on Pinza, beating Queen Elizabeth's horse Auriole into second place–shortly after the Queen had knighted him. It was with some irony that Richards' career came to an end the following year after an accident on one of the Queen's horses.

▶ Bill Shoemaker on Ferdinand edges out Chris McCarron on Alysheba to win the 1987 Breeders' Cup Classic.

◀ Britain's top jockey, Gordon Richards, winner of the most races in a career, jockeys' titles, and races in a flat racing season.

Top 10 **Most wins in a season by the annual money leader in the US**

	Jockey	Year	Wins
1	Steve Cauthen	1977	487
2	Bill Shoemaker	1953	485
3	Laffit Pincay, Jr.	1979	420
4	Chris McCarron	1980	405
5	Angel Cordero, Jr.	1982	397
6 =	Laffit Pincay, Jr.	1971	380
=	Bill Shoemaker	1954	380
8	Darrel McHargue	1978	375
9	Jose Santos	1988	370
10	Angel Cordero, Jr.	1983	362

Steve Cauthen rode his first winner just two weeks after his 16th birthday. He was still under 18 when he rode 487 winners in 1977. He won the Triple Crown at 18, and in 1979 moved to England, where he went on to win 10 Classics, including the Derby twice (1985 and 1987).

Top 10 Money-winning North American jockeys*

	Jockey	Prize money ($)
1	Chris McCarron	260,239,073
2	Pat Day	256,418,663
3	Laffit Pincay, Jr.	226,071,563
4	Jerry Bailey	218,820,137
5	Gary Stevens	202,224,804
6	Eddie Delahoussaye	190,427,188
7	Angel Cordero, Jr.	164,561,227
8	Kent Desormeaux	148,784,542
9	Jose Santos	143,494,382
10	Alexis Solis	143,394,762

* Up to and including the 2001 season

Source: NTRA Communications

Chris McCarron has won the Breeders' Cup Classic five times, each of the US Triple Crown races twice, and, in 2000, came close to winning the Epsom Derby when he finished fourth on Best of the Bests.

Top 10 US jockeys with most wins in a career*

	Jockey	Years riding	Wins
1	Laffit Pincay, Jr.	38	9,291
2	Bill Shoemaker	42	8,833
3	Pat Day	29	8,146
4	Russell Baze	28	7,658
5	David Gall	43	7,396
6	Chris McCarron	27	7,089
7	Angel Cordero, Jr.	35	7,057
8	Jorge Velasquez	33	6,795
9	Sandy Hawley	31	6,449
10	Larry Snyder	35	6,388

* As at the end of the 2001 season

Source: NTRA Communications

Laffit Pincay, Jr. was born in Panama in 1946 and rode his first winner in the US in 1966. He overtook Bill Shoemaker's all-time record on December 10, 1999, when, at the age of 52, he rode Irish Nip to victory at Hollywood Park. It was his 8,834th career win.

- Jockeys in the Epsom Derby
- National Hunt jockeys with most wins in a career
- Jockeys in the English Classics in the 1990s
- National Hunt jockeys with most wins in a season
- Jockeys in the English Classics

> The Derby is a national day out for aristocrats and artisans, gypsies and generals, viscounts and villains.
>
> **Tim Nelligan,** CEO of United Racecourses

Top 10 Jockeys in the Epsom Derby

	Jockey	First win	Last win	Total
1	Lester Piggott	1954	1983	9
2 =	Steve Donoghue	1915	1925	6
=	Jem Robinson	1817	1836	6
4 =	Fred Archer	1877	1886	5
=	John Arnull	1784	1799	5
=	Frank Buckle	1792	1823	5
=	Bill Clift	1793	1819	5
8 =	Sam Arnull	1780	1798	4
=	Willie Carson	1979	1994	4
=	Tom Goodison	1809	1822	4
=	Bill Scott	1832	1843	4
=	Charlie Smirke	1934	1958	4
=	Jack Watts	1887	1896	4

The most prestigious of all English Classics, the Derby is run over 1½ miles at Epsom Downs, Surrey, England, during the first week in June and is open to three-year-old colts and fillies.

Top 10 National Hunt jockeys with most wins in a career

	Jockey	Years	Wins
1	Richard Dunwoody	1983–99	1,699
2	Peter Scudamore	1978–95	1,678
3	Tony McCoy	1994–2002*	1,603
4	John Francome	1970–85	1,138
5	Stan Mellor	1952–72	1,035
6	Adrian Maguire	1991–2002*	1,024
7	Peter Niven	1984–2002*	1,002
8	Fred Winter	1939–64	923
9	Graham McCourt	1975–96	921
10	Bob Davies	1966–82	911

* As of end of 2001–02 season

Peter Niven and Adrian Maguire both passed the 1,000-win mark in 2001 and, by coincidence, they are the only two members of the "1,000 club" never to have won the National Hunt Jockey's title.

◀ Richard Dunwoody after winning the 1994 Grand National on the Martin Pipe–trained Minnehoma.

Top 10 Jockeys in the English Classics in the 1990s

	Jockey	1000 Guineas	2000 Guineas	Derby	Oaks	St. Leger	Wins
1 =	Frankie Dettori	1	2	0	2	2	7
=	Pat Eddery	1	1	1	1	3	7
3 =	Kieren Fallon	2	0	1	2	0	5
=	Michael Kinane	0	3	1	1	0	5
5	Willie Carson	2	0	1	1	0	4
6 =	John Reid	1	0	1	0	1	3
=	Walter Swinburn	2	0	1	0	0	3
8 =	George Duffield	0	0	0	1	1	2
=	Richard Hills	1	0	0	0	1	2
=	Michael Roberts	0	1	0	1	0	2

Pat Eddery was the only jockey to ride winners of all five Classics in the 1990s. The only person to train winners of all five Classics in the same period was Saeed bin Suroor. Milan-born Frankie Dettori is one of the most popular men in racing. He was born in 1970 and is the son of the Italian jockey Gianfranco Dettori, who won the English 2,000 Guineas in 1975 and 1976. Frankie followed in his father's footsteps and won the race in 1996 and 1999. The one Classic that still eludes him is the Derby.

Top 10 National Hunt jockeys with most wins in a season*

	Jockey	Years	Wins
1	Tony McCoy	2001–02	289
2	Tony McCoy	1997–98	253
3	Tony McCoy	1999–2000	245
4	Peter Scudamore	1988–89	221
5	Richard Dunwoody	1993–94	197
6	Tony McCoy	2000–01	191
7	Tony McCoy	1996–97	190
8	Tony McCoy	1998–99	186
9 =	Tony McCoy	1995–96	175
=	Peter Scudamore	1991–92	175

* Based on wins by champion jockeys

Tony McCoy rode his first winner at Thurles Racecourse, Tipperary, Ireland on March 26, 1991. He moved to England in 1994, won his first jockeys' title in 1995–96, and has won it every year since.

Top 10 Jockeys in the English Classics

	Jockey	First/last wins	1000 Guineas	2000 Guineas	Derby	Oaks	St. Leger	Wins
1	Lester Piggott	1954–92	2	5	9	6	8	30
2	Frank Buckle	1792–1827	6	5	5	9	2	27
3	Jem Robinson	1817–48	5	9	6	2	2	24
4	Fred Archer	1874–86	2	4	5	4	6	21
5 =	Bill Scott	1821–46	0	3	4	3	9	19
=	Jack Watts	1883–97	4	2	4	4	5	19
7	Willie Carson	1972–94	2	4	4	4	3	17
8 =	John Day	1826–41	5	4	0	5	2	16
=	George Fordham	1859–83	7	3	1	5	0	16
10	Joe Childs	1912–33	2	2	3	4	4	15

◀ Tony McCoy has been the most successful National Hunt jockey for the last seven seasons, and in 2002 he broke the all-time UK record for the most winners in a season.

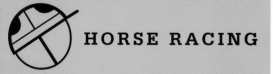

HARNESS RACING

- Money-winning drivers in harness racing
- Most wins by drivers
- Money-winning trotters in harness racing
- Money-winning pacers in harness racing
- Fastest winning heats in the Hambletonian
- Fastest winning heats in the Little Brown Jug

TROTTERS AND PACERS

Harness-racing horses pull a jockey on a two-wheeled "sulky" around an oval track. Unlike thoroughbred racehorses, standardbred harness-racing horses are trained to trot and pace, but do not gallop. A trotter is a horse whose diagonally opposite legs move forward together, while a pacer's legs are extended laterally and with a "swinging motion." Pacers usually travel faster than trotters.

Top 10 Money-winning drivers in harness racing

	Driver	Prize money ($)
1	John Campbell	201,811,667
2	Michel Lachance	139,383,533
3	Bill O'Donnell	94,745,044
4	Herve Filion	85,044,653
5	Jack Moiseyev	84,853,198
6	Cat Manzi	83,789,347
7	Doug Brown	78,587,951
8	Ron Waples	71,304,838
9	Steve Condren	70,433,069
10	Luc Ouellette	69,865,097

Source: US Trotting Association

Born at London, Ontario, in 1955, John Campbell was the first man to go past the $100 million mark in career earnings. He has won the Hambletonian five times, in 1987–88, 1990, 1995, and 1998, and has three times been the Driver of the Year. He had his first winner at the age of 17.

Top 10 Most wins by drivers

	Driver	Wins
1	Herve Filion	14,783
2	Walter Case, Jr.	10,124
3	Cat Manzi	9,236
4	Mike Lachance	9,043
5	Dave Magee	8,940
6	John Campbell	8,824
7	Dave Palone	8,234
8	Jack Moiseyev	8,090
9	Eddie Davis	7,977
10	Bill Parker, Jr.	7,698

Source: US Trotting Association

Herve Filion enjoyed a 37-year career and, with 407 wins in 1968, became the first driver to top 400 in a season. He went on to achieve the same feat—which only a handful of other drivers can claim to have done once—on 14 further occasions. He retired in 1995, at the age of 45.

Top 10 Money-winning trotters in harness racing

	Horse	Prize money ($)
1	Moni Maker	5,589,256
2	Peace Corps	4,137,737
3	Varenne	4,127,151
4	Ourasi	4,010,105
5	Mack Lobell	3,917,594
6	Reve d'Udon	3,611,351
7	Zoogin	3,513,324
8	Sea Cove	3,138,986
9	Ina Scot	2,897,044
10	Magician	2,875,150

Source: US Trotting Association

Moni Maker won six of 14 starts and $72,610 in prize money while only a two-year-old. She retired in 2000 and on February 10, 2002, whilst still only eight years of age, gave birth to her first foal, a bay filly—perhaps another champion trotter in the making.

Top 10 Money-winning pacers in harness racing

	Horse	Prize money ($)
1	Gallo Blue Chip	3,704,111
2	Nihilator	3,225,653
3	Artsplace	3,085,083
4	Presidential Ball	3,021,363
5	Matt's Scooter	2,944,591
6	On the Road Again	2,819,102
7	Riyadh	2,763,527
8	Red Bow Tie	2,625,325
9	Bettor's Delight	2,581,461
10	Beach Towel	2,570,357

Source: US Trotting Association

Gallo Blue Chip won $2.4 million of his career winnings in just one season, 1990. Inevitably, the three-year-old gelding went on to win the Harness Horse of the Year, outpolling Moni Maker by 152 votes to 40. He also won the Pacer of the Year award for 1990.

Top 10 Fastest winning heats in the Hambletonian

	Driver	Horse	Year	Time (min/sec)
1	Mike Lachance	Self Possessed	1999	1:51.6
2	John Campbell	Muscles Yankee	1998	1:52.4
3	Mike Lachance	Continental Victory	1996	1:52.8
4	Ron Pierce	American Winner	1993	1:53.2
5	Trevor Ritchie	Yankee Paco	2000	1:53.4
6	John Campbell	Mack Lobell	1987	1:53.6
7	Stefan Melander	Scarlet Knight	2001	1:53.8
8	John Campbell	Harmonious	1990	1:54.2
9	Mike Lachance	Victory Dream	1994	1:54.3
10 =	John Campbell	Ambro Goal	1988	1:54.6
=	Billy Fahy	Probe	1989	1:54.6*
=	Bill O'Donnell	Prakas	1985	1:54.6
=	Ron Waples	Park Avenue Joe	1989	1:54.6*

* Park Avenue Joe and Probe finished in a dead heat in the race-off and were declared joint winners.

First held in 1926 and won by Nat Ray, the Hambletonian is the season's top race for trotters. It has had several venues since its inauguration, but since 1981 has been held at The Meadowlands, East Rutherford, New Jersey.

Top 10 Fastest winning heats in the Little Brown Jug

	Driver	Horse	Year	Time (min/sec)
1	Mike Lachance	Western Dreamer	1997	1:51.2
2	John Campbell	Nick's Fantasy	1995	1:51.4
3	Mike Lachance	Bettor's Delight	2001	1:51.8
4	John Campbell	Life Sign	1993	1:51.0
5	Bill O'Donnell	Nihilator	1985	1:52.2
6 =	Mike Lachance	B. J. Scoot	1988	1:52.6
=	Mike Lachance	Magical Mike	1994	1:52.6
=	Jack Moiseyev	Armbro Operative	1996	1:52.6
=	Ron Pierce	Shady Character	1998	1:52.6
10	Bill O'Donnell	Barberry Spur	1986	1:52.8

The Little Brown Jug is the most prestigious race for three-year-old pacers. It has been held at the Delaware [Ohio] County Fairgrounds since 1946 and was first won by "Curly" Smart, who drove Ensign Hanover to victory in a time of 2:02.0. The winning horse must win two heats. Those times listed here are the fastest heats of winning horses.

▼ Harness racing at Moonee Valley, Melbourne, Australia.

OTHER SPORTS

At the Start

Human ingenuity has given rise to an infinite variety of sporting activities devised with the purpose of pitting individuals and teams against each other. Some, such as Australian rules football, represent national variations on games played elsewhere, while others are simple innovations—for example, table tennis developed from impromptu indoor games. Many sports, including cycling, Paralympic events, and bobsledding, have developed as new materials and technologies have been applied to established equipment. Yet others, such as darts, have been adapted from a form of self defense—the Pilgrim Fathers are known to have played darts aboard the *Mayflower* on their way to the New World in 1620.

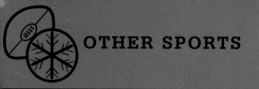
CYCLING

- Most wins in the three major Tours
- Most medals in the World Road Race Championship
- Oldest cycling classic races
- Medal-winning cycling countries at the Olympics
- Countries providing the most winners of the three major Tours

HISTORY REPEATED

The result of the 2001 Tour de France was a repeat of the previous year's race, when Lance Armstrong (US), Jan Ullrich (Germany), and Joseba Beloki (Spain) once again occupied first, second, and third places. The only other time this occurred was in 1978 and 1979, when Bernard Hinault (France), Joop Zoetemelk (Netherlands), and Joaquim Agostinho (Portugal) occupied the first three places in successive years.

Top 10 Most wins in the three major Tours*

	Cyclist/country	Tour	Giro	Vuelta	Years	Total
1	Eddy Merckx, Belguim	5	5	1	1968–74	11
2	Bernard Hinault, France	5	3	2	1978–85	10
3	Jacques Anquetil, France	5	2	1	1957–64	8
4 =	Fausto Coppi, Italy	2	5	0	1940–53	7
=	Miguel Induráin, Spain	5	2	0	1991–95	7
6 =	Gino Bartali, Italy	2	3	0	1938–48	5
=	Alfredo Binda, Italy	0	5	0	1925–33	5
=	Felice Gimondi, Italy	1	3	1	1965–76	5
9	Tony Rominger, Switzerland	0	1	3	1992–95	4
10 =	Lance Armstrong, US	3	0	0	1999–2001	3
=	Louison Bobet, France	3	0	0	1953–55	3
=	Giovanni Brunero, Italy	0	3	0	1921–26	3
=	Pedro Delgado, Spain	1	0	2	1986–89	3
=	Laurent Fignon, France	2	1	0	1983–89	3
=	Charly Gaul, Luxembourg	1	2	0	1956–59	3
=	Greg LeMond, US	3	0	0	1986–90	3
=	Fiorenzo Magni, Italy	0	3	0	1948–55	3
=	Philippe Thys, Belguim	3	0	0	1913–20	3

* The three major tours are: the Tour de France, launched in 1903 and won by Maurice Garin (France); the Tour of Italy (Giro d'Italia), first contested in 1909 and won by Luigi Ganna (Italy); the Tour of Spain (Vuelta de España), first held in 1935 and won by Gustave Deloor (Belgium)

Eddy Merckx won a record 33 stages in the Tour de France in 1969–75.

Top 10 Most medals in the World Road Race Championship*

	Cyclist/country	Years	G	S	B	Total
1 =	Jeannie Longo, France	1981–2001	5	2	1	8
=	Ketie von Oosten Hage, Holland	1966–78	2	3	3	8
3	Yvonne Reynders, Belgium	1959–76	4	2	1	7
4 =	Alfredo Binda, Italy	1927–32	3	0	1	4
=	André Darrigade, France	1957–60	1	1	2	4
=	Anna Konkina, Russia	1967–72	2	0	2	4
=	Greg LeMond, US	1982–89	2	2	0	4
=	Catherine Marsal, France	1989–97	1	2	1	4
=	Rik van Steenbergen, Belgium	1946–57	3	0	1	4
=	Rik van Looy, Belgium	1956–63	2	2	0	4

* Men's and women's

G – gold medals, S – silver medals, B – bronze medals

◀ Lance Armstrong of the US during the Prologue of the Tour De France 2001 in Dunkerque, France.

Top 10 Oldest cycling classic races

	Race	First held
1	Bordeaux–Paris	1891
2	Liège–Bastogne–Liège	1892
3	Paris–Brussels	1893
4	Paris–Roubaix	1896
5	Tour de France	1903
6	Tour of Lombardy	1905
7	Milan–San Remo	1907
8	Giro d'Italia (Tour of Italy)	1909
9	Tour of Flanders	1913
10	Grand Prix des Nations	1932

Regarded as the "Derby of Road Racing," the Bordeaux–Paris race lasted for around 16 hours, starting in darkness in the early hours of the morning. The first race, in 1891, was won by the UK's George Pilkington Mills. Originally for amateurs, it became a professional race and remained so until its last staging in 1989.

Top 10 Medal-winning cycling countries at the Olympics

	Country	G (men)	S (men)	B (men)	G (women)	S (women)	B (women)	Total
1	France	33	10	24	5	4	1	77
2	Italy	31	12	7	4	1	0	55
3	UK	10	22	17	0	0	1	50
4	Germany/West Germany	14	14	15	1	3	2	49
5	US	11	6	13	1	2	3	36
6	Netherlands	9	11	4	4	2	3	33
7 =	Australia	6	9	10	1	3	1	30
=	USSR/Russia	11	5	9	2	1	2	30
9	Belgium	6	7	10	0	0	0	23
10	Denmark	6	4	7	0	0	0	17

G – gold medals, S – silver medals, B – bronze medals

Since riders were not allowed to have assistance from outsiders during the road race in 1932, it is reported that the champion, Attilio Pavesi (Italy), carried with him the following: a bowl of soup, a bottle of water, sandwiches, spaghetti, cinnammon rolls, jam, and two spare tires.

Top 10 Countries providing the most winners of the three major Tours

	Country	Tour	Giro	Vuelta	Total
1	Italy	9	60	4	73
2	France	36	6	9	51
3	Spain	8	2	24	34
4	Belgium	18	7	7	32
5	Switzerland	2	2	5	9
6	US	6	1	0	7
7	Luxembourg	4	2	0	6
8	Netherlands	2	0	2	4
9	Ireland	1	1	1	3
10 =	East Germany	0	0	2	2
=	Germany/West Germany	1	0	1	2
=	Russia	0	2	0	2

▶ Spain's Miguel Induráin, the only man to win the Tour de France five years in succession, 1991–95.

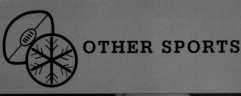
- Olympic medals in men's gymnastics

- Olympic medals in women's gymnastics

- Medal-winning countries in men's events at the Olympics

- Medal-winning countries in women's events at the Olympics

- Most individual World gymnastic titles

MAKING A TRIBUTE

When gymnast Vera Cáslavská returned home to Czechoslovakia from the 1968 Mexico Olympics, she gave her four gold medals away to the four Czech leaders, Dubcek, Svoboda, Cernik, and Smrkorsky, who had been in power at the time of the Soviet invasion in 1967.

GYMNASTICS

Top 10 Olympic medals in men's gymnastics

	Gymnast/country	Years	G	S	B	Total
1	Nikolai Andrianov, USSR	1972–80	7	5	3	15
2 =	Takashi Ono, Japan	1956–64	5	4	4	13
=	Boris Shakhlin, USSR	1956–64	7	4	2	13
4 =	Sawao Kato, Japan	1968–76	8	3	1	12
=	Alexei Nemov, Russia	1996–2000	4	2	6	12
6	Viktor Chukarin, USSR	1952–56	7	3	1	11
7 =	Aleksandr Ditiatin, USSR	1976–80	3	6	1	10
=	Akinori Nakayama, Japan	1968–72	6	2	2	10
=	Vitaly Scherbo, Unified Team/Belarus	1992–96	6	0	4	10
10 =	Eizo Kenmotsu, Japan	1968–76	3	3	3	9
=	Heikki Savolainen, Finland	1928–52	2	1	6	9
=	Yuri Titov, USSR	1956–64	1	5	3	9
=	Mitsuo Tsukahara, Japan	1968–76	5	1	3	9
=	Mikhail Voronin, USSR	1968–72	1	5	3	9

G – gold medals, S – silver medals, B – bronze medals

Aleksandr Ditiatin is the only gymnast to obtain medals in all eight events at one Olympiad, winning three golds, four silvers, and a bronze in Moscow in 1980.

Top 10 Olympic medals in women's gymnastics

	Gymnast/country	Years	G	S	B	Total
1	Larissa Latynina, USSR	1956–64	9	5	4	18
2	Vera Cáslavská, Czechoslovakia	1960–68	7	4	0	11
3 =	Polina Astahkova, USSR	1956–64	5	2	3	10
=	Ágnes Keleti, Hungary	1952–56	5	3	2	10
5 =	Nadia Comaneci, Romania	1976–80	5	3	1	9
=	Lyudmila Tourischeva, USSR	1968–76	4	3	2	9
7 =	Margit Korondi, Hungary	1952–56	2	2	4	8
=	Sofia Muratova, USSR	1956–60	2	2	4	8
9 =	Nelli Kim, USSR	1976–80	5	2	0	7
=	Olga Korbut, USSR	1972–76	4	2	0	7
=	Maria Goroshovskaya, USSR	1952	2	5	0	7
=	Karin Janz, East Germany	1968–72	2	3	2	7
=	Shannon Miller, US	1992–96	2	2	3	7

G – gold medals, S – silver medals, B – bronze medals

With 18 medals, Larissa Latynina holds the record for medals won by any athlete in any sport in Olympic history. Vera Cáslavská (1968) and Daniela Silivas, (Romania, 1988) are the only gymnasts to win medals in all six events at one Olympics.

◀ Vera Cáslavská (Czechoslovakia) in action during the vault competition at the 1968 Olympics in Mexico City. She won the gold medal for the event.

Top 10 Medal-winning countries in men's events at the Olympics

	Country	Gold medals	Silver medals	Bronze medals	Total
1	USSR/Unified Team/Russia	49	45	24	118
2	Japan	27	28	30	85
3	US	22	17	19	58
4	Switzerland	16	19	13	48
5	Germany/West Germany	12	7	11	30
6	Italy	13	7	9	29
7	Finland	8	5	12	25
8	China	9	10	4	23
9	France	4	9	9	22
10	Czechoslovakia	3	7	9	19

Gymnastics was first seen at the inaugural Modern Olympics in 1896 and has been contested at every Games since. Europeans dominated the first two Olympics in Athens in 1896 and Paris in 1900, but the St. Louis Games of 1904 were monopolized by the host country, who won 27 of the 33 gymnastics medals, including a clean sweep in nine of the 11 events. The other six medals were distributed evenly between Austria, Switzerland, and Germany.

Top 10 Medal-winning countries in women's events at the Olympics

	Country	Gold medals	Silver medals	Bronze medals	Total
1	USSR/Unified Team/Russia	42	34	32	108
2	Romania	18	15	19	52
3	Hungary	7	6	10	23
4	East Germany	3	10	7	20
5	US	4	6	9	19
6	Czechoslovakia	9	6	1	16
7	China	3	4	4	11
8	Sweden	1	1	1	3
9 =	Bulgaria	0	1	1	2
=	Germany/West Germany	1	1	0	2
=	Ukraine	1	1	0	2

Women's gymnastics was first seen at the 1928 Amsterdam Games, but for a team competition in combined exercises only—individual events were not introduced until the 1952 Helsinki Games. Rhythmic Gymnastics was introduced in Los Angeles in 1984, and is for women gymnasts only. The leading country is USSR/Unified Team/Russia, which has won nine of the 21 medals contested through to 2000. Aleksandra Tymoshenko (USSR/Unified Team) is the only person to win two Rhythmic Gymnastics medals (one gold and one bronze).

▶ Olga Korbut, the girl who reinvigorated the sport of gymnastics. She became the darling of the crowd at the 1972 Munich Games, and the judges liked her, too—she won two individual gold medals.

Top 10 Most individual World gymnastics titles

	Gymnast/country	Years	Golds
1	Vitaliy Scherbo, Belarus	1993–96	14
2	Larissa Latynina,* USSR	1956–64	12
3 =	Vera Cáslavská,* Czechoslovakia	1962–68	10
=	Boris Shakhlin, USSR	1956–64	10
5 =	Nikolai Andrianov, USSR	1972–80	9
=	Dimitry Bilozerchev, USSR	1983–88	9
=	Akinori Nakayama, Japan	1966–72	9
=	Daniela Silivas,* Romania	1985–89	9
=	Leon Stukelj, Yugoslavia	1922–28	9
10	Joseph Martinez, France	1903–09	7

* Women's champion

The World Championships were first held in Antwerp in 1903. In Olympic years, the Olympic champion is also declared World Champion.

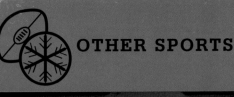
BADMINTON, TABLE TENNIS & SQUASH

- Most All-England badminton singles titles
- Most world table tennis titles
- Most world table tennis team titles
- Most British Open squash titles

Top 10 Most All-England badminton singles titles

	Player/country	Male/female	Years	Wins
1	Rudy Hartono, Indonesia	M	1968–76	8
2	Erland Kops, Denmark	M	1958–67	7
3 =	Frank Devlin, Ireland	M	1925–31	6
=	Judy Hashman (née Devlin), US	F	1961–67	6
5	Ralph Nicholls, England	M	1932–38	5
6 =	Eddy Choong, Malaysia	M	1953–57	4
=	Morten Frost, Denmark	M	1982–87	4
=	Wong Peng Soon, Malaysia	M	1950–55	4
=	Susi Susanti, Indonesia	F	1990–94	4
=	George Thomas, England	M	1920–23	4

First contested in 1899, the All-England Championships were the most prestigious badminton championships in the world prior to the launch of the World Championships in 1977. However, they have still retained their standing as a major event within the sport.

ALL-AROUNDER

Kitty McKane, winner of four All-England badminton titles between 1920 and 1924, was also the women's singles champion at Wimbledon on two occasions, in 1924 and 1926 (as Kitty Godfrey in the latter year).

Top 10 Most world table tennis titles

	Country	Singles	Men's doubles	Women's doubles	Mixed doubles	Total
1	Maria Mednyánszky, Hungary	5	0	7	6	18
2	Viktor Barna, Hungary/England	5	8	0	2	15
3	Angelica Rozeanu, Romania	6	0	3	3	12
4	Anna Sipos, Hungary	2	0	6	3	11
5 =	Gizi Farkas, Hungary	3	0	3	4	10
=	Miklós Szabados, Hungary	1	6	0	3	10
7	Bohumil Vána, Czechoslovakia	2	3	0	3	8
8 =	Ichiro Ogimura, Japan	2	2	0	3	7
=	Ferenc Sidó, Hungary	1	2	0	4	7
10	Deng Yaping, China	3	0	3	0	6

Viktor Barna won five singles titles between 1930 and 1935. He was prevented from making it six in a row by his regular doubles partner Miklós Szabados, who beat Barna in the 1931 final. He captured all three titles at the 1935 Championships in Wembley, England. His singles career was ended shortly afterwards when his playing arm was severely injured in a car crash. He made a comeback, though, and, representing England with Richard Bergmann, won the doubles in 1939.

Top 10 Most World table tennis team titles*

	Country	Swaythling Cup	Corbillon Cup	Total
1	China	13	14	27
2	Japan	7	8	15
3	Hungary	12	0	12
4	Czechoslovakia	6	3	9
5 =	Romania	0	5	5
=	Sweden	5	0	5
7 =	England	1	2	3
=	US	1	2	3
9 =	Germany	0	2	2
=	Korea/South Korea	0	2	2

* For the Swaythling Cup (men) and Corbillon Cup (women)

The Swaythling Cup was first contested in 1926 and is the men's team trophy at the World Championships, which is held every two years. It was donated by Lady Swaythling, the mother of Ivor Montagu, the first president of the International Table Tennis Federation. The Corbillon Cup is the ladies' equivalent of the Swaythling Cup and was presented in 1934 by Marcel Corbillon, president of the French Table Tennis Association.

Top 10 Most British Open squash titles

	Player/country	Male/female	Years	Wins
1	Heather McKay (née Blundell), Australia	F	1962–77	16
2 =	Jahangir Khan, Pakistan	M	1982–91	10
=	Janet Morgan, UK	F	1950–59	10
4 =	Susan Devoy, New Zealand	F	1984–92	8
=	Geoff Hunt, Australia	M	1969–81	8
6	Hashim Khan, Pakistan	M	1951–58	7
7 =	Jonah Barrington, UK	M	1967–73	6
=	Abdelfattah Amr Bey, Egypt	M	1933–38	6
=	Jansher Khan, Pakistan	M	1992–97	6
=	Michelle Martin, Australia	F	1993–98	6

Until the launch of the World Amateur Championships in 1967, the British Open was regarded as the unofficial World Championship. It was first held for women at Queen's Club in 1922, and for men in 1930, when C. R. Read was designated as "champion," though in the first match for the championship, also at Queen's Club, in 1931, he was beaten by Don Butcher.

▶ Pakistan's Jahangir Khan was the British Open winner ten times, and won the World Open title six times.

WEIGHT LIFTING, WRESTLING & JUDO

- ● Olympic medal-winning countries in weight lifting
- ● Countries setting the most world weight lifting records
- ● Olympic medal-winning countries in freestyle wrestling
- ● Olympic medal-winning countries in men's judo
- ● Olympic medal-winning countries in women's judo

A STARRING ROLE

The silver medalist in the 82.5 kg class (now light heavyweight) weightlifting competition at the 1948 London Olympics was Harold Sakata of the United States, who played the part of Oddjob in the James Bond movie, *Goldfinger*. He was also a one-time professional wrestler, using the name Tosh Togo.

Top 10 Olympic medal-winning countries in weight lifting

	Country	Gold medals	Silver medals	Bronze medals	Total
1	USSR/Unified Team/Russia	46	26	5	77
2	US	15	16	10	41
3	Bulgaria	11	16	7	34
4	Germany/West Germany	7	9	14	30
5	Poland	4	4	19	27
6	China	7	7	8	22
7	Hungary	2	7	10	19
8 =	France	9	2	4	15
=	Greece	7	5	3	15
=	Italy	5	5	5	15

Weight lifting made its debut in the first modern Olympics in 1896. It appeared again in 1904, and also at the Intercalated Games of 1906, but it has not been a regular sport since 1920. Women's weight lifting was added in Sydney in 2000, when China won four of the seven gold medals.

Top 10 Countries setting the most world weight lifting records*

	Country	Men	Women	Total
1	USSR/Russia	648	9	657
2	China	42	445	487
3	Bulgaria	226	26	252
4	US	60	7	67
5 =	France	51	0	51
=	Turkey	44	7	51
7	Poland	33	13	46
8	Germany/West Germany	44	0	44
9	Egypt	40	0	40
10	Japan	38	0	38

* Senior men's and women's world records only

Source: International Weightlifting Federation (IWF)

G – gold medals, S – silver medals, B – bronze medals

Vassily Alexeev (USSR) is one of the most prolific world record holders in any sport. Between January 20, 1970 and November 1, 1977, he set 80 world records. Weighing 327 lb (148 kg), he would have a 36-egg omelet for breakfast and half a dozen steaks for lunch.

Top 10 Olympic medal-winning countries in freestyle wrestling

	Country	G	S	B	Total
1	US	45	34	24	103
2	USSR/Unified Team/Russia	38	19	15	72
3	Turkey	16	11	7	34
4	Japan	16	9	8	33
5	Bulgaria	7	16	9	32
6 =	Sweden	8	10	8	26
=	Iran	5	9	12	26
8	Finland	8	7	10	25
9	South Korea/Korea	4	8	7	19
10	UK	3	4	10	17

G – gold medals, S – silver medals, B – bronze medals

Freestyle wrestling was first seen at the 1904 St. Louis Games and has been featured ever since, with the exception of 1912. Wilfred Dietrich (West Germany) is the only man to have won five Olympic wrestling medals (all freestyle). He won one gold (1960), two silvers (1956, 1960), and two bronzes (1964, 1968).

▶ Vassily Alexeev (Russia) on his way to winning the Super Heavyweight gold medal at the 1976 Montreal Olympics with a total lift of 1,411 lb (640 kg)—66 lb (30 kg) more than the silver medalist.

> I know exactly where I am going, I have a will to win, and I have the ability to keep up an incomparably more intensive training program.
>
> **Vassily Alexeev**

Top 10 Olympic medal-winning countries in men's judo

	Country	Gold medals	Silver medals	Bronze medals	Total
1	Japan	21	6	8	35
2	USSR/Unified Team/Russia	7	5	16	28
3	France	6	4	14	24
4	South Korea/Korea	5	9	8	22
5	Germany/West Germany	2	5	9	16
6	UK	0	5	7	12
7	Brazil	2	3	5	10
8	East Germany	1	2	6	9
9 =	Netherlands	4	0	4	8
=	US	0	3	5	8

Judo was first contested at the Tokyo Olympics in 1964. It was not included in 1968, but returned in 1972, and has been contested ever since.

The UK has always done well at judo, despite not having won an Olympic gold medal. Neil Adams won consecutive silver medals in 1980 and 1984. He was on course to win the UK's first judo gold in 1984, but with just three minutes to go in the final against Frank Wieneke of Germany, Adams glanced at the clock in the hall. Noticing his distraction, his opponent pounced and Adams was on the mat. He lost by an ippon for the first time in his career, and the gold medal slipped away.

Top 10 Olympic medal-winning countries in women's judo

	Country	Gold medals	Silver medals	Bronze medals	Total
1 =	Cuba	4	4	5	13
=	Japan	2	6	5	13
3	China	4	1	4	9
4 =	France	4	1	3	8
=	South Korea/Korea	2	2	4	8
6	Belgium	1	1	4	6
7	Spain	3	0	2	5
8 =	UK	0	2	2	4
=	Italy	0	1	3	4
10	Netherlands	0	0	3	3

Women's judo was first included as a demonstration sport at the 1988 Seoul Olympic Games, and became a full medal sport four years later.

Two of Spain's three gold medals came on home soil at the 1992 Barcelona Olympic Games. The judges were popular with the home crowd, particularly after the half-lightweight semifinal between local favorite Almundena Muñoz Martinez and tournament favorite Sharon Rendle of the UK. The referee awarded the contest to Rendle, but the judges overruled and gave the match to the Spanish competitor, who went on to win the gold medal by beating Japan's Noriko Mizoguchi.

ARCHERY, FENCING & SHOOTING

- Most men's world archery titles
- Olympic medal-winning countries in archery
- Men's individual Olympic shooting medal winners
- Individual Olympic fencing medal winners

LONG OLYMPIC CAREER

Danish fencer Ivan Osiier appeared in the Olympics before World War I and after World War II. He made his debut at London in 1908 and bowed out, also in the London Games, 40 years later. His medal haul consisted of just one silver, in 1912.

Top 10 Most men's world archery titles

	Archer/country	Gold medals	Silver medals	Bronze medals	Total
1	Richard McKinney, US	8	4	2	14
2	Einar Tang-Holbek, Denmark	3	7	3	13
3	Darrell Pace, US	7	4	0	11
4	Hans Deutgen, Sweden	5	3	1	9
5	Georges De Rons, Belgium	2	5	1	8
6	Oscar Kessels, Belgium	1	3	3	7
7 =	Frantisek Hadas, Czechoslavakia	3	2	1	6
=	Emil Heilborn, Sweden	2	2	2	6
=	Henry Kjellson, Sweden	2	0	4	6
=	Kyosti Laasonen, Finland	1	4	1	6
=	Joe Thornton, US	4	2	0	6

Source: FITA

Three of Richard McKinney's gold medals came in the individual event, and the others were as part of the US team, which dominated the team prize every year from 1959 to 1983. McKinney was in five of their winning lineups. His individual titles were in 1977, 1983, and 1985, the first two being with Championship-best scores. McKinney never won an Olympic gold medal.

Top 10 Olympic medal-winning countries in archery

	Archer/country	Gold medals	Silver medals	Bronze medals	Total
1	US	14	9	8	31
2	France	7	9	6	22
3	Korea/South Korea	11	6	4	21
4	Belgium	10	7	2	19
5	USSR/Unified Team	1	3	5	9
6	UK	2	2	4	8
7 =	China	0	3	0	4
=	Finland	1	1	2	4
=	Italy	0	1	3	4
10 =	Germany	0	1	1	2
=	Japan	0	1	1	2
=	Poland	0	1	1	2
=	Sweden	0	2	0	2
=	Ukraine	0	1	1	2

▶ The women's individual silver medal winner, Soo-Nyung Kim of Korea, in action during the 2000 Sydney Olympics.

> It is the very difficulty of hitting that round target with its bright and open countenance that makes archery so engrossing.
>
> **Alice B. Leigh,** on Ladies' Archery, 1894

Top 10 Men's individual Olympic shooting medal winners

	Competitor/country	Gold medals	Silver medals	Bronze medals	Total
1	Carl Osburn, US	5	4	2	11
2	Alfred Swahn, Sweden	3	3	3	9
3 =	Vilhelm Carlberg, Sweden	3	4	1	8
=	Otto Olsen, Norway	4	3	1	8
5 =	Willis Lee, US	5	1	1	7
=	Einar Liberg, Sweden	4	2	1	7
=	Léon Moreaux, France	2	2	3	7
8 =	Oscar Gomer Swahn, Sweden	3	1	2	6
=	Albert Helgerud, Norway	2	4	0	6
=	Johann Hübner von Holst, Sweden	2	3	1	6
=	Alfred Lane, US	5	0	1	6
=	Maurice Lecoq, France	1	1	4	6
=	Ole Lillö-Olsen, Norway	5	1	0	6
=	Harald Natvig, Norway	3	2	1	6
=	Louis Richardet, Switzerland	5	1	0	6

Alfred Lane won one of his gold medals in the Military Revolver Team event at the 1920 Antwerp Games. One of his teammates was veterinary professor James Howard Snook, who achieved notoriety when, in 1929, he was arrested for murdering his mistress, Theora Hix, by beating her to death with a hammer. On 28 February 1930, Snook went to his death in the Ohio Penitentiary electric chair.

Top 10 Individual Olympic fencing medal winners

	Competitor/country	Gold medals	Silver medals	Bronze medals	Total
1	Edoardo Mangiarotti, Italy	6	5	2	13
2	Aladár Gerevich, Hungary	7	1	2	10
3	Giulio Gaudini, Italy	3	4	2	9
4 =	Philippe Cattiau, France	3	4	1	8
=	Roger Ducret, France	3	4	1	8
6 =	Pál Kovács, Hungary	6	0	1	7
=	Gustavo Marzi, Italy	2	5	0	7
=	Ildikó Ságiné–Rejtö (née Uljaki–Rejtö),* Hungary	2	3	2	7
9 =	Elena Belova-Novikova,* Belarus	4	1	1	6
=	Georges Buchard, France	2	3	1	6
=	Giuseppe Delfino, Italy	4	2	0	6
=	Christian d'Oriola, France	4	2	0	6
=	Lucien Gaudin, France	4	2	0	6
=	Rudolf Kárpáti, Hungary	6	0	0	6
=	Gyözö Kulcsár, Hungary	4	0	2	6
=	Nedo Nadi, Italy	6	0	0	6
=	Vladimir Nazlymow, Russia	3	2	1	6
=	Daniel Revenu, France	1	0	5	6
=	Philippe Riboud, France	2	2	2	6
=	Viktor Sidiak, Belarus	4	1	1	6
=	Giovanna Trillini,* Italy	4	0	2	6

*Women competitors

Fernand de Montigny (Belgium) won five fencing medals; he also won a bronze as a member of the Belgian field hockey team in 1920.

OTHER SPORTS

- World Cup countries
- Goal-scorers in the final stages of the World Cup
- Players who have appeared in most World Cup tournaments
- Most-capped international players
- Countries in the Copa America

WEALTHIEST TEAMS

While five of the ten wealthiest soccer clubs in the world are from Italy, not one Italian club ranks in the top three. Those places are filled by Manchester United (England), Real Madrid (Spain), and Bayern Munich (Germany).

SOCCER

Top 10 World Cup countries*

	Country	Tournaments won	Played	Won	Drawn	Lost	For	Against	Points
1	Brazil	4	80	53	14	13	173	78	120
2	Germany#	3	78	45	17	16	162	103	107
3	Italy	3	66	38	16	12	105	62	92
4	Argentina	2	57	29	10	18	100	69	68
5	England	1	45	20	13	12	62	42	53
6	France	1	41	21	6	14	86	58	48
7	Spain	0	40	16	10	14	61	48	42
8	Yugoslavia	0	37	16	8	13	60	46	40
9	Uruguay	2	37	15	8	14	61	52	38
10 =	Netherlands	0	32	14	9	9	56	36	37
=	Sweden	0	38	14	9	15	66	60	37

* Based on two points for a win and one point for a draw; matches resolved on penalties are classed as a draw

\# Including West Germany

Brazil appeared in their first final in 1950 but lost to Uruguay on home soil. Their first triumph was in Sweden in 1958, when the world witnessed the emergence of the great Pelé.

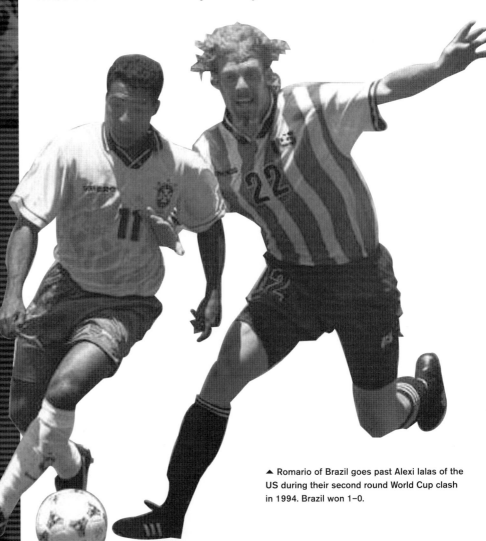

▲ Romario of Brazil goes past Alexi Ialas of the US during their second round World Cup clash in 1994. Brazil won 1–0.

DID YOU KNOW? Brazil is the only country to have appeared in the final stages of every World Cup since its launch in 1930.

Top 10 Goal-scorers in the final stages of the World Cup

	Player/country	Years	Goals
1	Gerd Müller, West Germany	1970–74	14
2	Just Fontaine, France	1958	13
3	Pelé, Brazil	1958–70	12
4 =	Jürgen Klinsman, Germany	1990–98	11
=	Sandor Kocsis, Hungary	1954	11
6 =	Teófilio Cubillas, Peru	1970–78	10
=	Grzegorz Lato, Poland	1974–82	10
=	Gary Lineker, England	1986–90	10
=	Helmut Rahn, West Germany	1954–58	10
10 =	Ademir, Brazil	1950	9
=	Roberto Baggio, Italy	1990–98	9
=	Gabriel Batistuta, Argentina	1994–98	9
=	Eusébio, Portugal	1966	9
=	Jairzinho, Brazil	1970–74	9
=	Paolo Rossi, Italy	1978–82	9
=	Karl-Heinz Rummenigge, West Germany	1978–86	9
=	Uwe Seeler, West Germany	1958–70	9
=	Leónidas da Silva, Brazil	1934–38	9
=	Vavà, Brazil	1958–62	9

Top 10 Players who have appeared in the most World Cup tournaments

	Player	Country	Years	Tournaments
1 =	Lothar Matthäus	West Germany/Germany	1982–98	5
=	Antonio Carbajal	Mexico	1950–66	5
3 =	Giuseppe Bergomi	Italy	1982–98	4
=	Frankie van der Elst	Belgium	1986–98	4
=	Diego Maradona	Argentina	1982–94	4
=	Pelé	Brazil	1958–70	4
=	Gianni Rivera	Italy	1962–74	4
=	Pedro Rocha	Uruguay	1962–74	4
=	Djalma Santos	Brazil	1954–66	4
=	Karl-Heinz Schnellinger	West Germany	1958–70	4
=	Enzo Scifo	Belgium	1986–98	4
=	Uwe Seeler	Germany	1958–70	4
=	Wladislaw Zmuda	Poland	1974–86	4
=	Andoni Zubizarreta	Spain	1986–98	4

Mexican goalkeeper Antonio Carbajal was the only man to appear in five World Cup tournaments until his record was equaled by Lothar Matthäus in 1998. In comparison to his German counterpart, Carbajal came nowhere near matching the achievements of Matthäus. He made his debut in a 4–0 defeat by Brazil in 1950 and bowed out in a goalless draw against Uruguay in London in 1966. He never progressed beyond the first stage and was only once on a winning team, against Czechoslovakia in 1962.

Top 10 Most-capped international players*

	Player	Country	Years	Caps
1	Claudio Suárez	Mexico	1992–2002	170
2 =	Mohamed Al-Deayea	Saudi Arabia	1990–2002	162
=	Hossam Hassan	Egypt	1985–2002	160
4 =	Cobi Jones	USA	1992–2002	153
=	Lothar Matthäus	West Germany/Germany	1980–2000	150
6 =	Mohammed Al-Khilaiwi	Saudi Arabia	1992–2001	143
=	Thomas Ravelli	Sweden	1981–97	143
8	Majed Abdullah	Saudi Arabia	1978–94	140
9	Peter Schmeichel	Denmark	1987–2001	129
10 =	Marcelo Balboa	USA	1988–2000	128
=	Jorge Campos	Mexico	1991–2002	128

* As of April 23, 2002

The first man to make 100 international appearances was England's Billy Wright, who played his 100th game against Scotland in London in 1959.

Top 10 Countries in the Copa America*

	Country	Tournaments won	P	W	D	L	F	A	Pts
1	Argentina	14	161	102	30	29	390	154	234
2	Uruguay	14	172	98	26	48	364	189	222
3	Brazil	6	155	88	27	40	359	179	203
4	Paraguay	2	145	57	29	59	228	257	143
5	Chile	0	154	53	24	77	241	276	139
6	Peru	2	124	44	28	52	181	206	116
7	Colombia	1	90	32	19	39	110	159	83
8	Bolivia	1	96	19	20	57	90	248	58
9	Ecuador	0	102	14	19	69	108	280	47
10	Mexico	0	28	11	8	9	37	32	30

* Based on two points for a win and one point for a draw in all matches played in the final stages

The first South American Championship was staged in 1916 and is now held every two years. The only other countries to have competed are Costa Rica, Honduras, Japan, Venezuela, and the United States.

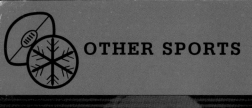

OTHER SPORTS

SKIING

- Men's alpine skiing World Cup titles

- Women's alpine skiing World Cup titles

- Medal-winning countries in men's alpine events at the Olympics

- Medal-winning countries in women's alpine events at the Olympics

> I'm not there to hear the crowd yelling or to achieve glory or to earn money. I'm there to ski a perfect race.
>
> Jean-Claude Killy

Top 10 Men's alpine skiing World Cup titles

	Skiier/country	O	D	GS	SG	S	C	Total
1	Ingemar Stenmark, Sweden	3	0	8	0	8	0	19
2 =	Marc Girardelli, Luxembourg	5	2	1	0	3	4	15
=	Pirmin Zurbriggen, Switzerland	4	2	3	4	0	2	15
4	Hermann Maier, Austria	3	2	3	4	0	0	12
5 =	Phil Mahre, US	3	0	2	0	1	3	9
=	Alberto Tomba, Italy	1	0	4	0	4	0	9
7	Gustavo Thoeni, Italy	4	0	2	0	2	0	8
8	Kjetil Andre Aamodt, Norway	1	0	1	1	1	3	7
9	Jean-Claude Killy, France	2	1	2	0	1	0	6
10 =	Luc Alphand, France	1	3	0	1	0	0	5
=	Franz Klammer, Austria	0	5	0	0	0	0	5
=	Karl Schranz, Austria	2	2	1	0	0	0	5
=	Andreas Wenzel, Liechtenstein	1	0	0	0	0	4	5

O – Overall; D – Downhill; GS – Giant Slalom; SG – Super-G; S – Slalom; C – Combined

The World Cup was launched in the 1966–67 season. It is a winter-long series of races, with champions being declared in five categories in addition to an overall champion.

Top 10 Women's alpine skiing World Cup titles

	Skiier/country	O	D	GS	SG	S	C	Total
1	Annemarie Moser-Pröll, Austria	6	7	3	0	0	1	17
2	Vreni Schneider, Switzerland	3	0	5	0	6	0	14
3	Katja Seizinger, Germany	2	4	0	5	0	0	11
4	Erika Hess, Switzerland	2	0	1	0	5	1	9
5 =	Michela Figini, Switzerland	2	4	1	1	0	0	8
=	Hanni Wenzel, Liechtenstein	2	0	2	0	1	3	8
7	Maria Walliser, Switzerland	2	2	1	1	0	1	7
8 =	Renate Goetschl, Austria	1	2	0	1	0	2	6
=	Carole Merle, France	0	0	2	4	0	0	6
=	Lisa-Marie Morerord, Switzerland	1	0	3	0	2	0	6
=	Anita Wachter, Austria	1	0	2	0	0	3	6

O – Overall; D – Downhill; GS – Giant Slalom; SG – Super-G; S – Slalom; C – Combined

Annemarie Moser-Pröll won her seven downhill titles within a period of nine years (1971–79), including five in succession between 1971 and 1975. She won 62 World Cup races in her career. Her best season was in 1975, when she won the Downhill, Giant Slalom, and Overall titles.

▶ The greatest female slalom skier of all time, Vreni Schneider of Switzerland.

◀ Champion skier Ingemar Stenmark of Sweden. Stenmark has won a record 19 World Cup titles.

Top 10 Medal-winning countries in men's alpine events at the Olympics

	Country	Gold medals	Silver medals	Bronze medals	Total
1	Austria	17	15	20	52
2	Switzerland	6	11	9	26
3	France	19	5	7	22
4	Norway	7	7	6	20
5	Italy	7	5	2	14
6	US	3	5	2	11
7	Germany/West Germany	3	3	1	7
8	Sweden	2	0	3	5
9	Liechtenstein	0	1	3	4
10 =	Canada	0	0	2	2
=	Luxembourg	0	2	0	2

Austria has produced some great champions over the years, including Toni Sailer, who won three golds at the 1956 Olympics, but none can match the renown of Franz Klammer. He may have won only one Olympic gold medal, in the downhill on home soil in Innsbruck in 1976, but such was the popularity of Klammer that when he was left out of the team in 1980, the Austrian coach had to appear on national television and publicly explain to the people of Austria his reasons for excluding their hero from the team.

Top 10 Medal-winning countries in women's alpine events at the Olympics

	Country	Gold medals	Silver medals	Bronze medals	Total
1	Austria	9	14	11	34
2	Germany/West Germany	10	9	8	27
3	Switzerland	10	7	7	24
4	US	7	9	3	19
5	France	4	8	6	18
6	Italy	5	3	5	13
7	Canada	4	1	3	8
8 =	Liechtenstein	2	1	2	5
=	Sweden	2	2	1	5
10	Croatia	3	1	0	4

Two of Austria's gold medals were won by Petra Kronberger in 1992. She first won the Alpine Combined after coming from behind with a strong second run in the slalom section. She followed that victory with another gold, in the Slalom event, again having to come from behind after finishing third after the first run, to capture first place.

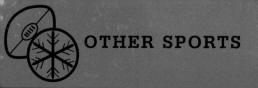
SKATING & BOBSLEDDING

- Olympic figure skating medal winners
- Most World figure skating titles
- Olympic speed skating medal winners
- Olympic bobsled medal-winning countries

MULTITALENTED

Three members of the US gold-medal four-man bob team at the 1932 Winter Olympics each had a small claim to fame: Billy Fiske was the first American to join the British Royal Air Force, in 1939; Edward Eagan became the first and only man to win gold medals at both Summer and Winter Olympics—he was the light heavyweight boxing champion in 1920; and Clifford "Tippy" Gray wrote over 3,000 songs, including "If You Were the Only Girl in the World."

Top 10 Olympic figure skating medal winners*

	Skater/country	Male/female	Years	Gold	Silver	Bronze	Total
1	Gillis Grafström, Sweden	M	1920–32	3	1	0	4
2 =	Andrée Brunet (née Joly), France	F	1924–32	2	0	1	3
=	Pierre Brunet, France	M	1924–32	2	0	1	3
=	Artur Dmitriev, USSR/Russia	M	1992–98	2	1	0	3
=	Sonja Henie, Norway	F	1928–36	3	0	0	3
=	Irina Rodnina, USSR	F	1972–80	3	0	0	3
7 =	Lyudmila Belousova, USSR	F	1964–68	2	0	0	2
=	Dick Button, US	M	1948–52	2	0	0	2
=	Yekaterina Gordeyeva, USSR/Russia	F	1988–94	2	0	0	2
=	Sergei Grinkov, USSR/Russia	M	1988–94	2	0	0	2
=	Oksana Grishuk, Russia	F	1994–98	2	0	0	2
=	Yevgeny Platov, Russia	M	1994–98	2	0	0	2
=	Oleg Protopopov, USSR	M	1964–68	2	0	0	2
=	Karl Schäfer, Austria	M	1932–36	2	0	0	2
=	Katarina Witt, East Germany	F	1984–88	2	0	0	2
=	Aleksandr Zaitsev, USSR	M	1976–80	2	0	0	2

* Minimum qualification: 2 gold medals

Top 10 Most World figure skating titles

	Skater/country	Men	Women	Pairs	Dance	Total
1 =	Sonja Henie, Norway	0	10	0	0	10
=	Irina Rodnina, USSR	0	0	10	0	10
=	Ulrich Salchow, Sweden	10	0	0	0	10
4 =	Herma Planck (née Szabo), Austria	0	5	2	0	7
=	Karl Schäfer, Austria	7	0	0	0	7
6 =	Aleksandr Gorshkov, USSR	0	0	6	0	6
=	Lyudmila Pakhomova, USSR	0	0	0	6	6
=	Aleksandr Zaitsev, USSR	0	0	6	0	6
9 =	Dick Button, US	5	0	0	0	5
=	Lawrence Demmy, UK	0	0	0	5	5
=	Carol Heiss, US	0	5	0	0	5
=	Jean Westwood, UK	0	0	0	5	5

> Tony Nash did not win because I gave him a bolt. Tony Nash won because he was the best driver.
>
> **Eugenio Monti,** Italian bobsled driver, after sportingly donating a bolt to the British driver

Top 10 Olympic speed skating medal winners

	Skater/country	Male/female	Gold	Silver	Bronze	Total
1 =	Karin Kania (née Enke), East Germany	F	3	4	1	8
=	Gunda Niemann-Stirnemann (formerly Niemann-Kleeman), Germany	F	3	4	1	8
3 =	Ivar Ballangrud, Norway	M	4	2	1	7
=	Andrea Ehrig (née Mitscherlich, formerly Schöne), East Germany	F	1	5	1	7
=	Claudia Pechstein, Germany	F	4	1	2	7
=	Clas Thunberg, Finland	M	5	1	1	7
7 =	Bonnie Blair, US	F	5	0	1	6
=	Roald Larsen, Norway	M	0	2	4	6
=	Lydia Skoblikova, USSR	F	6	0	0	6
10 =	Marc Gagnon, Canada	M	3	0	2	5
=	Yevgeny Grischin, USSR	M	4	1	0	5
=	Eric Heiden, US	M	5	0	0	5
=	Knut Johannesen, Norway	M	2	2	1	5
=	Johann-Olaf Koss, Norway	M	4	1	0	5
=	Chung Lee Kyung, Korea	F	4	0	1	5
=	Rintje Risma, Netherlands	M	0	2	3	5
=	Christa Rothenberger-Luding, East Germany	F	2	2	1	5

Eric Heiden's five gold medals all came at Lake Placid in 1980 and, because of the United States boycott of the Moscow Summer Games, he can claim to be the only individual US Olympic champion of 1980. In addition to his Olympic golds, Heiden won seven World Championship gold medals and one silver. After ending his skating career, he turned to cycling and entered the 1986 Tour de France.

Top 10 Olympic bobsled medal-winning countries

	Country	G	S	B	Total
1	Switzerland	9	10	9	28
2	Germany/ West Germany	7	9	7	23
3	US	6	4	6	16
4	East Germany	5	4	3	12
5	Italy	4	4	3	11
6	UK	1	1	2	4
7 =	Austria	1	2	0	3
=	USSR	2	0	1	3
9 =	Belgium	0	1	1	2
=	Canada	2	0	0	2

G – gold medals, S – silver medals, B – bronze medals

The four-man event made its debut at the 1924 Games. The two-man bobsled event was introduced at the 1932 Olympics, and has been held at every Games since then, with the exception of 1960—there was no bob run at Squaw Valley. The two-woman bobsled event was held for the first time at the 2002 Olympics, and was won by the United States.

▶ The veteran Wolfgang Hoppe leading the Germany I four-man bobsled team during the 1987 World Championships in St. Moritz, Switzerland.

BOWLING, TRIATHLON, FIELD HOCKEY, HURLING, GAELIC FOOTBALL & HANDBALL

- First PBA bowlers to roll a perfect 300 game on national television
- Fastest Hawaii Ironmans
- Olympic medal-winning countries in field hockey
- Hurling teams
- Gaelic football teams
- World Championship medal-winning countries in handball

The 10 First PBA bowlers to roll a perfect 300 game on national television

	Bowler	Opponent (score)	Venue	Year
1	Jack Biondolillo	Les Schissler (216)	Akron, Ohio	1967
2	John Guenther	Don Johnson (189)	San Jose, California	1969
3	Jim Stefanich	Glenn Carlson (243)	Alameda, California	1974
4	Pete McCordic	Wayne Webb (249)	Torrance, California	1987
5	Bob Benoit	Mark Roth (255)	Grand Prairie, Texas	1988
6	Mike Aulby	David Ozio (279)	Wichita, Kansas	1993
7	Johnny Petraglia	Walter Ray Williams, Jnr. (179)	Toledo, Ohio	1994
8	Butch Soper	Bob Benoit (236)	Reno, Nevada	1994
9	C. K. Moore	Parker Bohn III (192)	Austin, Texas	1996
10	Bob Learn, Jr.	Johnny Petraglia (279)	Erie, Pennsylvania	1996

Source: PBA (Professional Bowlers' Association)

▼ John Teahy of Tipperary (right) and Pat Dwyer of Kilkenny in the 1991 All-Ireland Hurling final at Croke Park. "Tipp" won 1–16 to 0–15 as they overtook Kilkenny to become the then second most successful team behind Cork.

LUCKY ENTRY

The United Kingdom won a surprise field hockey bronze medal at the 1984 Los Angeles Olympics by beating one of the pretournament favorites, Australia, in their playoff match. The United Kingdom qualified for the Games only as a result of the Soviet boycott.

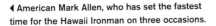

◀ American Mark Allen, who has set the fastest time for the Hawaii Ironman on three occasions.

Top 10 Fastest Hawaii Ironmans

	Triathlete/country	Year	Time (hr:min:sec)
1	Luc Van Lierde, Belgium	1996	8:04:08
2	Mark Allen, US	1993	8:07:45
3	Mark Allen, US	1992	8:09:08
4	Mark Allen, US	1989	8:09:15
5	Luc Van Lierde, Belgium	1999	8:17:17
6	Mark Allen, US	1991	8:18:32
7	Greg J. Welch, Australia	1994	8:20:27
8	Mark Allen, US	1995	8:20:34
9	Peter Reid, Canada	2000	8:21:01
10	Peter Reid, Canada	1998	8:24:20

The most famous of all triathlons, the Hawaii Ironman was first held at Waikiki Beach, Hawaii, in 1978, but has been held at Kailua-Kona since 1981. The competitors have to complete, or attempt to complete, a 2.4-mile (3.86-km) swim, a 112-mile (180-km) cycle race, and a full marathon of 26 miles 385 yards. The fastest time for women is 8:55:28, by Paula Newby-Fraser of Zimbabwe, in 1992.

Top 10 Olympic medal-winning countries in field hockey*

	Country	G (men)	S (men)	B (men)	G (women)	S (women)	B (women)	Total
1 =	India	8	1	2	0	0	0	11
=	Netherlands	2	2	3	1	0	3	11
3 =	Australia	0	3	3	3	0	0	9
=	Germany/West Germany	2	3	2	0	2	0	9
5 =	UK	3	1	3	0	0	1	8
=	Pakistan	3	3	2	0	0	0	8
7	Spain	0	2	1	1	0	0	4
8	South Korea	0	1	0	0	2	0	3
9 =	US	0	0	1	0	0	1	2
=	USSR	0	0	1	0	0	1	2

G – gold medals, S – silver medals, B – bronze medals

* Based on total medals won in the men's and women's events

Hockey made its Olympic debut in London in 1908, but was not seen again until 1920. The women's competition was introduced in 1980.

Between 1928 and 1960, India played 30 consecutive hockey matches in the Olympic Games without losing or drawing. In that time, they scored 197 goals and conceded just eight. Their run came to an end in the 1960 final, when they were beaten 1–0 by Pakistan, also ending their sequence of six consecutive titles. They regained the title four years later but had to wait until 1980 for their record eighth, and last, Olympic title.

Top 10 Hurling teams*

	Team	Years	Wins
1	Cork	1890-1999	28
2	Kilkenny	1904-2000	26
3	Tipperary	1887-2001	25
4	Limerick	1897-1973	7
5 =	Dublin	1889-1938	6
=	Wexford	1910-96	6
7 =	Galway	1923-88	4
=	Offaly	1981-98	4
9	Clare	1914-97	3
10	Waterford	1948-59	2

* Based on wins in the All-Ireland Final

Source: Gaelic Athletic Association

The All-Ireland Hurling final is played at Croke Park, Dublin, on the first Sunday in September each year. It was first contested in 1887, and won by Tipperary. The winners play for the McCarthy Cup.

Top 10 Gaelic football teams*

	Team	Years	Wins
1	Kerry	1903-2000	32
2	Dublin	1891-1995	22
3	Galway	1925-2001	9
4	Meath	1949-99	7
5	Cork	1890-1990	6
6 =	Cavan	1933-52	5
=	Down	1960-94	5
=	Wexford	1893-1918	5
9 =	Kildare	1905-28	4
=	Tipperary	1889-1920	4

* Based on wins in the All-Ireland Final

Source: Gaelic Athletic Association

The All-Ireland Gaelic Football Final is played at Croke Park, Dublin on the third Sunday in September each year. It was first contested in 1887, when it was won by Limerick. The finalists play for the Sam Maguire Cup.

Top 10 World Championship medal-winning countries in handball*

	Country	G	S	B	Total
1 =	USSR/Russia	7	5	1	13
=	Yugoslavia	2	4	7	13
3	Sweden	4	3	4	11
4 =	Czechoslovakia	2	3	3	8
=	East Germany	3	2	3	8
=	Hungary	1	4	3	8
=	Romania	5	1	2	8
8	Germany/ West Germany	3	1	3	7
9 =	Denmark	1	3	1	5
=	France	2	2	1	5

* Based on medals won in the World Championships

G – gold medals, S – silver medals, B – bronze medals

The handball World Championships was first held for men in 1938 and for women in 1949. On both occasions, the events were played outdoors, but it is now chiefly an indoor sport.

AUSTRALIAN RULES FOOTBALL

- Most AFL Premierships
- Annual leading goal kickers with the most goals
- Most leading goal kicker medals
- Brownlow medal winners receiving the most votes
- Fewest seasons taken to win the AFL

Top 10 Most AFL Premierships

	Club	First win	Last win	Total
1 =	Carlton	1906	1995	16
=	Essendon	1897	2000	16
3	Collingwood	1902	1990	14
4	Melbourne	1900	1964	12
5	Richmond	1920	1980	10
6	Hawthorn	1961	1991	9
7	Fitzroy	1898	1944	8
8	Geelong	1925	1963	6
9	North Melbourne/ Kangaroos	1975	1999	4
10	South Melbourne/ Sydney	1909	1933	3

The Victoria Football League (VFL) was formed on October 2, 1896 with eight clubs: Carlton, Collingwood, Essendon, Fitzroy, Geelong, Melbourne, South Melbourne, and St. Kilda. Over the years, non-Victoria State teams joined the League and the inevitable change of name from the VFL to the Australian Football League (AFL) came about in 1990. Freemantle and Port Adelaide are the only current clubs not to have won the title.

Top 10 Annual leading goal kickers with the most goals*

	Player/club	Year	Goals
1	Peter Hudson, Hawthorn	1970	146
2	Peter Hudson, Hawthorn	1971	140
3	Jason Dunstall, Hawthorn	1992	139
4	Bob Pratt, South Melbourne	1934	138
5	Peter McKenna, Collingwood	1972	130
6	Jason Dunstall, Hawthorn	1989	128
7	Peter Hudson, Hawthorn	1968	125
8 =	Gary Ablett, Geelong	1993	124
=	Jason Dunstall, Hawthorn	1988	124
10	Doug Wade, Geelong	1969	122

* Based on goals scored by the season's leading goal kicker

Source: Australian Football League

Probably the greatest forward of all time, Peter Hudson averaged 5.64 goals per game, which is a League record. He was prevented from scoring in just five games throughout his career.

AUSSIE RULES

"Aussie" Rules is the main code of football in Victoria, Western Australia, South Australia, Tasmania, and the Northern Territory, and also has a strong following in the Australian Capital Territory. It is also played in Queensland and New South Wales. Up to 1992, all winners of the AFL had come from Victoria, but that run was ended by the West Coast Eagles of Perth.

Top 10 Most leading goal kicker medals

	Player	Club(s)	Years	Wins
1	Dick Lee	Collingwood	1907–10, 1914, 1916–17, 1919	8
2	Gordon Coventry	Collingwood	1926–30, 1933	6
3	John Coleman	Essendon	1949–53	5
4 =	Peter Hudson	Hawthorn	1968, 1970–71, 1977	4
=	Tony Lockett	St. Kilda, Sydney	1987, 1991, 1996, 1998	4
=	Doug Wade	Geelong, North Melbourne	1962, 1967, 1969, 1974	4
7 =	Gary Ablett	Geelong	1993–95	3
=	Jason Dunstall	Hawthorn	1988–89, 1992	3
=	Fred Fanning	Melbourne	1944–45, 1947	3
=	John Peck	Hawthorn	1963–65	3

Source: Australian Football League

The player kicking the most goals in the home and away rounds receives the John Coleman medal, presented in honor of the former Essendon player and later coach, whose career was cut short by injury after 537 goals in just 98 games. It was first awarded in 1897 and won by Eddy James of Geelong with 22 goals.

◀ Veteran player Bob Pratt: he kicked 138 goals for South Melbourne in the 1934 season, a tally that was to stand as a record for 36 years.

Top 10 Brownlow medal winners receiving the most votes

	Player	Club	Year	Votes
1	Graham Teasdale	South Melbourne	1977	59
2	Graham Moss	Essendon	1976	48
3 =	Des Fothergill	Collingwood	1940*	32
=	Herbie Matthews	South Melbourne	1940*	32
=	Robert Harvey#	St. Kilda	1998	32
6	Greg Williams	Carlton	1994	30
7	Roy Wright	Richmond	1954	29
8 =	Shane Crawford#	Hawthorn	1999	28
=	Alistair Lord	Geelong	1962	28
10 =	Gordon Collis	Carlton	1964	27
=	Keith Greig	North Melbourne	1973	27
=	Keith Greig	North Melbourne	1974	27
=	Dick Reynolds	Essendon	1937	27

* Shared title

Active in 2001

The Charles Brownlow medal was instituted in 1924. It is awarded to the "fairest and best" player in the League's home and away series. The field umpires decide after each game who was the best player on the field, awarding him three points, two points to the second best, and one to the third. In 1976 and 1977, the voting was changed so that the two field judges were each allocated six points per game, which explains why the figures for numbers one and two are so high.

Top 10 Fewest seasons taken to win the AFL*

	Club	First year in League	First title	Span (seasons)
1	Essendon	1897	1897	1
2	Fitzroy	1897	1898	2
3	Melbourne	1897	1900	4
4 =	Brisbane#	1996	2001	6
=	Collingwood	1897	1902	6
=	West Coast	1987	1992	6
7	Adelaide	1991	1997	7
8	Carlton	1897	1906	10
9 =	Richmond	1908	1920	13
=	South Melbourne	1897	1909	13

* Previously the VFL

The Brisbane Lions were formed in 1996 following a merger of Fitzroy Lions and Brisbane Bears

Time taken is based on first season in the League and a team's first title. St. Kilda had to wait the longest for their first triumph. As founder members in 1897, they did not win their first title until 1966, after a wait of 70 seasons.

▼ One of the best-known players in the 1980s and 1990s was Gary Ablett of Geelong, seen here in action against Essendon during the 1988 season.

SPORTING WORLD

- Sport whose participants have the largest average heart
- Most popular participation activities in the UK
- Highest-earning sportsmen
- Most popular participation activities in the United States
- Highest-earning sports movie

Top 10 Sport whose participants have the largest* average heart

	Sport
1	Tour de France cyclists
2	Marathon runners
3	Rowers
4	Boxers
5	Sprint cyclists
6	Middle-distance runners
7	Weightlifters
8	Swimmers
9	Sprinters
10	Decathletes

* Based on average medical measurements

The size of the heart of a person who engages regularly in a demanding sport enlarges according to the strenuousness of the sport.

Top 10 Most popular participation activities in the UK

	Sport/pastime	(%)*
1	Walking	65
2	Swimming	42
3	Snooker/pool/billiards	22
4	Aerobics/yoga	19
5	Cycling	17
6	Darts	13
7	Golf	12
8	Bowling/skittles	11
9 =	Badminton	9
=	Running/jogging	9
=	Weightlifting/weight training	9

* Based on percentage of population participating in activity

Source: Office for National Statistics

Top 10 Highest-earning sportsmen

	Name*	Sport	Team	Income 2000 ($)
1	Michael Shumacher, Germany	Auto racing	Ferrari	59,000,000
2	Tiger Woods	Golf	–	53,000,000
3	Mike Tyson	Boxing	–	48,000,000
4	Michael Jordan	Basketball	Chicago Bulls	37,000,000
5	Grant Hill	Basketball	Detroit Pistons	26,000,000
6	Dale Earnhardt†	Stock car racing	–	24,500,000
7	Shaquille O'Neal	Basketball	LA Lakers	24,000,000
8 =	Oscar De La Hoya	Boxing	–	23,000,000
=	Lennox Lewis, UK	Boxing	–	23,000,000
10	Kevin Garnett	Basketball	Minnesota Timberwolves	21,000,000

* All US unless otherwise stated

† Killed February 18, 2001 during the Daytona 500

Used with permission of Forbes magazine

Forbes' annual analysis of celebrity income includes many of the world's highest-earning athletes. Among those falling outside the Top 10 are boxers such as George Foreman ($20,100,000) and tennis player Andre Agassi ($17,500,000). The extended list includes several non-Americans, among them Australian golfer Greg Norman ($15,000,000) and Czech-born tennis player Martina Hingis ($11,000,000), the highest-earning woman among this elite group. She is closely followed by Anna Kournikova and Venus Williams (both $10,000,000), Serena Williams ($7,500,000), and Lindsay Davenport ($6,000,000). The earnings of many represent their cumulative income from the sport itself and from sponsorship deals: Tiger Woods' contract with Nike, for example, is reported to be worth $40 million over five years.

Top 10 Most popular participation activities in the United States

	Activity	% change since previous year	Number participating (2000)
1	Exercise walking	+0.6	81,300,000
2	Swimming	+2.3	59,300,000
3	Camping	-2.3	49,900,000
4	Fishing	+4.5	48,800,000
5	Exercising with equipment	-4.4	43,200,000
6	Bicycle riding	+0.3	42,500,000
7	Bowling	+1.6	42,300,000
8	Billiards/pool	+0.1	32,200,000
9 =	Aerobics	+3.5	27,200,000
=	Basketball	-8.1	27,200,000

Source: National Sporting Goods Association

The annual NSGA survey includes people over age seven who participated in each activity on more than one occasion. From 1995 to 2000, skateboarding experienced the greatest increase in the number of participants, while windsurfing sustained the sharpest decline.

Top 10 Highest-earning sports movies

	Movie/year of release	Sport	World box office income ($)
1	Rocky IV (1985)	Boxing	300,500,000
2	Jerry Maguire (1996)	Football	273,600,000
3	Space Jam (1996)	Basketball	225,400,000
4	The Waterboy (1998)	Football	190,200,000
5	Days of Thunder (1990)	Stock car racing	165,900,000
6	Cool Runnings (1993)	Bobsledding	154,900,000
7	A League of Their Own (1992)	Baseball	130,500,000
8	Remember the Titans (2000)	Football	130,000,000
9	Rocky III (1982)	Boxing	122,800,000
10	Rocky V (1990)	Boxing	120,000,000

While three of the hugely successful Rocky movies appear in the Top 10, the original (made in 1976) and its sequel *Rocky II* (1979) failed to earn enough globally to merit an entry. Sylvester Stallone was paid a reported $16 million for acting, writing, and directing *Rocky IV*–more than half its total budget.

▼ Rocky Balboa (Sylvester Stallone) gunning for the Russian fighter Ivan Drago (Dolph Lundgren) in the sports movie blockbuster *Rocky IV*.

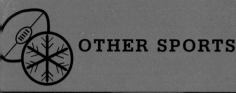

AWARDS

- Most Associated Press Athlete of the Year Awards
- First back-to-back winners of the Associated Press Athlete of the Year Award
- Last BBC Sports Personality of the Year Award winners
- Latest winners of the Jesse Owens International Trophy
- Sports represented by the James E. Sullivan Award
- First Sullivan Award winners to become Olympic champions

ATHLETE OF THE YEAR

Pioneered in 1931 by the Associated Press, the annual Athlete of the Year Award, unlike the Sullivan Award, can be awarded to amateur or professional athletes and a person can win it more than once. It also differs in that a separate award is made to women athletes. Babe Didrikson Zaharias, Maureen Connolly, and Michael Jordan all won the award three years in succession.

Top 10 Most Associated Press Athlete of the Year Awards

	Athlete	Sport	Years	Total
1	Babe Didrikson Zaharias	Track & field/Golf	1932, 1945–47, 1950, 1954	6
2	Chris Evert	Tennis	1974–75, 1977, 1980	4
3 =	Patty Berg	Golf	1938, 1943, 1955	3
=	Maureen Connolly	Tennis	1951–53	3
=	Michael Jordan	Basketball	1991–93	3
=	Tiger Woods	Golf	1997, 1999–2000	3
7 =	Tracy Austin	Tennis	1979, 1981	2
=	Donald Budge	Tennis	1937–38	2
=	Althea Gibson	Tennis	1957–58	2
=	Billy Jean King	Tennis	1967, 1973	2
=	Sandy Koufax	Baseball	1963, 1965	2
=	Carl Lewis	Track & field	1983–84	2
=	Nancy Lopez	Golf	1978, 1985	2
=	Alice Marble	Tennis	1939–40	2
=	Joe Montana	Football	1989–90	2
=	Martina Navratilova	Tennis	1983, 1986	2
=	Byron Nelson	Golf	1944–45	2
=	Wilma Rudolph	Track & field	1960–61	2
=	Monica Seles	Tennis	1991–92	2
=	Kathy Whitworth	Golf	1965–66	2
=	Mickey Wright	Golf	1963–64	2

The first winner of the men's award in 1931 was baseball player Peper Martin; the first women's winner was swimmer Helene Madison, also in 1931.

The 10 First back-to-back winners of the Associated Press Athlete of the Year Award

	Athlete	Sport	Years
1	Donald Budge	Tennis	1937–38
2	Alice Marble	Tennis	1939–40
3	Byron Nelson	Golf	1944–45
4	Babe Didrikson Zaharais	Golf	1945–46
5	Maureen Connolly	Tennis	1951–52
6	Althea Gibson	Tennis	1957–58
7	Wilma Rudolph	Track & field	1960–61
8	Mickey Wright	Golf	1963–64
9	Kathy Whitworth	Golf	1965–66
10	Chris Evert	Tennis	1974–75

> It's ironic; I used to ride my bike to make a living.
> Now I just want to live so that I can ride.
>
> **Lance Armstrong**

The 10 Last BBC Sports Personality of the Year Award winners

	Year	Winner/sport
1	2001	David Beckham, Football
2	2000	Steve Redgrave, Rowing
3	1999	Lennox Lewis, Boxing
4	1998	Michael Owen, Football
5	1997	Greg Rusedski, Tennis
6	1996	Damon Hill, Motor racing
7	1995	Jonathan Edwards, Track & field
8	1994	Damon Hill, Motor racing
9	1993	Linford Christie, Track & field
10	1992	Nigel Mansell, Motor racing

First presented in 1954, when it was won by athlete Chris Chataway, the annual award is based on a poll of BBC (British Broadcasting Corporation) television viewers. Muhammed Ali was voted Sports Personality of the Century in 1999.

The 10 Latest winners of the Jesse Owens International Trophy

	Year	Winner/sport
1	2001	Marion Jones, Track & field
2	2000	Lance Armstrong, Cycling
3	1999	Marion Jones, Ttrack & field
4	1998	Haile Gebrselassie, Track & field
5	1997	Michael Johnson, Track & field
6	1996	Michael Johnson, Track & field
7	1995	Johann Olav Koss, Speed skating
8	1994	Wang Junxia, Track & field
9	1993	Vitaly Scherbo, Gymnastics
10	1992	Mike Powell, Track & field

The Jesse Owens International Trophy has been presented by the International Amateur Athletic Association since 1981, when it was won by speed skater Eric Heiden, and is named in honor of US athlete Jesse (James Cleveland) Owens (1913–80). Michael Johnson and Marion Jones are the only sports personalities to have won the award twice.

Top 10 Sports represented by the James E. Sullivan Award

	Sport	Awards
1	Track & field	37
2	Swimming	9
3	Football	4
4	Diving	3
=	Speed skating	3
=	Wrestling	3
7	Basketball	2
=	Golf	2
=	Sculling	2
10 =	Baseball	1
=	Figure skating	1
=	Gymnastics	1
=	Tennis	1

Source: Amateur Athletic Union

The award is made annually to the sportsman or woman who has contributed most to good sportsmanship. The trophy is in memory of James E. Sullivan, the president of the Amateur Athletic Union (AAU) from 1906 to 1914.

The 10 First Sullivan Award winners to become Olympic champions

	Athlete	Award year	Sport	Event	Olympic year
1	Jim Bausch	1932	Track & field	Decathlon	1932
2	Glenn Morris	1936	Track & field	Decathlon	1936
3	Bob Mathias	1948	Track & field	Decathlon	1948
4	Ann Curtis	1944	Swimming	400-meter freestyle	1948
5	Bob Richards	1951	Track & field	Pole vault	1952
6	Horace Ashenfelter	1952	Track & field	Steeplechase	1952
7	Dick Button	1949	Ice skating	Men's figures	1952
8	Pat McCormick	1956	Swimming	Springboard diving	1956
9	Glenn Davis	1958	Track & field	400-meter hurdles	1960
10	Rafer Johnson	1960	Track & field	Decathlon	1960

Button, McCormick, and Davis, like several other athletes, also won Olympic golds prior to winning their Sullivan Awards.

◀ Lance Armstrong won the Tour de France three years in succession, 1999–2001, after successfully combating cancer.

A

ABA *see* American Basketball Association
Ablett, Gary 199
AFL *see* Australian Football League
Agassi, Andre 62–3
Agostini, Giacomo 140
Alexeev, Vassily 187
all-time greats 106–7, 120–1
Allen, Mark 197
alpine skiing 192–3
American Basketball Association (ABA) 110
American football 66–81
American League baseball 84, 87
American-born boxers 49
Anderson, Gary 69, 72–3
appearances
  baseball 87
  basketball 100, 101
  Davis Cup 62
  ice hockey 116, 126
  Ryder cup 26
  Super Bowl 69
  World Cup soccer 191
archery 188–9
arenas 102–3, 122–4
Armstrong, Lance 181, 203
assists 104–5, 106, 119
Associated Press Athlete of the Year Awards 202
athletes
  awards 202
  Olympics 145
  world championships 16–17
  world mile record 20–1
ATP record breakers 64–5
Auerbach, Red 109
Augusta course 32
Australian Football League (AFL) Premierships 198–9
Australian Open tennis 60–1
Australian Rules football 198–9
auto sports 128–41
  bikes 140–1
  CART 132–3
  drivers 133–5, 137

auto sports *cont.*
  endurance races 138–9
  Formula One 136–7
  Indianapolis 500 134–5
  NASCAR 130–1
  rallying 138–9
  records 130–7
awards 202–3
  baseball 94–5
  basketball 108–9
  ice hockey 122–3

B

back-to-back winners 133
badminton 184
Bagwell, Hal 51
Ballesteros, Seve 27
ballparks 96–7
Bannister, Roger 21
Barber, Tiki 70–1
bare-knuckle champions 45
Barnes, Randy 151
baseball 82–97
  averages 86, 89, 92
  ballparks 96–7
  batsmen 88–9
  Championship Series 86–7
  divisional winners 86–7
  managers 94–5
  pitchers 85–7, 90–1, 93
  records 84–5, 92–5
  single-season records 92–3
  teams 96–7
  World Series records 84–5
basketball 98–113
  all-time greats 106–7
  arenas 102–3
  averages 101, 104–5, 107, 112
  awards 108–9
  coaches 108–9
  college 112–13
  drafts 108–9
  playoffs 100–1
  records 104–5
  teams 102–3
batsmen 86, 88–9, 92
BBC Sports Personality Award 203

Beamon, Bob 11
Belmont Stakes 169
Big "Five Bowl" wins 80
bikes 140–1, 180–1
Biondi, Matt 159
bobsledding 195
Bonds, Barry 93
Borg, Bjorn 61
Boston Marathon 23
Bourque, Ray 117
bowling 196
Bowman, Scotty 123
boxing 40–51
  champions 42–50
  firsts 48–9
  greats 46–7
  heavyweight 42–5
  records 50–1
  titles 50–1
Boxing World Champions 46
Bozeman, Cedric 112
Braid, James 35
Breeders Cup 170–1
British Open
  golf 30–1, 34–5
  squash 185
Brown, Jim 77
Brownlow medal winners 199
Bubka, Sergey 16

C

canoeing 164–5
capped international players 191
captains 63
career earnings 29, 65
cars *see* auto sports
CART 132–3
Cáslacská, Vera 182, 183
Chamberlain, Wilt 104
champions
  boxing 42–50
  jockeys 172–3
  Olympics 144–5
Championship fights 42
Championship games 70–1
Championship Series 86–7
Charles, Ezzard 51

Cleveland Browns 70
coaches
  basketball 108–9
  football 76–7
  ice hockey 122–3, 126–7
Cobb, Ty 88–9
College basketball 112–13
College football 80–1
College World Series titles 94
Connors, Jimmy 65
consecutive boxing defences 46
constructors 137, 139
Cooper, Cynthia 110
Copa America 191
Cotton Bowl 80
countries at Olympics 146–53, 155
countries of birth, Major League players 95
countries winning medals
  basketball 111
  bobsledding 195
  cycling 181
  gymnastics 183
  ice hockey 125
  Olympics 145–53, 155, 186–8, 197
  watersports 161–2, 165, 193
Courier, Jim 62–3
Court, Margaret 61
cycling 180–1

D

Dählie, Bjorn 153
Davis Cup 62–3
Day, Pat 171
Daytona races 130, 138, 140
Diaggio, J 96, 97
divisional winners, baseball 86–7
drivers
  auto sports 133–5, 137, 139
  harness racing 176
Dunwoody, Richard 175
Dwyer, Pat 196

E

earnings 29, 65, 200–2
Edwards, Jonathon 14
Ender, Kornelia 161
endurance races 138–9
engines 135
English Classics 175
Epsom Derby 174
ERA, baseball 86, 90
European Championship
    medals 124
European PGA Tour 28
Evert-Lloyd, Chris 56–7

F

fastest runners 12–13,
    20–1
fencing 189
Ferrari, Enzo 136
field goals 100, 105, 106
field hockey 197
Fiery, Theo 124
Fighter of the Year award 47
fights 51
figure skating 194
Fischer, Birgit 164
flat-races 172
football 66–81
    Australian Rules 198–9
    Championship games
        70–1
    coaches 76–7
    college 80–1
    drafts 77, 108–9
    franchises 78–9
    Gaelic 197
    post-season games 70–1
    records 68–9, 71–5
    season records 74–5
    soccer 190–1
    Super Bowl 68–9
    teams 78–9
Formula One records
    136–7
four-minute mile 20, 21
four-round totals 31, 35
Foyt, A. J. 132
franchises 78–9
free throws 100, 106
freestyle 159
French Open tennis 60
Frey, Konrad 149

G

Gaelic football 197
goals
    football 191, 198
    ice hockey 116–17,
        119–20
goaltenders 116–17, 118, 120
Godfrey, Kitty (nee McKane)
    184
gold medals
    ice hockey 124
    Olympics 145
    track & field medals 10–11
    water sports 161
    world championships 16
golf 24–39
    British Open 30–1,
        34–5
    Majors 30–1
    miscellaneous records
        38–9
    money winners 28–9
    Ryder Cup 26–7
    tournament winners 28–9
    US Masters 32–3
    US Open & US PGA
        36–7
Graf, Steffi 65
Grand Prix races 136, 137
Grand Slam Championships
    54–5
Green, Maurice 13
Gretzky, Wayne 119
Grey-Thompson, Tanni
    154
Griffith-Joyner, Florence
    12–13
Gullikson, Tom 62–3
Guttmann, Sir Ludwig 154
gymnastics 182–3

H

Hagler, Marvin 46–7
Hambletonian 178
handball 197
harness racing 176–7
Hart Trophy 122
Hawaii Ironmans 197
Hearns, Thomas 48–9
heart size 200
heaviest boxers 42–3
heavyweight boxing 42–5

Heismann Trophy winners
    77
Hermandez, Roberto 12
high jump 14–15
highest-scoring sets 63
hits 89, 92
hockey 114–27, 197
hole in one 32
holes, longest 38
homers 92
home runs 84, 89, 93, 97
Hoppe, Wolfgang 195
horse racing 166–77
    Breeders Cup 170–1
    champion jockeys 172–3
    harness racing 176–7
    Triple Crown 168–9
    United Kingdom 174–5
hurling 197

I

IAAF Grand Prix titles 16–17
ice hockey 114–27
    all-time greats 120–1
    awards 122–3
    coaches 122–3, 126–7
    NCAA 126–7
    playoffs 116–17
    records 116–19
    season record-breakers
        118–19
    stadiums 122–3
    Stanley Cup 116–17
    world 124–5
ice rinks 125
Ickk, Jacky 138
Indianapolis 500 134–5
Induráin, Miguel 181
innings pitched 91
International Boxing Hall of
    Fame 47
Isle of Man 141

J

Jesse Owens International
    Trophy 203
jockeys 169–70, 172–5
Johnson, Magic 100, 101
Johnson, Michael 16
Jones, Robert Tyre 32
Jordon, Michael 101
judo 187

K

Kentucky Derby 168
Khan, Jahangir 185
Kim, Soo-Nyung 189
knockouts 51
Kong, Linghui 151
Korbut, Olga 183

L

LA Lakers 103
Ladies' Plate 58
Latynina, Larissa 144–5
Le Mans 138
League Championship Series
    Pennants 87
Leonard, Sugar Ray
    46–7
Lewis, Lennox 45
Lewis, Ray 70–1
Little Brown Jug 178
Little League World Series
    94
London Marathon
    22–3
long jump 15
longest holes 38
Louis, Joe 50

M

McCoy, Tony 174–5
Mack, Connie 95
Major League Baseball (MLB)
    84, 89, 95, 96
Majors 30–1
Malone, Karl 107
marathons 22–3
Marciano, Rocky 43
Marino, Dan 75
medals
    see also gold medals
    archery 188
    Australian Rules football
        198–9
    basketball 111
    bobsledding 195
    cycling 180, 181
    fencing 189
    field hockey 197
    gymnastics 182–3
    handball 197
    ice hockey 124–5
    judo 187

medals cont.
Olympics 125, 144–53,
155, 182, 186–8, 197
Paralympics 155
shooting 189
skiing 193
track & field events 10–11,
16–17
water sports 158, 161–2,
164–5, 193
weight lifting 186
winning countries 145–53,
155, 186–8, 197
winter Olympics 152–3
wrestling 186
men's events
boxing world title 48, 49
gymnastics 182–3
high jump 15
judo 187
long jump 15
Olympics 144, 152–3,
158–9
record breakers 18, 19
running 12–13
skiing 192–3
swimming 158–9
tennis 54–60, 64–5
track & field gold medals
10, 11
water sports 158–61,
163–4
winter Olympics 152–3
world mile record 21
Messier, Mark 121
milers 20–1
Miller, Nate 48–9
Millerg, Kurt 127
MLB see Major League
Baseball
models, World Rally
Championships 139
money winners
auto sports 131, 132
golf 28–9
harness racing 176
jockeys 170, 173
Moonee Valley, Melbourne
177
Morris, Tom Sr. 31
Most Valuable Player (MVP)
award 108–9

motor sports see auto sports
Muhammad, Ali 44, 45
MVP see Most Valuable
Player

N
NASCAR 130–1
National Basketball
Association (NBA) 100–9
National Championships,
football 81
National Hockey League
(NHL) 118–23
National Hunt 174, 175
National League baseball 84,
87
Navratilova, Martina 59
NBA see National Basketball
Association
NCAA 112–13, 126–7
Nelson, Azumah 49
New York City Marathon 23
New York Yankees 85
NFL 76–9
NFL-NFC Championships 71
NHL see National Hockey
League
North American jockeys 173

O
Ohno, Apolo Anton "Chunky"
153
Olazabel, Jose-Maria 30–1
oldest World Heavyweight
champions 43
Olympic records 10
Olympic torch 148
Olympics 142–55
archery 188
basketball 111
bobsledding 195
boxing 47
champions 10–15, 47,
144–5, 203
fencing 189
gymnastics 182
ice hockey 125
judo 187
medals 125, 144–53, 155,
182, 186–8, 197
Paralympics 154–5
poster 147

Olympics cont.
shooting 189
skating 194–5
skiing 193
track & field events 10–15
water sports 158–9, 162,
165
weight lifting 186
winning countries 145–53,
155, 186–8, 197
winter games 152–3
Orange Bowl 81
Orosco, Jesse 90
Oslo 20
outdoor world records 18–19
Owens, Jesse 19, 149, 203

P
pacers 176
Paralympics 154–5
passes 73
payrolls 102
PBA see Professional
Bowlers Association
Petty, Richard 131
pitchers 85–7, 90–1, 93
playoffs 100–1, 116–17
points
basketball 100, 102, 104,
106, 110
college basketball 113
football 68, 73, 75, 78
ice hockey 117–18, 121,
127
poles 133, 134
Pontian Silverdome 79
popular participation activities
200, 201
Portis, Clinton 81
post-season football 70–1
Pratt, Bob 199
President's Trophy 122
Professional Bowlers
Association (PBA) 196
Prokopec, Luke 86

QR
Qualcomm Stadium 97
Queensberry Rules 48
race circuits 131, 133
rallying 138–9
rebounds 107

receptions 69, 73, 75
records
auto sports 130–7
baseball 84–5, 92–5
basketball 104–5
boxing 50–1
football 68–9, 71–5
golf 30–1
ice hockey 116–19
seasons 74–5, 92–3,
104–5, 118–19
swimming 159
tennis 61, 64–5
track & field 18–19
water sports 159–61
weight lifting 186
Rice, Jerry 69
Richards, Gordon 173
Rocky IV 201
Rookie award 108
Rose Bowl 80–1
rounds, lowest 37
rowing 164–5
Roy, Patrick 117
runners 12–13, 20–1
runners-up, Majors 31
runs 84, 89, 92, 93
Rushcutter's Bay 163
Ruth, B 85
Ryder cup 26–7

S
St. Andrews 38
St. Louis, Missouri 147
Sainz, Carlos 139
Salt Lake City 155
Sampras, Pete 55, 62–3
Sampson, Jamal 112
Schneider, Vreni 193
Schumacher, Michael
137
season records 74–5, 92–3,
104–5, 118–19
Secretariat 168
Senna, Ayrton 137
shirt numbers 103
Shoemaker, Bill 173
shooting 189
Shula, D. 77
shutouts 120
single-season records 92–3,
104–5

singles
see also tennis
Australian Open 61
French Open 60
Grand Slam 54
US Open 57
Wimbledon 59
skating 194–5
skiing 162–3, 192–3
Smith, Emmitt 74
Snead, Sam 36, 37
soccer 190–1
Soldier Field 79
sophomores 112
Sorenstam, Annika 29
Sotomayer, Javier 15
speed skating 195
speed winners 130, 134
Splitz, Mark 159
sports movies 201
Sports Personality Award 203
squash 185
stadiums 79, 97, 122–3
Stanley Cup 116–17, 122, 123
starting positions 135
starts 134
Stenmark, Ingemar 193
Stockton, John 105
strikeouts 84, 91, 92
Sugar Bowl 80–1
Sullivan Award 203
summer Paralympics 155
Super Bowl 68–9
swimming 158–9
Sydney 145, 155

T
table tennis 184–5
Taylor, J. H. 35
Teahy, John 196
teams
baseball 96–7
basketball 102–3
Davis Cup 62
football 78–9
tennis 52–65
Australian Open 61
Davis Cup 62–3
French Open 60
Grand Slam
Championships 54–5

tennis cont.
record breakers 61, 64–5
table 184–5
US Open 56–7
Wimbledon 58–9
The Ring 46
Thorpe, Ian 161
torch 148
touchdowns 72, 75
Tour de France 180
tournament winners 28–9
Tours, cycling 180, 181
track & field events 8–23
see also athletes
fastest runners 12–13
gold medals 10–11, 16
jump events 14–15
marathons 22–3
medals 10–11, 16–17
Olympic champions 10–11
records 18–19
World Champions 16–17
world mile record 20–1
trainers 168, 169, 171
triathlon field hockey 197
Triple Crown 91, 168–9
triple jumpers 15
trotters 176
two country Olympic event 146

U
UK see United Kingdom
undefeated professional boxing records 43
United Kingdom (UK) 172, 174–5, 200
United States (US)
champion jockeys 173
popular participation activities 201
runners 21
winter Olympics 153
US see United States
US Masters 30–1, 32–3
US Open
golf 30–1, 36–7
tennis 56–7
US PGA 30–1, 36–7
US Seniors Tour 28
US Tour 28
US Women's Open 39

V
valuable football players 76
Vardon, Harry 35
Vardon Trophy 39

W
Wagner, Katrina 164
water sports 156–65
canoeing 164–5
records 160–1
rowing 164–5
skiing 162–3
swimming 158–9
water-skiing 162–3
World Champions 160–1
yachting 162–3
Webb, Karrie 38–9
weight lifting 186
Wilkins, Lenny 108, 109
Wimbledon 58–9
winners
see also countries winning medals
auto sports 130–4, 135, 137
baseball 85, 94, 96
cycling 180
Davis Cup 62
football 68, 78, 80
golf 26, 27, 31–8, 39
harness racing 176–7
horse racing 168, 170, 171
ice hockey 126
World Heavyweight fights 45
winning heats 177
Winston Cup 131
winter Olympic games 152–3
winter Paralympics 155
WNBA see Women's National Basketball Association
women's events
golf 29, 38
gymnastics 182–3
high jump 14
judo 187
long jump 15
Olympics 144, 152–3, 158
record breakers 18, 19
running 12–13

women's events cont.
skiing 192–3
swimming 158
tennis 54–60, 64–5
track & field gold medals 10, 11
water sports 158, 160–1, 163, 165
winter Olympics 152–3
world mile record 20
Women's National Basketball Association (WNBA) 110
Women's Open 39
Woods, Tiger 6, 33, 34–5
World Championships
basketball 111
boxing 47, 48–9, 50
ice hockey 125
track & field 16–17
water sports 160–1
World Cup
football 190, 191
golf 39
skiing 192–3
World figure skating 194
World gymnastics titles 183
World Heavyweight fight 42–5
World ice hockey 124–5
World mile record 20–1
World Motorcycling titles 141
World Rally Championships 139
World Road Race Championship 180
World Series 84–5, 95
World Swimming Championships 161
World table tennis titles 185
World Trials Championship 141
wrestling 186
WTA World record breakers 64–5

XYZ
yachting 162–3
yards 69, 73, 74
youngest British Open winners 35

ACKNOWLEDGMENTS

Dorling Kindersley would like to thank the following for their contributions: Picture Research Franziska Marking, Carolyn Clerkin; Picture Library Hayley Smith; Jacket Editor Jane Oliver-Jedrzejak; Jacket Designer Dean Price; Proofreading Christine Heilman. Index by Indexing Specialists, Hove, Brighton

PICTURE CREDITS

Picture researcher: Franziska Marking
Additional picture research: Carolyn Clerkin

The publisher would like to thank the following for their kind permission to reproduce their photographs: (Abbreviations key: t=top, b=bottom, r=right, l=left, c=center)

2: Empics Ltd/Rob Tringali, Jr. (cr), Getty Images/Tony Duffy (c), Getty Images/Gary M. Prior (l); 3: Empics Ltd/Neal Simpson (c), Getty Images/Mike Powell (l); 5: Getty Images/Clive Mason; 6: Getty Images/Andrew Redington; 8–9: Getty Images/Scott Barbour; 11: Getty Images/Tony Duffy (bl); 12: Getty Images/Tony Duffy (br); 13: Getty Images/Andy Lyons (tl); 14: Getty Images/Clive Brunskill (bc); 15: Empics Ltd/Andy Heading; 16: Getty Images/Shaun Botterill (br); 17: Getty Images/Gary M. Prior; 19: Empics Ltd; 21: Getty Images/Clive Brunskill (tl); 21: Empics Ltd/Alpha (bl); 23: Empics Ltd/Andy Heading; 24–25: Empics Ltd/Jon Buckle; 26: Empics Ltd/Tony Marshall; 27: Getty Images/Stephen Munday; 28: Empics Ltd/Tony Marshall; 29: Getty Images/Scott Halleran (r), Empics Ltd/Don Morley (tl); 30: Empics Ltd/Tony Marshall (l); 30–31: Getty Images/Steve Munday (b); 31 Getty Images/Hulton Getty Archive (tl); 32: Empics Ltd/Tony Marshall (l); 32–33: Getty Images/Andrew Redington (b); 34–35: Empics Ltd/Mike Egerton (b), Empics Litd/Tony Marshall (l); 35: Getty Images/Hulton Getty Archive (tl); 36–37: Getty Images/David Cannon (bc); 36: Empics Ltd/Tony Marshall (l); 38–39: Getty Images/Scott Halleran (bc); 38: Empics Ltd/Tony Marshall (l); 40–41: Empics Ltd/Tony Marshall; 42: Empics Ltd/Neal Simpson; 43: Empics Ltd/Topham Picturepoint; 44: Empics Ltd/Neal Simpson; 45: Action Plus (b), Empics Ltd/Nick Potts (tl); 46: Empics Ltd/Neal Simpson (l); 46–47: Empics Ltd/Bob Tringali; 48: Empics Ltd/Neal Simpson; 49: Getty Images/Holly Stein (tl), Getty Images/John Gichigi (b); 50: Empics Ltd/Neal Simpson; 51: Empics Ltd/S&G; 52–53: Getty Images/Al Bello; 54: Getty Images/Gary M. Prior; 55: Empics Ltd/Alpha (tl), Getty Images/Gary M. Prior (bl); 56: Getty Images/Gary M. Prior; 57: Getty Images; 58: Getty Images/Gary M. Prior; 59: Action Images/Chris Barry (b), Getty Images (tl); 60: Getty Images/Gary M. Prior; 61: Getty Images (br), Getty

Images/Tony Duffy (tl); 62: Getty Images/Gary M. Prior (l); 62–63: Getty Images/Clive Brunskill (bc); 64: Getty Images/Gary M. Prior; 65: Empics Ltd/Mike Egerton (b), Getty Images (tl); 66–67: Getty Images/Al Bello; 68: Getty Images/Al Bello; 69: Getty Images/Brian Bahr (br), Getty Images/Matthew Stockman (tl); 70: Empics Ltd/Frank Peters (br), Getty Images/Al Bello; 71: Empics Ltd/ Matthew Ashton; 72: Getty Images/Al Bello, Getty Images/Matthew Stockman (br); 74: Getty Images/Al Bello (br); 75: Getty Images/Jed Jacobsohn; 76: Getty Images/ Al Bello; 77: Empics Ltd/Tony Tomsic (br), Getty Images/Brian Masck (tl); 78: Getty Images/Al Bello (l); 78–79: Empics Ltd/Rob Tringali, Jr. (b); 79: Getty Images/Tom Pidgeon (tl); 80: Getty Images/Al Bello; 81: Getty Images/Robert Laberge; 82–83: Empics Ltd/Rob Tringali, Jr.; 84: Empics Ltd/Rob Tringali, Jr. (l); 85: Getty Images/Hulton Getty Archive (tl), Empics Ltd/Rob Tringali, Jr. (bl); 86: Getty Images/Jeff Gross (br), Empics Ltd/Rob Tringali, Jr. (l); 88: Empics Ltd/Rob Tringali, Jr. (l), Hulton Getty Archive/Howard Muller (br); 89: Empics Ltd/SportsChrome (tl); 90: Empics Ltd/Rob Tringali, Jr.; 91: Getty Images/Doug Pensinger (bl); 92: Empics Ltd/Rob Tringali, Jr. (l); 93: Getty Images/Jed Jacobsohn (bl); 94: Empics Ltd/Rob Tringali, Jr. (l); 94–95: Corbis/Bettmann; 96: Empics Ltd/Rob Tringali, Jr.; 97: Getty Images/Allsport/Hulton Getty (br), Empics Ltd/Michael Zito, Empics Ltd/SportsChrome (tl); 98–99: Getty Images/Rocky Widner/NBAE; 101: Empics Ltd/Steve Lipofsky (tl), Empics Ltd/Steve Lipofsky (br); 103: Corbis/Bettmann; 105: Empics Ltd/Steve Lipofsky; 107: Empics Ltd/Steve Lipofsky; 109: Empics Ltd/Steve Lipofsky (tl), Empics Ltd/Steve Lipofsky (br); 110: Getty Images/Todd Warshaw (br); 111: Getty Images/David Leah; 114–115: Empics Ltd/Aubrey Washington; 116: Getty Images/Mike Powell; 117: Empics Ltd/Rob Tringali, Jr. (bc), Getty Images/Elsa (tl); 118: Getty Images/Mike Powell; 119: Empics Ltd/SportsChrome (tl), Getty Images/Mike Powell (bc); 120: Getty Images/Mike Powell; 121: Corbis/Bettmann; 122: Getty Images/Mike Powell; 123: Getty Images/ Sylvia Pecota; 124: Getty Images/Brian Bahr, Getty Images/Mike Powell; 126: Getty Images/Mike Powell; 127: Getty Images; 128–129: Empics Ltd/John Marsh; 130: Empics Ltd/Steve Mitchell; 131: Getty Images/Allen Steele; 132: Empics Ltd/Steve Etherington (br), Empics Ltd/Steve Mitchell (l); 134: Empics Ltd/Steve Mitchell; 135: Getty Images/Mark Thompson; 136: Empics Ltd/Steve Mitchell; 137: Getty Images/Pascal Rondeau (tl); 138: Empics Ltd/Steve Mitchell; 138–139: Getty Images/Pascal Rondeau; 140: Empics Ltd/S&G (br), Empics/Steve Mitchell (l); 142–143: Getty Images/Adam Pretty; 145: Getty Images/Hulton Getty Archive (bl), Getty Images/SOCOG (tl); 147: Getty Images/IOC Olympic Museum; 149: Empics Ltd (tl), Empics (br); 151: Getty Images/Mike Powell (tl), Empics Ltd/Jon

Buckle (br); 153: Getty Images/Clive Mason (b); Todd Warshaw (tl); 154: Empics Ltd/Adam Pretty (br); 156–157: Getty Images/Bob Martin; 159: Getty Images/Hulton Getty Archive (tl); Getty Images/Mike Powell (b); 161: Empics Ltd/Topham Picturepoint (tl), Getty Images/Al Bello (bc); 163: Getty Images/Hamish Blair; 164: Getty Images/Darren England (r); 166–167: Empics Ltd/John Marsh; 168: Empics Ltd/Chris Turvey; 169: Getty Images/Doug Pensinger; 170: Empics Ltd/Chris Turvey; 171: Getty Images/Doug Pensinger; 172: Empics Ltd/Chris Turvey; 173: Getty Images/Mike Powell (b), Empics Ltd/S&G (tl); 174: Empics Ltd/Chris Turvey (l); 174–175: Getty Images/Julian Herbert; 175: Getty Images/Mike Cooper (tl); 176: Empics Ltd/Chris Turvey; 177: Empics Ltd/Hamish Blair; 178–179: Empics Ltd/Tony Marshall; 180: Getty Images/Mike Powell; 181: Getty Images/Pascal Rondeau (tl), Getty Images/Vandystadt (br); 182: Getty Images/ Mike Powell; 183: Getty Images (tl), Getty Images (bl); 184: Getty Images/Mike Powell; 185: Action Plus; 186: Getty Images/Mike Powell; 187: Getty Images; 188: Getty Images/Mike Powell; 189: Empics Ltd/Tony Marshall; 190: Getty Images/Chris Cole (br), Getty Images/Mike Powell (l); 192: Getty Images/ Mike Powell; 193: Empics Ltd/Alpha (bc), Getty Images/Hulton Getty Archive (tl); 194: Getty Images/Mike Powell; 195: Getty Images/Mike Hewitt; 196: Getty Images/Simon Bruty (br), Getty Images/Mike Powell; 197: Getty Images/Mike Powell; 198: Getty Images/Mike Powell; 199: Getty Images/Allsport Australia (r), Getty Images/Sean Garnsworthy tl; 200: Getty Images/Mike Powell; 201: Kobal Collection/MGM/UA; 202: Getty Images/Mike Powell; 203: Getty Images/Doug Pensinger.

Jacket photography: front: Getty Images/Clive Brunskill; back: Empics Ltd/Chris Cole (tl), Empics Ltd/Neal Simpson (tr), Empics Ltd/Steve Mitchell (br), Empics Ltd/Tony Marshall (bl).

All other images © Dorling Kindersley.
For further information see: www.dkimages.com

AUTHORS' ACKNOWLEDGMENTS

Ian and Russell would like to thank the following for all their help:

Ray Fletcher
Aylla Macphail
David Middleton, National Rugby League, Australia
Ann Morrison
Dafydd Rees
Debbie Smiley, US Trotting Association
David Wright, Southport Sports Quiz League